Matthew Henry, William Bates

An account of the life and death of Mr. Philip Henry, minister of the gospel near Whitchurch in Shropshire,

Who died June 24, 1696, in the sixty fifth year of his age ; with Dr. Bates's dedication

Matthew Henry, William Bates

An account of the life and death of Mr. Philip Henry, minister of the gospel near Whitchurch in Shropshire,
Who died June 24, 1696, in the sixty fifth year of his age ; with Dr. Bates's dedication

ISBN/EAN: 9783337714468

Printed in Europe, USA, Canada, Australia, Japan

Cover: Foto ©ninafisch / pixelio.de

More available books at **www.hansebooks.com**

AN

ACCOUNT

OF THE

LIFE AND DEATH

OF

Mr PHILIP HENRY,

MINISTER OF THE GOSPEL NEAR WHITCHURCH,
IN SHROPSHIRE.

Who died June 24, 1696, in the Sixty-fifth year of his age.

WITH

Dr *BATES*'s DEDICATION.

EDINBURGH:

PRINTED BY J. RUTHVEN & SONS.

1797.

TO HIS MUCH HONOURED FRIEND,

SIR *HENRY ASHURST*, Bart.

SIR,

THE ministers of the gospel are, in the scripture-language, Stars in the right hand of Christ, to signify their diffusive light, and beneficial influences. As in the future state of the resurrection, some Stars shall differ from others in glory; so in the present state of the regeneration, some ministers are distinguished from others, by a brighter eminence in their endowments, and a more powerful emanation of light in their preaching. Of this select number was Mr Philip Henry, in whom there was a union of those real excellencies of parts, learning, and divine graces, that signalized him among his brethren. This does evidently appear in the narrative of his life, drawn by one very fit to do it: as having had entire knowledge of him, by long and intimate conversation; and having, by his holy instructions, and the impression of his example, been made partaker of the same sanctifying Spirit. The describing the external actions of saints, without observing the holy principles and affections from whence they derived their life and purity, is a defective and irregular representation of them. 'Tis as if an account were given of the riches and fœcundity of the earth, from the flowers and fruits that grow upon it, without considering the mines of precious metals contained in its bosom. Now only an inward christian that has felt the power of religion in his heart, can, from the reflection upon himself, and his uncounterfeit experience, discover the operations of grace in the breasts of others.

Mr Henry was dedicated to the service of Christ by his mother in his tender age. His first love and desires (when he was capable to make a judicious choice) were set upon God. He entered early into the ministry, and consecrated all the powers of his soul, understanding, memory, will, and affections, with his time

and

The Dedication.

and strength, to the service of Christ. And such was the grace and favour of God to him, that he lost no days in his flourishing age, by satisfying the voluptuous appetites; nor in his declining age by diseases and infirmities, but incessantly applied himself to his spiritual work. He was called to a private place in Wales, but his shining worth could not be shaded in a corner. A confluence of people from other parts attended on his ministry. Indeed the word of truth that dies in the mouths of the cold and carelefs, (for they are not all saints that serve in the sanctuary) had life and spirit in his preaching; for it proceeded from a heart burning with zeal for the honour of Christ and salvation of souls. Accordingly he suited his discourses to the wife and the weak; and imitated the prophet, who contracted his stature to the dead body of the widow's son, applying his mouth to the mouth of the child, to inspire the breath of life into him. The poor and despised were instructed by him, with the same compassionate love and diligence as the rich, notwithstanding the civil distinction of persons, which will shortly vanish for ever; for he considered their souls were of the same precious and immortal value. In the administration of the Lord's, Supper, he exprest the just temperament of sweetness and severity: with melting compassion he invited all relenting and returning sinners to come to Christ, and receive their pardon sealed with his blood: but he was so jealous of the honour of Christ, that he deterred, by the most fearful consequences, the rebellious that indulged their lusts, from coming to partake of the feast of the unspotted Lamb. He was not allured by temporal advantage (which is the mark of a mercenary) to leave the first place, where by the divine disposal he was seated.

When the fatal Bartholomew-day came, though he had fair hopes of preferment, by his attendance upon the King and Duke of York, in their early age, of which the remembrance might have been revived; yet he was guided by a superior spirit, and imitated the

self-

self-denial of Moses (a duty little understood, and less practised, by the earthly-minded) "rather choosing to "suffer affliction with the people of God, than to en- "joy the good things of this world." As the light of heaven, when the air is stormy and disturbed, does not lose the rectitude of its rays; so his enlightened conscience did not bend in compliance with the terms of conformity, but he obeyed its sincere judgment.

After his being expelled from the place of his publick ministry, his deportment was becoming a son of peace. He refused not communion with the church of England, in the ordinances of the gospel, so far as his conscience permitted. Yet he could not desert the duty of his office, to which he was, with sacred solemnity set apart. He was faithful to improve opportunities for serving the interest of souls, notwithstanding the severities inflicted on him. And after the restoring our freedom of preaching, he continued in the performance of his delightful work, till death put a period to his labours.

After this account of him as a minister of Christ, I will glance upon his carriage as a christian. His conversation was so holy and regular, so free from taint, that he was unaccusable by his enemies: they could only object his nonconformity as a crime. But his vigilant and tender conscience discovered the spots of sin in himself, which so affected his soul, that he desired repentance might accompany him to the gate of heaven: an excellent testimony of humility, the inseparable character of a saint. His love to God was supreme, which was declared by his chosen hours of communion with him every day. The union of affections is naturally productive of union in conversation. Accordingly our Saviour promises, " He that loveth me, shall " be loved of my Father; and I will love him, and " will manifest myself to him:" and he repeats the promise, " If a man love me, he will keep my words: " and my Father will love him, and we will come to " him, and make our abode with him." To his special

cial and singular love to God, was joined a universal love to men: he did good to all according to his ability. His forgiving of injuries, that rare and difficult duty, was eminently conspicuous in the sharpest provocations. When he could not excuse the offence, he would pardon the offender, and strive to imitate the perfect model of charity expreſt in our suffering Saviour, who, in the extremity of his sufferings, when resentments are most quick and sensible, prayed for his cruel persecutors. His filial trust in God was correspondent to God's fatherly providence to him. This was his support in times of trial, and maintained an equal temper in his mind, and tenor in his conversation. In short, he led a life of evangelical perfection, most worthy to be honourably preserved in the memory of future times. The following narrative of it, if read with an observing eye, how inſtructive and affecting will it be to ministers, and apt to transform them into his likeness!

Thus, Sir, I have given a short view of the life of that man, for whom you had such a high veneration and dear love. It argues a clearer spirit and a diviner temper than is usual in persons of conspicuous quality, when holiness is so despicably mean in the esteem of carnal men, to value it above all titles and treasures, and the perishing pride of this world. I am perswaded it will be very pleasing to you, that your name and excellent Mr Henry's, are joined in the same papers.

I am,

SIR,

Your very humble and faithful servant,

WILLIAM BATES.

PREFACE.

THAT which we aim at in this undertaking, and which we would set before us, at our entrance upon it is, not so much to embalm the memory of this good man (though that also is blessed) as to exhibit to the world a pattern of that primitive christianity, which all that knew him well, observed to be exemplified in him, while he lived; and when they saw the end of his conversation, as it were with one consent, desired a public and lasting account of, or rather demanded it, as a just debt owing to the world, by those into whose hands his papers came, as judging such an account likely to conduce much to the glory of God's grace, and to the edification of many, especially of those that were acquainted with him. He was one whom the Divine Providence did not call out (as neither did his own inclination lead him) to any very public scene of action: he was none of the forward men of the age, that make themselves talked of: the world scarce knew that there was such a man in it. But in his low and narrow sphere he was a burning and shining light, and therefore we think his pious example is the more adapted to general use, especially consisting not in the extasies and raptures of zeal and devotion, which are looked upon rather as admirable than imitable; but in the long series of an even, regular, prudent, and well-ordered conversation, which he had in the world, and in the ordinary business of it, with simplicity and godly sincerity; not with fleshly wisdom, but by the grace of God.

It hath been said, that quiet and peaceable reigns, though they are the best to live in, yet they are the worst to write of, as yielding least variety of matter for the historian's pen to work upon: but a quiet and peaceable life, in all godliness and honesty, being the sum and substance of practical christianity, the recommending of the example of such a life, in the common and familiar instances of it; together with the kind and gracious providences of God attending it, may be, if not as diverting to the curious, yet every whit as useful and instructive to the pious readers.

If any suggest, that the design of this attempt is to credit and advance a party, let them know, that Mr Henry was a man of no party, but true catholick christianity (not debauched by bigotry, nor leavened by any private opinions or interests) was his very temper and genius.

Ac-

Preface.

According to the excellent and royal laws of this holy religion, his life was led with a strict and conscientious adherence to truth and equity; a great tenderness and inoffensiveness to all mankind; and a mighty tincture of sincere piety and devotedness to God: and according to those sacred rules we shall endeavour, in justice to him, as well as to our reader, to represent him in the following account; and if any thing should drop from our pen, which might justly give offence to any, (which we promise industriously to avoid,) we desire it may be looked upon as a false stroke; and so far not truly representing him, who was so blameless and harmless, and without rebuke.

Much of our materials for this structure we have out of his own papers, (especially his diary,) for by them his picture may be drawn nearest to the life, and from thence we may take the truest idea of him, and of the spirit he was of. Those notes being intended for his own private use in the review, and never communicated to any person whatsoever; and appearing here (as they ought to do) in their own native dress, the candid reader will excuse it, if sometimes the expressions should seem abrupt; they are the genuine, unforced, and unstudied breathings of a gracious soul; and we hope will be rather the more acceptable to those, who, through grace, are conscious to themselves of the same devout and pious motions; for as in water face answers to face, so doth one sanctified and renewed soul to another; and (as Mr Baxter observes in his Preface to Mr Clark's Lives) God's graces are much the same in all his holy ones; and therefore we must not think that such instances as these are extraordinary rarities; but God hath in wonderful mercy raised up many, by whose graces even this earth is perfumed and enlightened. But if one star be allowed to differ from another star in glory; perhaps our reader will say, when he hath gone through the following account, that Mr Henry may be ranked among those of the first magnitude.

AN

AN
ACCOUNT
OF THE
LIFE AND DEATH
OF
Mr *PHILIP HENRY*, &c:

CHAP. I:
Mr Philip Henry's *Birth, Parentage, early Piety, and Education at School.*

HE was born at Whitehall, in Weftminfter, on Wednefday 24th Auguft 1631, being Bartholomew-day. I find ufually, in his diary, fome pious remark or other upon the annual return of his birthday: as in one year he notes, that the Scripture mentions but two who obferved their birth-day with feafting and joy, and they were neither of them copies to be written after, viz. Pharaoh, Gen. xl. 20. and Herod, Mat. xiv. 6. " But (faith he) I rather ob-
" ferve it as a day of mourning and humiliation, be-
" caufe fhapen in iniquity, and conceived in fin."
And when he had compleated the thirtieth year of his age, he noted this, " So old, and no older, Alex-
" ander was when he had conquered the great world;
" but (faith he) I have not yet fubdued the little
" world, myfelf." At his thirty-third year he hath this humble reflection; " A long time lived to fmall
" purpofe, What fhall I do to redeem it?" And at another, " I may mourn as Cæfar did when he reflec-
" ted upon Alexander's early atchievements, that
" others, younger than I am, have done much more

A than

than I have done for God, the God of my life." And (to mention no more) when he had lived forty-two years, he thus writes; " I would be loth to live it " over again, left, inftead of making it better, I fhould " make it worfe; and befides, every year. and day " fpent on earth is loft in heaven." This laſt note minds me of a paffage I have heard him tell of a friend of his, who being grown into years, was afked how old he was, and anfwer'd, On the wrong fide of fifty: which (faid Mr Henry) he fhould not have faid ; for if he was going to heaven, it was the right fide of · fifty.

He always kept a will by him ready made; and it was his cuſtom yearly, upon the return of his birthday, to review, and (if occafion were) to renew and alter it: for it is good to do that at a fet time, which it is very good to do at fome time. The laſt will he made bears date, " This 24th day of Auguft 1695, " being the day of the year on which I was born " 1631, and alfo the day of the year on which by law " I died, as did alfo near two thoufand faithful mini- " fters of Jefus Chriſt, 1662 ;" alluding to that claufe in the Act of Uniformity, which difpofeth of the places and benefices of minifters not conforming, as if they were naturally dead.

His father's name was John Henry, the fon of Henry Williams of Britton's Ferry, betwixt Neath and Swanfey, in Glamorganfhire. According to the old Welfh cuftom, (fome fay conformable to that of the ancient Hebrews, but now almoft in all places laid afide,) the father's Chriſtian name was the fon's firname. He had left his native country, and his father's houfe very young, unprovided for by his relations ; but it pleafed God to blefs his ingenuity and induſtry with a confiderable income afterwards, which enabled him to live comfortably himfelf, to bring up his children well, and to be kind to many of his relations ; but public events making againſt him at his latter end, when he died he left little behind him for his children,

but

but God gracioufly took care of them. Providence brought this Mr John Henry, when he was young, to be the Earl of Pembroke's gentleman, whom he ferved many years: the Earl, coming to be Lord Chamberlain, preferred him to be the King's fervant: he was firft made keeper of the orchard at Whitehall, and afterwards page of the back ftairs to the King's fecond fon, James Duke of York, which place obliged him to a perfonal attendance upon the Duke in his chamber. He lived and died a courtier, a hearty mourner for his royal mafter King Charles the Firft, whom he did not long furvive. He continued, during all the wartime, in his houfe at Whitehall, though the profits of his places ceafed. The King paffing by his door, under a guard, to take water, when he was going to Weftminfter, to that which they call'd his trial, inquired for his old fervant, Mr John Henry, who was ready to pay his due refpects to him, and prayed God to blefs his Majefty, and to deliver him out of the hands of his enemies, for which the guard had like to have been rough upon him.

His mother was Mrs Magdalen Rochdale, of the parifh of St Martins-in-the-Fields, in Weftminfter. She was a virtuous, pious gentlewoman, and one that feared God above many: fhe was altogether dead to the vanities and pleafures of the court, though fhe lived in the midft of them. She looked well to the ways of her houfehold; prayed with them daily, catechized her children, and taught them the good knowledge of the Lord betimes. I have heard him fpeak of his learning Mr Perkins his fix principles when he was very young; and he often mentioned, with thankfulnefs to God, his great happinefs in having fuch a mother, who was to him as Lois and Eunice were to Timothy, acquainting him with the fcriptures from his childhood; and there appearing in him early inclinations both to learning and piety, fhe devoted him in his tender years to the fervice of God in the work of the miniftry. She died of a confumption 6th March 1645, leaving behind her only this fon and five daughters. A little before fhe died, fhe had this faying, " My " head is in heaven, and my heart is in heaven; it is " but one ftep more, and I fhall be there too."

His fufceptors in baptifm were Philip Earl of Pembroke (who gave him his name, and was kind to him as long as he lived, as was alfo his fon Philip after him) James Earl of Carlifle, and the Countefs of Salifbury.

Prince Charles and the Duke of York being fomewhat near of an age to him, he was in his childhood very much an attendant upon them in their play, and they were often with him at his father's houfe, and were wont to tell him what preferment he fhould have at court, as foon as he was fit for it. He kept a book to his dying day, which the Duke of York gave him: and I have heard him bewail the lofs of two curious pictures, which he gave him likewife. Archbifhop Laud took a particular kindnefs to him when he was a child, becaufe he would be very officious to attend at the water-gate (which was part of his father's charge in Whitehall) to let the Archbifhop through when he came late from council, to crofs the water to Lambeth.

Thefe circumftances of his childhood he would fometimes fpeak of among his friends, not as glorying in them, but taking occafion from thence to blefs God for his deliverance from the fnares of the court, in the midft of which it is fo very hard to maintain a good confcience and the power of religion, that it hath been faid (though bleffed be God, it is not a rule without exception) *Exeat ex aulo qui velit effe pius.* The breaking up and fcattering of the court, by the calamities of 1641, as it dafhed the expectations of his court-preferments, fo it prevented the danger of court-entanglements: and though it was not, like Mofes's, a choice of his own, when come to years, to quit the court; yet when he was come to years, he always expreffed a great fatisfaction in his removal from it, and bleffed God, who chofe his inheritance fo much the better for him.

Yet

The Life of Mr Philip Henry.

Yet it may not be improper to obferve here what was obvious, as well as amiable to all who convers'd with him; viz. that he had the moſt ſweet and obliging air of courteſy and civility that could be; which ſome attributed in part to his early education at court. His mien and carriage was always ſo very decent and reſpectful, that it could not but win the hearts of all he had to do with. Never was any man further from that rudeneſs and moroſeneſs which ſome ſcholars, and too many that profeſs religion, either wilfully affect, or careleſly allow themſelves in, ſometimes to the reproach of their profeſſion. 'Tis one of the laws of our holy religion, exemplified in the converſation of this good man, to honour all men. Sanctify'd civility is a great ornament to chriſtianity. It was a ſaying he often uſed, " Religion doth not deſtroy good manners;" and yet he was very far from any thing of vanity in apparel, or formality of compliment in addreſs; but his converſation was all natural and eaſy to himſelf and others, and nothing appeared in him which even a ſevere critick could juſtly call affected. This temper of his tended very much to the adorning of the doctrine of God our Saviour; and the general tranſcript of ſuch an excellent copy would do much towards the healing of thoſe wounds which religion had received in the houſe of her friends by the contrary. But to return to his ſtory :----

The firſt Latin ſchool he went to was at St Martins' church, under the teaching of a Mr Bonner. Afterwards he was removed to Batterſey, where a Mr Wells was his ſchool-maſter. The grateful mention which in ſome of his papers he makes of theſe that were the guides and inſtructors of his childhood and youth, brings to mind that French proverb to this purpoſe: " To father, teacher, and God all-ſufficient, " none can render equivalent."

But in the year 1643, when he was about twelve years old, he was admitted into Weſtminſter-ſchool, in the fourth form, under Mr Thomas Vincent, then

uſher,

usher, whom he would often speak of, as a most able, diligent school-master; and one who grieved so much at the dullness and non-proficiency of any of his scholars, that, falling into a consumption, I have heard Mr Henry say of him, That he even killed himself with false Latin.

A while after, he was taken into the upper school, under Mr Richard Busby (afterwards Dr Busby) and in October 1645 he was admitted King's scholar, and was first of the election, partly by his own merit, and partly by the interest of the Earl of Pembroke.

Here he profited greatly in school-learning, and all his days retained his improvements therein to admiration. When he was in years, he would readily, in discourse, quote passages out of the classick authors that were not common, and had them *ad unguem*, and yet rarely us'd any such things in his preaching, (tho' sometimes, if very apposite, he inserted them in his notes.) He was very ready and exact in the Greek accents, the quantities of words, and all the several kinds of Latin verse; and often pressed it upon young scholars, in the midst of their university-learning, not to forget their school authors.

Here and before, his usual recreation at vacant times was, either reading the printed accounts of publick occurrences, or attending the courts at Westminsterhall, to hear the trials and arguments there, which I have heard him say, he hath often done to the loss of his dinner, and oftner of his play.

But *paulo majora canamus*—Soon after those unhappy wars begun, there was a daily morning-lecture set up at the Abby-Church, between six and eight of the clock, and preached by seven worthy members of the Assembly of Divines in course, *viz.* Mr Marshal, Mr Palmer, Mr Herl, Dr Staunton, Mr Nye, Mr Whitaker, and Mr Hill. It was the request of his pious mother to Mr Busby, that he would give her son leave to attend that lecture daily; which he did, not abating any thing of his school exercise, in which he kept pace with the rest; but only dispensing with his

ab-

absence for that hour: and the Lord was pleased to make good impressions on his soul, by the sermons he heard there. His mother also took him with her every Thursday to Mr Case's lecture at St Martins. On the Lord's days he sat under the powerful ministry of Mr Stephen Marshall, in the morning, at New-Chapel; in the afternoon at St Margarets, Westminster (which was their parish church:) in the former place Mr Marshall preached long from Phil. ii. 5, 6, &c. in the latter, from John viii. 36. of our freedom by Christ. This minister, and this ministry, he would, to his last, speak of with great respect, and thankfulness to God, as that by which he was, through grace, in the beginning of his days begotten again to a lively hope. I have heard him speak of it, as the saying of some wise men at that time, That if all the Presbyterians had been like Mr Steven Marshall, and all the Independents like Mr Jeremiah Burroughs, and all the Episcopal men like Archbishop Usher, the breaches of the church would soon have been heal'd. He also attended constantly upon the monthly fasts at St Margarets, where the best and ablest ministers of England preached before the then House of Commons; and the service of the day was carried on with great strictness and solemnity, form eight in the morning till four in the evening. It was his constant practice, from eleven or twelve years old, to write (as he could) all the sermons he heard, which he kept very carefully, transcribed many of them fair over after, and notwithstanding his many removes, they are yet forthcoming.

At these monthly fasts (as he himself hath recorded it) he had often sweet meltings of soul in prayer, and confession of sin, (particularly once with special remark, when Mr William Bridge of Yarmouth prayed) and many warm and lively truths came home to his heart, and he daily increased in that wisdom and knowledge which is to salvation. Read his reflections upon this, which he wrote many years after:

"If

"If ever any child (faith he) fuch as I then was, between the tenth and fifteenth years of my age, enjoy'd line upon line, precept upon precept, I did. And was it in vain? I truft not altogether in vain. My foul rejoiceth and is glad at the remembrance of it; the word diftilled as the dew, and dropt as the rain: I lov'd it and lov'd the meffengers of it; their very feet were beautiful to me. And, Lord, what a mercy was it, that, at a time when the poor countries were laid wafte, when the noife of drums and trumpets, and the clattering of arms was heard there, and the way to Zion mourn'd, that then my lot fhould be where there was peace and quietnefs, where the voice of the turtle was heard, and there was great plenty of gofpel-opportunities? Blefs the Lord, O my foul! as long as I live, I will blefs the Lord, I will praife my God while I have my being. Had it been only the reftraint that it laid upon me, whereby I was kept from the common fins of other children and youths; fuch as curfing, fwearing, fabbath-breaking, and the like; I were bound to be very thankful: but that it prevailed through grace effectually to bring me to God, how much am I indebted, and what fhall I render!"

Thus you fee how the dews of Heaven foftened his heart by degrees.—From thefe early experiences of his own.

1. He would blame thofe who laid fo much ftrefs on people's knowing the exact time of their converfion, which he thought was with many not poffible to do. Who can fo foon be aware of the day-break, or of the fpringing up of the feed fown? The work of grace is better known in its effects than in its caufes.

He would fometimes illuftrate this by that faying of the blind man to the Pharifees, who were fo critical in examining the recovery of his fight: This and t'other I know not concerning it, but "this one thing I know, "that whereas I was blind, now I fee; John ix. 25."

2. He

2. He would bear his testimony to the comfort and benefit of early piety, and recommend it to all young people, as a good thing to bear the yoke of the Lord Jesus in youth. He would often witness against that wicked Proverb, " A young Saint, an old Devil;" and would have it said rather, " A young Saint, an " old Angel." He observed it concerning Obadiah (and he was a courtier) that he " feared the Lord " from his youth, 1 Kings xviii. 12.; and it is said of him, ver. 3. that he " feared the Lord greatly." Those that would come to fear God greatly, must learn to fear him from their youth. No man did his duty so naturally as Timothy did (Phil. ii. 20.) who from a child knew the Holy Scriptures: he would sometimes apply to this that common saying, " He that would " thrive, must rise at five;" and in dealing with young people, how earnestly would he press this upon them: I tell you, " You cannot begin too soon to be religi-" ous, but you may put it off too long." Manna must be gathered early; and he that is the first, must have the first. He often inculcated Eccl. xii. 1. " Remem-" ber thy Creator in the days of thy youth," or, as in the original, " the days of thy choice:" thy choice days, and thy chusing days.

I remember a passage of his in a lecture sermon, in the year 1674, which much affected many; he was preaching on that text, Matt. xi. 30. " My yoke is " easy;" and after many things insisted upon, to prove the yoke of Christ an easy yoke, he at last appealed to the experiences of all that had drawn in that yoke: " Call now, if there be any that will answer you, and " to which of the saints will you turn?" turn to which you will, and they will all agree that they have found " wisdom's ways pleasantness," and " Christ's com-" màndments not grievous: and (saith he) I will here " witness for one, who through grace have in some " poor measure been drawing in this yoke now above " thirty years, and I have found it an easy yoke, and " like my choice too well to change."

3. He would also recommend it to the care of parents, to bring their children betimes to public ordinances. He would say, that they are capable sooner than we are aware, of receiving good by them. The scripture takes notice more than once of the little ones in the solemn assemblies of the faithful, Deut. xxix. 11. Ezra x. 1. Acts xxi. 5. If we lay our children by the pool-side, who knows but the blessed Spirit may help them in, and heal them. He used to apply that scripture to this, Cant. i. 8. Those that would have communion with Christ, must not only go forth by the footsteps of the flock themselves, but feed their kids too; their children or other young ones that are under their charge, " beside the Shepherd's tents."

4. He would also recommend to young people the practice of writing sermons. He himself did it, not only when he was young, but continued it constantly till within a few years before he died, when the decay of his sight obliging him to the use of spectacles, made writing not so ready to him as it had been. He never wrote short-hand, but had an excellent art of taking the substance of a sermon in a very plain and legible hand, and with a great deal of ease. And the sermons he wrote he kept by him, in such method and order, that by the help of indexes, which he made to them, he could readily turn almost to any sermon that ever he heard, where he noted the preacher, place, and time; and this he called " hearing for the time " to come." He recommended this practice to others, as a means to engage their attention in hearing, and to prevent drowsiness, and to help their memories after hearing, when they come either to meditate upon what they have heard themselves, or to communicate it to others; and many have had reason to bless God for his advice and instruction herein: he would advise people sometimes to look over the sermon-notes that they had written, as a ready way to revive the good impressions of the truths they had heard, and would blame those who made waste-paper of them;

for

for (faith he) "the day is coming, when you will ei-
"ther thank God for them, or heartily wish you had
"never written them."

But it is time we return to Westminster-school, where, having begun to learn Christ, we left him in the successful pursuit of other learning, under the eye and care of that great master Dr Busby; who, on the account of his pregnancy and diligence, took a particular kindness to him, call'd him his child, and would sometimes tell him he should be his heir; and there was no love lost betwixt them. Dr Busby was noted for a very severe school-master, especially in the beginning of his time. But Mr Henry would say sometimes, that as in so great a school there was need of a strict discipline, so for his own part, of the four years he was in the school, he never felt the weight of his hand but once, and then (faith he in some of the remarks of his youth which he wrote long after,) I deserved it; for being monitor of the chamber, and according to the duty of his place, being sent out to seek one that played truant; he found him out where he had hid himself, and at his earnest request promised to make an excuse for him, and to say he could not find him; which (faith he in a penitential reflection upon it afterwards) I wickedly did. Next morning the truant coming under examination, and being asked whether he saw the monitor, said, Yes, he did: at which Dr Busby was much surprised, and turned his eye upon the monitor, with these words, " what, thou my
" son!" and gave him correction, and appointed him to make a penitential copy of Latin verses, which when he brought he gave him sixpence, and received him into his favour again.

Among the mercies of God to him in his youth (and he would say 'twere well if parents would keep an account of those for their children, till they come to be capable of doing it for themselves, and then to set them upon the doing of it,) he hath recorded a remarkable deliverance he had here at Westminster-school,

school, which was this: It was customary there, among the studious boys, for one or two, or more, to sit up the former part of the night at study, and when they went to bed, about midnight to call others; and they others at two or three a clock, as they desired. His request was to be called at twelve, and being awaked, desired his candle might be lighted, which stuck to the bed's head; but he dropt asleep again, and the candle fell, and burnt part of the bed and bolster ere he awaked; but, through God's good providence, seasonable help came in, the fire soon quenched, and he received no harm. This gave him occasion long after to say, "It is of the Lord's mercies that we are not consumed."

When he was at Westminster-school he was employed by Dr Busby, as some others of the most ingenious and industrious of his scholars were, in their reading of the Greek authors, to collect, by his direction, some materials for that excellent Greek grammar which the Doctor afterwards published.

But be the school ever so agreeable, youth is desirous to commence man by a removal from it: this step he took in the sixteenth year of his age. It was the ancient custom of Westminster-school, that all the King's scholars who stood candidates for an election to the University, were to receive the Lord's Supper the Easter before, which he did with the rest, in St Margaret's church, at Easter 1647; and he would often speak of the great pains which Dr Busby took with his scholars that were to approach to that solemn ordinance, for several weeks before, at stated times; with what skill and seriousness of application, and manifest concern for their souls, he opened to them the nature of the ordinance, and of the work they had to do in it; and instructed them what was to be done in preparation for it; and this he made a business of, appointing them the religious exercises instead of their school exercises. What success this had, through the grace of God, upon young Mr Henry (to whom the doctor

had

had a particular regard) read from his own hand:
" There had been treaties (faith he) before, between
" my foul and Jefus Chrift, with fome weak overtures
" towards him; but then, then I think it was that the
" match was made, the knot tied: then I fet myfelf,
" in the ftrength of divine grace, about the great work
" of felf-examination, in order to repentance; and
" then I repented; that is, folemnly and ferioufly,
" with fome poor meltings of foul; I confeffed my
" fins before God, original and actual, judging and
" condemning myfelf for them, and cafting away from
" me all my tranfgreffions, receiving Chrift Jefus the
" Lord, as the Lord my righteoufnefs, and devoting
" and dedicating my whole felf abfolutely and unre-
" fervedly to his fear and fervice. After which, com-
" ing to the ordinance, there, there I received him
" indeed, and he became mine, I fay mine. Blefs the
" Lord, O my foul!"

Dr Bufby's agency, under God, in this bleffed work, he makes a very grateful mention of, in divers of his papers; " The Lord recompenfe it (faith he) a thou-
" fand fold, into his bofom."

I have heard him tell how much he furprifed the doctor the firft time he waited upon him after he was turned out by the Act of Uniformity; for when the doctor afked him, " Pr'ythee (child) what made thee
" a nonconformift?" " Truly, Sir, (faith Mr Henry,)
" you made me one;" for you taught me thofe things that hindered me from conforming.

" Encouraged by this experience, I have myfelf
" (faith he in one of his papers) taken like pains with
" divers others at their firft admiffion to the Lord's
" table, and have, through grace, feen the comfort-
" able fruits of it, both in mine own children, and
" others. To God be the glory."

Mr Jeremy Dyke's book of the Sacrament, I have heard him fay, was of great ufe to him at that time, in his preparation for that ordinance.

Thus was this great concern happily fettled before
his

his launching out into the world, which through grace he had all his days more or lefs the comfort of, in an even ferenity of mind, and a peaceful expectation of the glory to be revealed.

May 17, 1647, he was chofen from Weftminfter-fchool to Chrift-church in Oxford, *jure loci*, with four others, of which he had the fecond place. At his election he was very much countenanced and fmiled upon by his god-father the Earl of Pembroke, who was one of the electors.

CHAP. II.
His Years fpent at Oxford.

THough he was chofen to the Univerfity in May, yet being then young, under fixteen, and in love with his fchool-learning, he made no great hafte thither. 'Twas in December following, 1647, that he removed to Oxford. Some merciful providences in his journey (he being a young traveller) affected him much, and he ufed to fpeak of them, with a fenfe of God's goodnefs to him in them, according to the impreffions then made by them; and he hath recorded them with this thankful note, " That there may be a great mer-" cy in a fmall matter :" as the care that was taken of him by ftrangers, when he fainted and was fick in his inn the firft night, and his cafual meeting with Mr Annefly, fon to the Vifcount Valentia (who was chofen from Weftminfter-fchool at the fame time that he was) when his other company, going another way, had left him alone, and utterly at a lofs what to do. Thus, the fenfible remembrance of old mercies may anfwer the intention of new ones, which is to engage our obedience to God, and to encourage our dependance on him.

Being come to Oxford, he was immediately entered commoner of Chrift-church, where Dr Samuel Fell

was

was then dean; the tutor affigned to him and the reft of that election was Mr Underwood, a very learned, ingenious gentleman.

His godfather, the Earl of Pembroke, had given him ten pounds to buy him a gown, to pay his fees, and to fet out with. This in his papers he puts a remark upon, as a feafonable mercy in regard of fome ftraits, which providence, by the calamity of the times, had brought his father to. God had taught him from his youth that excellent principle, which he adhered to all his days, that " every creature is that to us, and " no more, than God makes it to be;" and therefore, while " many feek the ruler's favour," and fo expect to " make their fortunes," as they call it, feeing " every man's judgment proceedeth from the Lord;" it is our wifdom to feek his favour, who is the ruler of rulers, and that is an effectual way to make fure our happinefs.

To the proper ftudies of this place he now vigoroufly addreffed himfelf; but ftill retaining a great kindnefs for the claffick authors, and the more polite exercifes he loved fo well at Weftminfter-fchool.

He was admitted ftudent of Chrift-church March 24, 1647-8, by Dr Henry Hammond, that great man, then Sub-Dean, who call'd him his god-brother, the Earl of Pembroke being his god-father alfo, and Prince Henry the other, who gave him his name.

The vifitation of the Univerfity by the Parliament happened to be in the very next month after. Oxford had been for a good while in the hands of the Parliament, and no change made; but now the Earl of Pembroke, and feveral others thereunto appointed, came hither to fettle things upon a new bottom. The account Mr Henry in his papers gives of this affair, is to this purpofe: The fole queftion which the vifitors propos'd to each perfon, high and low, in every College, that had any place of profit, was this, " Will you fub-
" mit to the power of the Parliament in this prefent
" vifitation?" to which all were to give in their anfwer

fwer in writing, and accordingly were either difplaced or continued. Some cheerfully complied, others abfolutely refufed (among whom he would fometimes tell of one that was but of his ftanding, who gave in this bold anfwer, " I neither can, nor will fubmit to the " power of the Parliament in this prefent vifitation; " I fay I cannot, I fay I will not," (J. C.) Others anfwered doubtfully, pleading youth and ignorance in fuch matters. Mr Henry's anfwer was, " I fubmit to " the power of the Parliament in the prefent vifitation, " as far as I may with a fafe confcience and without " perjury." His reafon for the laft falvo was, becaufe he had taken the oaths of allegiance and fupremacy a little before, at his admiffion; which he was (according to the character of the good man, that he fears an oath) very jealous of doing any thing to contradict or infringe; which hath made him fometimes fignify fome diflike of that practice of adminiftring oaths to fuch as were fcarce paft children, who could hardly be fuppofed to take them with judgement, as oaths fhould be taken. However, this anfwer of his fatisfied; and by the favour of the Earl of Pembroke he was continued in his ftudent's place. But great alterations were made in that, as well as in other Colleges, very much (no queftion) to the hinderance and difcouragement of young fcholars, who came hither to get learning, not to judge of the rights of government. Dr Samuel Fell, the Dean, was removed, and Dr Edward Reynolds, afterwards Bifhop of Norwich, was put in his room: Dr Hammond, and all the canons, except Dr Wall, were difplaced, and Mr Wilkingfon, Mr Pocock, and others of the Parliament friends, were preferred to their places. His thoughts of this, in the reflection long after, was, that milder methods might have done better, and would have been a firmer eftablifhment to the new intereft: but confidering that many of thofe who were put out (being in expectation of a fudden change, which came not of many years after) were exafperating in their carriage towards the vifitors; and that the Parliament

(who

(who at this time rode mafters) had many of their own friends ready for Univerfity-preferments, (which Oxford, having been from the beginning a garrifon for the king, they had been long kept out of) and thefe they were concerned to oblige, it was not ftrange if they took fuch ftrict methods. And yet nothing being required but a bare fubmiffion, which might be interpreted but as crying Quarter, he thought, withal, that it could not be faid the terms were hard, efpecially (faith he) if compar'd with thofe of another nature impofed fince.

Among other ftudent-mafters removed, his tutor, Mr Underwood, was one, which he often bewail'd as ill for him, for he was a good fcholar, and one that made it his bufinefs to look after his pupils, who were very likely, by the bleffing of God, to have profited under his conduct: but upon the removal of Mr Underwood, he, with fome others, were turned over to Mr Finmore, who was then in with that intereft which was uppermoft, and was afterwards prebendary of Chefter; a perfon (as he notes) able enough, but not willing to employ his abilities for the good of thofe that were committed to his charge; towards whom he had little more than the name of a tutor. This he lamented as his infelicity, at his firft fetting out. But it pleas'd God to give him an intereft in the affections of a young man, an under-graduate then, but two or three years his fenior from Weftminfter, a Mr Richard Bryan, who took him to be his chamber-fellow while he continued at Oxford, read to him, looked over his ftudies, and directed him in them. Of this gentleman he makes a very honourable mention, as one who was, through God's bleffing, an inftrument of much good to him. Mr John Fell alfo, the Dean's fon (afterward himfelf dean of Chrift-church, and bifhop of Oxford) taking pity on him, and fome others that were neglected, voluntarily read to them for fome time; a kindnefs which he retain'd a very grateful fenfe of, and for which he much honour'd that learned and worthy perfon. C Here

Here he duly performed the college-exercises, disputations every day, in term-time; themes and verses once a week, and declamations when it came to his turn; in which performances he frequently came off with very great applause: and many of his manuscripts, which remain, shew how well he improved his name there.

And yet in some reflections I find under his hand, written long after (wherein he looks back upon his early days) he chargeth it upon himself, that for a good while after he came to the university (though he was known not to be inferior to any of his standing, in publick exercises, yet) he was too much a stranger to that hard study which afterwards he became acquainted with, and that he lost a deal of time which might have been better improved. Thus he is pleased to accuse himself of that which (for ought I ever heard) no one else did, or could accuse him of. But the truth is, in all the secret accounts he kept of himself, he appears to have had a very quick and deep sense of his own failings and infirmities, in the most minute instances,— the loss of time, weakness and distractions in holy duties; not improving opportunities of doing good to others, and the like; lamentably bewailing these imperfections, and charging them upon himself, with as great expressions of shame and sorrow, and self-abhorrence; and crying out as earnestly for pardon and forgiveness in the blood of Jesus, as if he had been the greatest of sinners: for though he was a man that walked very closely, yet withal he walked very humbly with God, and lived a life of repentance and self-denial. This minds me of a sermon of his, which one might discern came from the heart, on that scripture, Rom. vii. 24. " O wretched man that I am, who shall deliver me from " the body of this death!" a strange complaint (saith he) to come from the mouth of one who had learned in every state to be content. Had I been to have given my thoughts (said he) concerning Paul, I should have said, O blessed man that thou art, that hast been in the
third

third heaven, a great apoſtle, a ſpiritual father to thouſands, &c. and yet a wretched man all this while, in his own account and eſteem. He never complains thus of the bonds and afflictions that did abide him, the priſons that were frequent, the ſtripes above meaſure; but the body of death, that is, the body of ſin, that was it he groaned under. How feelingly did he obſerve from thence, " That the remainders of indwelling " corruption are a very grievous burthen to a gracious " ſoul."

But to return: It may not be amiſs to ſet down the cauſes to which he aſcribes his loſs of time when he came firſt to the univerſity. One was, that he was young, too young, and underſtood not the day of his opportunities, which made him afterwards adviſe his friends not to thruſt their children forth too ſoon from ſchool to the univerſity, though they may ſeem ripe, in reſpect of learning, till they have diſcretion to manage themſelves: while they are children, what can be expected but that they ſhould mind childiſh things? Another was, that coming from Weſtminſter-ſchool, his attainments in ſchool-learning were beyond what generally others had that came from other ſchools; ſo that he was tempted to think there was no need for him to ſtudy much, becauſe it was ſo eaſy to him to keep pace with others; which, he ſaith, was the thing Dr Caldecott, chaplain to the Earl of Pembroke, and his great friend, warned him of at his coming to Oxford. Another was, that there were two ſorts of perſons his contemporaries, ſome of the new ſtamp, that came in by the viſitation, and were divers of them ſerious, pious young men, but of ſmall ability, comparatively, for learning, and thoſe for that reaſon he deſired not to have much fellowſhip with. But there were others that were of the old ſpirit and way, enemies to the parliament, and the reformation they made; and theſe were the better ſcholars, but generally not the better men. With them for a while he ſtruck in, becauſe of their learning, and converſed moſt with them: but he soon found it a snare to him, and that it took him off from the life of religion, and communion with God, *Elanguescere mox cepit* (saith he in a Latin narrative of his younger years) *pristinæ pietatis ardor*, &c. but " for ever praised be the riches of God's free grace " (saith he, in another account) that he was pleased " still to keep his hold of me; and not to let me alone " when I was running from him, but set his hand " again the second time, (as the expression is, Isaiah " xi. 11.) to snatch me as a brand out of the fire." His recovery from this snare he would call a kind of second conversion; so much was he affected with the preventing grace of God in it, and sensible of a double bond to be for ever thankful, as well as of an engagement to be watchful and humble. 'Twas a saying of his, " He that stumbleth and doth not fall, gets ground " by his stumble."

At the latter end of the year 1648 he had leave given him to make a visit to his father at Whitehall, with whom he staid some time: there he was Jan. 30. when the King was beheaded, and with a very sad heart saw that tragical blow given. Two things he used to speak of, that he took notice of himself that day, which I know not whether any of the historians mention. One was, that at the instant when the blow was given, there was such a dismal, universal groan, among the thousands of people that were within sight of it (as it were with one consent) as he never heard before; and desired he might never hear the like again, nor see such a cause for it. The other was, that immediately after the stroke was struck, there was, according to order, one troop marching from Charing-cross towards King-street, and another from King-street towards Charing-cross, purposely to disperse and scatter the people, and to divert the dismal thoughts which they could not but be fill'd with, by driving them to shift every one for his own safety. He did upon all occasions testify his abhorrence of this unparallel'd action, which he always said was a thing that could not be justify'd,

and

and yet he faid he faw not how it could be called a national fin; for, as the king urged upon his trial, it was certain that not one man of ten in the kingdom did confent to it*: nor could it be call'd the fin of the Long Parliament, for far the greateft part of them were all that time, while the thing was in agitation, imprifon'd and kept under a force, and fcarce twenty-feven of the forty that were left to carry the name of a parliament, did give their vote for it; which the commiffioners for the trying of the king's judges, in the year 1660, (fome of whom had been themfelves members of the Long Parliament) urged again and again, in anfwer to that plea which the prifoners ftood fo much upon, that what they did was by authority of the parliament: but 'tis manifeft it was done by a prevailing party in the army, who (as he us'd to exprefs it) having beaten their plowfhares into fwords, could not fo eafily beat their fwords into plowfhares again, as having fought more for victory and dominion, than for peace and truth; but how far thefe men were acted and influenced by another fort of people behind the curtain, the world is not altogether ignorant. For fome years after King Charles II. came in, he obferved the yearly day of humiliation for this fin, defiring that God would not lay the guilt of blood to the charge of the nation: but afterwards finding to what purpofes it was generally obferved, and improved even to the reproach and condemning not only of the innocent but of fome of the excellent ones of the land; and noting that there is no precedent in fcripture of keeping annual days of humiliation for particular fins, efpecially after the immediate judgment is at an end, Zech. viii. 19. Heb. x. 2, 3. he took no farther notice of it; But in his diary, he adds this tender remark, (according to the fpirit he was of) " yet good men, no doubt, may obferve it to
" the

---

* See the bifhop of Chichefter's fermon before the king 30 Jan. 1697. where he faith, he did not fee how it could be call'd a national fin.

" the Lord," Rom. xiv. 6. Thus he judged not, and why then fhould he be judged?

In the year 1650-1 he took his batchelor of arts degree, and he hath recorded the goodnefs of God in raifing him up friends who helped him out in the expences. Such kindneffes have a peculiar fweetnefs in them to a good man, who fees and receives them as the kindnefs of God, and the tokens of his love.

He would often mention it with thankfulnefs to God, what great helps and advantages he had then in the univerfity, not only for learning, but for religion and piety. Serious godlinefs was in reputation; and befides the public opportunities they had, there were many of the fcholars that us'd to meet together for prayer, and Chriftian conference, to the great confirming of one another's hearts in the fear and love of God, and the preparing of them for the fervice of the church in their generation. I have heard him fpeak of the prudent method they took then about the univerfity-fermons on the Lord's day in the afternoon, which us'd to be preached by the fellows of colleges in their courfe; but, that being found not fo much for edification, Dr Owen and Dr Goodwin performed that fervice alternately, and the young mafters that were wont to preach it, had a lecture on Tuefday appointed them. The fermons he heard at Oxford he commonly wrote, not in the time of hearing, but afterwards, when he came home, in his reflection upon them, which he found a good help to his memory.

In December 1652, he proceeded mafter of arts, and in January following preached his firft fermon at South-Hinckfey in Oxfordfhire, on John viii. 34. " Whofo-" ever committeth fin, is the fervant of fin." On this occafion he writes in his diary, what was the breathing of his heart towards God, " The Lord make ufe of " me as an inftrument of his glory, and his churches " good, in this high and holy calling!"

His great parts and improvement, notwithftanding his extraordinary modefty and humility, had made him

fo

The Life of Mr PHILIP HENRY.

so well known in the university, that in the following act, in July 1653, he was chosen out of all the masters of that year, to be junior of the act, that is, to answer the philosophy questions in vesperiis, which he did with very great applause; especially for the very witty and ingenious oration which he made to the university upon that occasion. His questions were, 1. *An licitum sit carnibus vesci?* aff. 2. *An institutio academiarum sit utilis in Republica?* aff. 3. *An ingenium pendeat ab humoribus corporis?* aff. At the act in 1654 he was chosen Magister Replicans, and answered the philosophy questions *in comitiis*, with a like applause. His questions then were, 1. *An melius sit sperare quam frui?* neg. 2. *An maxima animi delectatio sit a sensibus?* neg. 3. *An utile sit peregrinari?* aff.

Dr Owen, who was then vice-chancellor, hath spoken with great commendation of these performances of Mr Henry's to some in the university afterwards, who never knew him otherwise than by report: and I have heard a worthy divine (who was somewhat his junior in the university, and there a perfect stranger to him) say, how much he admired these exercises of his, and loved him for them; and yet how much more he admired, when he afterwards became acquainted with him in the country, that so curious and polite an orator should become so profitable and powerful a preacher, and so readily lay aside the enticing words of man's wisdom, which were so easy to him.

There is a copy of Latin verses of his in print, among the poems which the university of Oxford published upon the Peace concluded with Holland in the year 1654, which shew him to be no less a poet than an orator.

He hath noted it of some pious young men, that before they removed from the university into the country, they kept a day of fasting and humiliation for the sins they had been guilty of, in that place and state. And in the visits he made afterwards to the university, he inserts into his book, as no doubt God did into his,— " a tear dropt over my university-sins."

CHAP.

CHAP. III.

His removal to Worthenbury *in* Flintſhire; *his Ordination to the Miniſtry, and his Exerciſe of it there.*

WOrthenbury is a little town by Dee ſide, in that Hundred of Flintſhire which is ſeparated ſome miles from the reſt of the county, and known by the name of Engliſh Mialors, becauſe though it is reputed in Wales, as pertaining to Flintſhire, yet in language and cuſtoms it is wholly Engliſh, and lies moſtly between Cheſhire and Shropſhire. Worthenbury was of old a parochial chapel, belonging to the rectory of Bangor, but was ſeparated from it in the year 1658, by the truſtees for uniting and dividing of pariſhes, and was made a pariſh of itſelf. But what was then done, being vacated by the king's coming in, it then came to be *in ſtatu quo,* and continued an appurtenant to Bangor, till, in the ſecond year of the reign of King William and Queen Mary, it was again, by act of Parliament, ſeparated, and made independant upon Bangor. That was the only act that paſſed the royal aſſent with the act of recognition, at the beginning of the ſecond parliament of this reign. The principal family in Worthenbury pariſh is that of the Puleſtons of Emeral. The head of the family was then John Puleſton, ſerjeant at law, one of the judges of the common-pleas.

This was the family to which Mr Henry came from Chriſt-church, preſently after he had compleated his maſter's degree, in 1653; ordered into that remote, and unto him unknown corner of the country, by that o-ver-ruling Providence which determineth the times before appointed, and the bounds of our habitation.

The judge's lady was a perſon of more than ordinary parts and wiſdom; in piety inferior to few, but in learning ſuperior to moſt of her ſex, which I could give inſtances of from what I find among Mr Henry's

papers,

papers, particularly an elegy she made upon the death of the famous Mr John Selden, who was her great friend.

This was the lady whose agency first brought Mr Henry into this country. She wrote to a friend of her's, Mr Francis Palmer, student of Christ-church, to desire him to recommend to her a young man to be in her family, and to take the over-sight of her sons (some of whom were now ready for the University) and to preach at Worthenbury on the Lord's days; for which a very honourable encouragement was promised. Mr Palmer proposed it to his friend Mr Henry, who was willing for one half year to undertake it, provided it might be required of him to preach but once on the Lord's day, and that some other supply might be got for t'other part of the day, he being now but twenty-two years of age, and newly entered upon that great work. Provided also, that he should be engaged but for half a year, as little intending to break off so soon from an academical life, which he delighted in so much. But preferring usefulness before his own private satisfaction, he was willing to make trial for a while in the country, as one that sought not his own things, but the things of Jesus Christ, to whose service in the work of the ministry he had entirely devoted himself, bending his studies wholly that way. In the latter part of his time at Oxford, as one grown weary of that which he used to say he found little to his purpose, he employed his time mostly in searching the scriptures, and collecting useful scripture-observations, which he made very familiar to him, and with which he was " throughly furnished for this good work." He got a Bible interleaved, in which he wrote short notes upon texts of scriptures as they occurred. He would often say, " I read other books, that I may be " the better able to understand the scripture."

It was a stock of scripture knowledge that he set up with, and with that he traded to good advantage. Though he was so great a master in the eloquence of Cicero,

Cicero, yet he preferred far before it that of Apollos, who was " an eloquent man, and mighty in the fcrip-" tures, Acts xviii. 24."

He bid very fair at that time for Univerfity-preferment, fuch was the reputation he had got at the late act, and fuch his intereft in Dr Owen: but the " fal-" vation of fouls" was that which his heart was upon, to which he poftponed all his other interefts.

In September 1653 he came down to Emeral, from whence a meffenger was fent on purpofe to Oxford to conduct him thither. Long after, when it had pleafed God to fettle him in that country, and to build him up into a family, he would often reflect upon his coming into it firft; what a ftranger he then was, and how far it was from his thoughts ever to have made his home in thofe parts: and paffing over the brook that parts between Flintfhire and Shropfhire, would fometimes very affectionately ufe that word of Jacob's, " With my ftaff I paffed over this Jordan, and now I " am become two bands."

At Emeral he prayed in the family, was tutor to the young gentlemen, and preached once a day at Worthenbury; other help being procured for the other part of the day, according to his requeft, out of a fear, being fo young, to take the whole work upon him. But it foon happened, that one Lord's day, the fupply that was expected failed; and fo he was neceffitated, rather than there fhould be a vacancy, to preach twice, in which he found the promife fo well fulfilled, " as " the day is, fo fhall the ftrength be;" and, " to him " that hath (i. e. that hath, and ufeth what he hath) " fhall be given, and he fhall have abundance;" that, to the great fatisfaction of his friends there, from thenceforward he waved looking out for other help than what came from above, and would fometimes fpeak of this as an inftance, that " we do not know what we can " do, till we have tried."

Here he applied himfelf to a plain and practical way of preaching, as one truly concerned for the fouls of

thofe

those he spoke to. He would say sometimes, " we stu-
" dy how to speak that you may understand us." And
" I never think I can speak plain enough when I am
" speaking about souls and their salvation." I have heard
him say, he thought it did him good, that for the first
half year of his being at Worthenbury, he had few or
no books with him, which engaged him (in studying
sermons) to a closer search of the scripture and his own
heart. What success his labours had in that parish,
which, before he came to it (I have been told) was accounted one of the most loose and prophane places in
all the country, may be gathered from a letter of the
Lady Puleston's to him, at the end of the first half year
after his coming to Emeral, when he was uncertain of
his continuance there, and inclinable to return to set-
tle at Christ-church. Take the letter at large:

" Dear Mr HENRY,
" The indisposition that my sadness hath bred,
" and the stay of Mrs V. here yesterday, hindered my
" answering your last expressions. As to ordering the
" conversation, and persevering to the practice of those
" good intents, taken up while one is in pursuit of a
" mercy, you and I will confer as God gives oppor-
" tunity, who also must give the will and the deed,
" by his Spirit, and by the rule of his word. As to
" begging that one thing for you, God forbid (as Sa-
" muel said) that I should cease to pray, &c. This I
" am sure, that having wanted hitherto a good mini-
" ster of the word among us, I have oft, by prayer and
" some tears, above five years besought God for such
" a one as yourself; which having obtained, I cannot
" yet despair, seeing he hath given us the good means,
" but he may also give us the good end. And this I
" find, that your audience is increased three for one
" in the parish (though in winter, more than formerly
" in summer,) and five for one out of other places.
" And I have neither heard of their being in the ale-
" house on our Lord's day, nor ball-playing that day,
" which

"which before you came was frequent (except that day that young Ch. preached:) I think I can name four or five in the parish, that of formal Chriſtians, are becoming, or become real: but you know all are not wrought on at firſt, by the word. (Some come in no misfortune like other men, and this is the cauſe they be ſo holden with pride, &c.) Hypocrites alſo have converted converſion itſelf: yet God may have reſerved thoſe that have not bowed the knee to Baal, &c. and may call them at the latter part of the day, though not in this half year. It is a good ſign, moſt are loth to part with you: and you have done more good in this half year than I have diſcerned theſe eighteen years: but, however, whether they will hear, or whether they will forbear, you have delivered your own ſoul. I have prayed, and do pray, ſeeing God hath ſent you, that you may be for his glory, and not for our condemnation."

It is eaſy to imagine what an encouragement this was to him thus at his firſt ſetting out to ſee of the travel of his ſoul, and what an inducement it was to him not to leave thoſe among whom God had thus owned him. However, that ſpring he returned to Oxford. The Lady Puleſton ſoon after came to him thither, with her five ſons, of whom ſhe placed the two eldeſt under his charge, in the College. In the following vacation he went to London to viſit his relations there; and there in October he received a letter from Judge Puleſton, with a very ſolemn and affectionate requeſt, ſubſcribed by the pariſhioners of Worthenbury, earneſtly deſiring his ſettlement among them, as their miniſter, which he was perſwaded to comply with, having fixed to himſelf that good rule, in the turns of his life, to "follow Providence, and not to force it:" ſo in the winter following he came down again, and ſettled with them. He continued in his ſtudent's place in Chriſt-church for two or three years, attending the ſervice of it once a year; but diſpoſing of moſt of the profit of it for the uſe of poor ſcholars there.

The

The tithe of Worthenbury belonged to Emeral family, paying some rent to the rector of Bangor; this tithe Judge Puleston was willing to give (clear of that charge) to the minister of Worthenbury for ever: but such was the peculiar and extraordinary kindness he had for Mr Henry, upon the experience of his merits, that he chose rather, by deed of indenture, bearing date 6 October 1655, between himself and Mr Henry, "In
" consideration of his being pleased to undertake the
" cure of souls, and to preach and teach, and perform
" other duties of divine service in the parish-church
" of Worthenbury (so the deed runs) to give, grant,
" and confirm for himself and his heirs, unto the said
" Philip Henry, the yearly rent of one hundred pounds,
" charged upon all his messuages, lands, and tene-
" ments in the several counties of Flint, Denbigh, and
" Chester, to be paid quarterly, until such times as
" the said Philip Henry shall be promoted or preferred
" to some other spiritual or ecclesiastical living or pre-
" ferment," with power of distress in case of non-payment. A hundred a year was more than Worthenbury tithes were worth at that time; and the manner of the gift freed the maintenance from much of that loss and incumbrance which commonly attends the gathering of tithe.

He still continued for some years in Emeral family, where he laid out himself very much for the spiritual good of the family, even of the meanest of the servants, by catechizing, repeating the sermons, and personal instruction, and he had very much comfort in the countenance and conversation of the Judge and his Lady. Yet he complains sometimes in his diary of "the snares
" and temptations that he found in his way there;" especially because some of the branches of the family, who did not patrizare, were uneasy at his being there, which made him willing to remove to a house of his own; which, when Judge Puleston perceived, in the year 1657, out of his abundant and continued kindness to him, he did, at his own proper cost and charges,

build

build him a very handsome house in Worthenbury, and settled it upon him by a lease, bearing date March 6th 1657, for threescore years, " if he should so long " continue minister at Worthenbury, and not accept of " better preferment."

He hath noted in his diary, that the very day that the workmen began the building of that house, Mr Mainwaring of Malpas preached the lecture at Bangor, from Psalm cxxvii. 1. " Except the Lord build the " house, they labour in vain that build it." There never was truth (saith he) more seasonable to any than this was to me: it was a word upon the wheels. He hath recorded it as his great care, that his affections might be kept loose from it, and that it might not encroach upon God's interest in his heart. When it was finished, he thus writes: " I do from my heart bless God, " that no hurt or harm befel any of the workmen in " the building of it."

Thus was his maintenance settled at Worthenbury. In the year 1659, he was, by a writing of Judge Puleston's, collated, nominated, and presented to the church of Worthenbury, and (the powers that then were having so appointed) he had an approbation thereof from the commissioners for approbation of publick preachers.

Some little opposition was made to his settlement at Worthenbury by Mr Fogg, then rector of Bangor, because he conceived it an intrenchment upon his right to Worthenbury, and thought it might prejudice his recovering of it by course of law. I only mention this for the sake of the note he hath upon it in his diary, which is this; " I do earnestly desire that the judge " may give Mr Fogg all reasonable satisfaction, that " there may be no appearance of wrong to him, or " any other, in this thing." And when Mr Fogg insisted upon it, that he would have Mr Henry give it under his hand, that he desired the consent of the said Mr Fogg to be minister of Worthenbury; he yielded to do it for peace-sake, and from thenceforward there

The Life of Mr PHILIP HENRY.

was an intimate and entire friendship between Mr Fogg and him.

Being thus settled at Worthenbury, his next care was touching ordination to the work of the ministry, to which he would see his call very clear, before he solemnly devoted himself to it. And though afterwards in the reflection (especially when he was silenced) it was some trouble to him, that he had so long deferred to be ordained, (and he would often, from the consideration of that, press those who intended the ministry not to put it off) yet as the times then were, there was something a reason for it.

The nearest acting class of presbyters was in the Hundred of Bradford, north in Shropshire, wherein Mr Porter of Whitchurch was the leading man, of whom Mr Baxter gives so high a character in his life, part 3. page 94. and who was one of those whom he recommended to the Lord Chancellor as fit to be made a bishop, part 2. p. 283. This class was constituted by ordinance of Parliament in April 1647; the members of it, then, were the aforesaid Mr Porter, Mr Boughy of Hodnet, Mr Houghton of Prees, Mr Parsons of Wem, and Mr John Bisby; and afterwards Mr Malden of Newport; Mr Binney of Ightfield, and Mr Steel of Hanmer (though in Flintshire) were taken in to them, and acted with them. This class, in twelve years time, publickly ordained sixty-three ministers. Mr Henry was very desirous to have been ordained at Worthenbury, *plebe præsente*, which he thought most agreeable to the intention, but the ministers were not willing to set such a precedent: however, that was one thing which occasioned the delay, so that he was not ordained till 16 Sept. 1657.

The way and manner of his ordination was according to the known directory of the assembly of divines, and the common usage of the presbyterians; and yet he having left among his papers a particular account of that solemnity, and some of the workings of his soul towards God in it, I hope it may be of some use, both

for

for inſtruction and quickening to miniſters, and for the information of ſuch as are perhaps wholly ſtrangers to ſuch a thing, to give ſome account of the whole tranſaction.

He made addreſſes to the preſbytery, in order to his ordination, July 6. at Prees, when he ſubmitted to trial; and inquiry was made, in the firſt place, concerning his experience of the work of grace in his heart; in anſwer to which he gave a reaſon of the hope that was in him, with meekneſs and fear; that the ſpirit of grace had been dealing with him when he was young, and he hoped had diſcovered to him his need of Chriſt, and had bowed his will in ſome meaſure to cloſe with him upon his own terms, &c. His ſkill in the original languages of the ſcripture was then tried; and he read and conſtrued two verſes in the Hebrew Bible, and two in the Greek Teſtament: he was then examined in logick and natural philoſophy, next in divinity, what authors he had read, and what knowledge he had touching the mediation of Chriſt, &c. And his ſkill in the ſcripture was tried, by propounding to him a difficult text to give his ſenſe of; a caſe of conſcience was alſo put to him to be reſolved, and inquiry made into his acquaintance with church-hiſtory. Laſtly, a queſtion was given him to provide a theſis upon againſt next meeting, which was this, *An Providentia Divina extendat ſe ad omnia?* Aff. On this queſtion he exhibited his theſis, Auguſt 3. and defended it. Several of the miniſters oppoſed, and Mr Porter moderated. He then produced two certificates, which he left with the regiſter of the claſs, one from Oxford, ſubſcribed by Dr Wilkinſon, Dr Langley, &c. the other from the neighbour miniſters, Mr Steel, Mr Fogg, &c. both teſtifying of his converſation, &c. " The Lord forgive me (faith he in " his diary upon this) that it hath not been more " exemplary as it ought for piety and induſtry." Amen, Lord in Chriſt. The day for ordination was appointed to be Sept. 16. at Prees, of which notice was given at Worthenbury by a paper, read in the church, and afterwards

wards affixed to the church-door the Lord's day before, signifying also, " That if any one could produce
" any just exceptions against the doctrine or life of the
" said Mr Henry, or any sufficient reason why he
" might not be ordained, they should certify the same
" to the classis, or the scribe, and it should be heard
" and considered."

On the day of ordination there was a very great assembly gathered together. Mr Porter began the public work of the day with prayer, then Mr Parsons preached on 1 Tim. i. 12. " I thank Christ Jesus, who hath
" enabled me, for that he counted me faithful, putting
" me into the ministry." Putting men into the ministry is the work of Jesus Christ. After sermon, Mr Parsons, according to the usual method, required of him a confession of his faith, which he made as follows:

" The ground and rule of my faith towards God, is
" the Scripture of the Old and New Testament: I be-
" lieve they were written by holy men, immediately
" inspired by the Holy Ghost; having found the effica-
" cy of them in some measure upon my own heart,
"-I believe they are further able to make me wise to
" salvation.

" Concerning God, I believe that he is, and that he
" is the rewarder of those that diligently seek him.

" The trinity of persons in the unity of the God-
" head, I receive and own as a truth, I admire and
" adore as a mystery; though no man hath seen God
" at any time, yet the only-begotten Son, which is in
" the bosom of the Father, he hath declared him, and
" what he hath declared concerning him, that I be-
" lieve. I believe that God is a Spirit,. for the Son hath
" said, God is a Spirit. I believe that he hath life in
" himself, and that he hath given to the Son to have
" life in himself. I believe all things were made by
" him, and without him was not any thing made that
" was made. I believe by his providence he preserves,
" guides, and governs all the creatures, according to

" the

"the purpose of his own will to his own glory; for the
"Father worketh hitherto, and the Son also worketh.
"I believe he made man upright after his own
"image and likeness, which image consisted in know-
"ledge, righteousness, and true holiness, but man by
"sin lost it.

"I believe we were all in the loins of our first pa-
"rents, and that they stood and fell as publick persons,
"and upon that account justly, without any colour of
"wrong, we bear our share, both in the guilt of their
"disobedience, and also the corruption of nature fol-
"lowing thereupon; so that we come into the world
"children of wrath, and heirs of the curse, one as
"well as another; enemies to God, hating him, and
"hated of him: averse to what is good, and prone to
"all manner of evil. Though all are born in this con-
"dition, yet there are some that do not die in it.

"I believe there is a Mediator, and there is but one
"Mediator between God and men, the man Christ
"Jesus. Those whom the Father hath from everlasting
"pitched his love upon, and given to Christ, not be-
"cause of works or faith foreseen, but merely of his
"free grace; for those I believe Christ was sent forth
"into the world, made of a woman, made under the
"law; for their sakes he sanctified himself, and be-
"came obedient to death, even the death of the cross;
"wherefore God also highly exalted him; and having
"raised him from the dead on the third day, set him
"at his own right hand, where he ever lives, to make
"intercession for those for whom he shed his blood.
"All these elect redeemed ones I believe are in due
"time, sooner or later, in their lives, effectually called,
"washed, sanctified, justified in the name of the Lord
"Jesus, and by the Spirit of our God.

"I believe the righteousness of Christ alone, appre-
"hended by faith, is the matter of our justification
"before God; and that no flesh can stand in his sight
"upon any other terms, for he is the Lord our Righ-
"teousness, and in him only the Father is well pleased.

I be-

"I believe the work of sanctification, managed by the Spirit, who dwelleth in us, though in respect of parts it be complete, for the whole man is renewed; yet in respect of degrees it is not fully perfected till we come to glory; and I believe all that are justified shall be glorified, for we are kept by the power of God, through faith unto salvation.

"I believe the gathering in and building up of saints, is the special end why pastors and teachers are appointed in the church: and that Jesus Christ, according to his promise, will be with them, in that work, to the end of the world.

"The two sacraments of the New Testament, baptism and the Lord's supper, I receive and own as signs and seals of the covenant of grace; the former instituted by our Lord Jesus, as a sign and seal of our engraffing into him, due, of right, to all the infants of believing parents, and but once to be administred; the other instituted by our Lord Jesus in the night wherein he was betrayed, to shew forth his death, and to seal the benefits purchased thereby to his church and people, and to be often repeated.

"When the body returns to the dust, I believe the soul returns to God that gave it; and that immediately it receives from him the sentence, according to what hath been done in the flesh; either, Come, inherit the kingdom;---or, Depart, accursed, into everlasting fire.

"I believe, besides this, a day of general judgment in the end of the world, wherein we must all appear before the tribunal of Jesus Christ; and that our bodies, being raised by an Almighty power from the dust, shall be united to the same souls again, and shall partake with them in the same condition, either of happiness or misery, to all eternity. Those that have done good shall come forth unto the resurrection of life; and those that have done evil, to the resurrection of damnation."

This is the sum and substance of my faith, into which

which I was baptized, and in which, by the grace of God, I will live and die.

Mr Parſons then propoſed certain queſtions to him, according to the inſtructions in the directory, to which he return'd anſwer as followeth:

Queſtion 1. *What are your ends in undertaking the work and calling of a miniſter?*

Anſwer. As far as upon ſearch and inquiry I can hitherto find, though there be that within me that would ſeek great things for myſelf (if indeed they were to be found in this calling) yet with my mind I ſeek them not. But the improvement of the talent which I have received in the ſervice of the goſpel, for the glory of God, and the ſalvation of ſouls, I hope is in my eye; if there be any thing elſe, I own it not, I allow it not; while ſo many ſeek their own, it is my deſire, and ſhall be my endeavour, to ſeek the things of Jeſus Chriſt.

Queſt. 2. *What are your purpoſes, as to diligence and induſtry in this calling?*

Anſw. I do purpoſe and reſolve, by the help of God, to give myſelf wholly to theſe things; to prayer, reading, meditation, inſtant preaching in ſeaſon and out of ſeaſon, wherein I ſhall very gladly ſpend and be ſpent, if by any means I may both ſave myſelf and them that hear me. And when at any time I fail herein, I deſire God by his Spirit, and my chriſtian friends, neighbours, and brethren, by ſeaſonable reproof and admonition, to put me in mind of this engagement now made in the preſence of this great congregation.

Queſt. 3. *Do you mean to be zealous and faithful in the defence of truth and unity, againſt error and ſchiſm?*

Anſw. I believe what the Spirit hath foretold, that in the laſt days perilous times ſhall come, wherein men will not endure ſound doctrine, but after their own luſts ſhall heap unto themſelves teachers. 'Tis my reſolution, by the grace of Chriſt, to watch in all things; to contend earneſtly for the faith, to hold faſt the form

of

The Life of Mr PHILIP HENRY.

of found and wholfome words, even the words of our Lord Jefus, and the doctrine which is according to godlinefs, in meeknefs, as I am able, inftructing thofe that oppofe themfelves: and for peace and unity, if my heart deceive me not, I fhall rather chufe to hazard the lofs of any thing that is moft dear to me, than be any way knowingly acceffary to the difturbance of thefe in the churches of Chrift.

Queft. 4. *What is your perfwafion of the truth of the reformed religion?*

Anfw. My perfwafion is, that the bifhop of Rome is that man of fin, and fon of perdition whom the Lord Jefus will confume with the fpirit of his mouth, and whom he will deftroy by the brightnefs of his coming. And the feparation which our firft reformers made, I do heartily rejoice in, and blefs God for, for had we ftill continued to partake with him in his fins, we fhould in the end have partaked with him alfo in his plagues.

Queft. 5. *What do you intend to do when the Lord fhall alter your condition, and bring a family under your charge?*

Anfw. When the Lord fhall pleafe in his Providence to bring me into new relations, I hope he will give me grace to fill them up with duty; it is my purpofe to wait upon him, and to keep his way, to endeavour in the ufe of means, that all that are mine may be the Lord's.

Queft. 6. *Will you in humility and meeknefs fubmit to admonition and difcipline?*

Anfw. I believe it to be a duty incumbent upon all that profefs the name of Chrift, to watch over one another, and that when any is overtaken in a fault thofe that are fpiritual are to fet him in joynt again with the fpirit of meeknefs. It fhall be my endeavour in the ftrength of Jefus Chrift to walk without rebuke, and when at any time I ftep afide, (for who is there that lives and fins not) I fhall account the fmitings of my brethren kindnefs, and their wounds faithful.

Queft.

Queſt. 7. *What if troubles, perſecutions, and diſcouragements ariſe, will you hold out to the end notwithſtanding?*

Anſw. Concerning this I am very jealous over my own heart, and there is cauſe. I find a great want of that zeal and courage for God, which I know is required in a miniſter of the goſpel, neverthelefs, I perſwade myſelf that no temptation ſhall befall me but ſuch as is common to man, and that God who is faithful, will not ſuffer me to be tempted above that which I am able, but that with the temptation he will alſo make a way to eſcape, that I may be able to bear it. I promiſe faithfulneſs to the death, but I reſt not at all in my promiſe to God, but in his to me----When thou goeſt thro' the fire, and through the water, I will be with thee.

When this was done, Mr Parſons prayed ; and in prayer, he and the reſt of the preſbyters (Mr Porter, Mr Houghton, Mr Malden, and Mr Steel) laid their hands upon him, with words to this purpoſe, " whom " we do thus in thy name ſet apart to the work and " office of the miniſtry." After him, there were five more, after the like previous examinations and trials, profeſſions and promiſes, at the ſame time in like manner ſet apart to the miniſtry.

Then Mr Malden of Newport cloſed with an exhortation directed to the newly-ordained miniſters, in which (faith Mr Henry in his diary) this word went near my heart : " As the nurſe puts the meat firſt in-
" to her own mouth, and chews it, and then feeds the
" child with it, ſo ſhould miniſters do by the word ;
" preach it over before-hand to their own hearts, it
" loſes none of the virtue hereby, but rather probably
" gains. As that milk nouriſheth moſt which comes
" warm, from the warm breaſt ; ſo that ſermon which
" comes warm from a warm heart. Lord quicken me
" to do thy will in this thing."

The claſſis gave him, and the reſt, inſtruments in parchment, certifying this, which it may ſatisfy the curioſity of ſome to read the form of :----

" Whereas

"Whereas Mr Philip Henry of Worthenbury, in
"the county of Flint, master of arts, hath addressed
"himself unto us, authorized by an ordinance of both
"Houses of Parliament, of the 29th of August 1648,
"for the ordination of ministers, desiring to be or-
"dained a presbyter, for that he is chosen and appoint-
"ed for the work of the ministry at Worthenbury in
"the county of Flint, as by a certificate now remaining
"with us, touching that his election and appointment,
"appeareth. And he having likewise exhibited a
"sufficient testimonial of his diligence and proficiency
"in his studies, and unblameableness of his life and
"conversation, he hath been examined according to
"the rules for examination in the said ordinance ex-
"pressed; and thereupon approved, there being no
"just exception made, nor put in against his ordina-
"tion and admission. These may therefore testify to
"all whom it may concern, that upon the sixteenth
"day of September 1657, we have proceeded so-
"lemnly to set apart for the office of a presbyter, and
"work of the ministry of the gospel, by laying on of
"our hands with fasting and prayer; by virtue where-
"of we do declare him to be a lawful and sufficiently
"authorized minister of Jesus Christ: and having good
"evidence of his lawful and fair calling, not only to
"the work of the ministry, but to the exercise there-
"of at the chapel of Worthenbury in the county of
"Flint, we do hereby send him thither, and actually
"admit him to the said charge, to perform all the
"offices and duties of a faithful pastor there; exhort-
"ing the people in the name of Jesus Christ willingly
"to receive and acknowledge him as the minister of
"Christ, and to maintain and encourage him in the
"execution of his office, that he may be able to give
"up such an account to Christ of their obedience to
"his ministry, as may be to his joy, and their ever-
"lasting comfort. In witness whereof, we, the presby-
"ters of the fourth class in the county of Salop,
"commonly called Bradford North Class, have here-
"unto

The Life of Mr PHILIP HENRY.

" unto set our hands, this 16th day of September, in
" the year of our Lord God, 1657.

  Tho. Porter, moderator for the time.
  Andrew Parsons, minister of Wem.
  Aylmar Haughton, minister of Prees.
  John Malden, minister of Newport.
  Richard Steel, minister of Hanmer.

I have heard it said by those who were present at this solemnity, that Mr Henry did, in his countenance, carriage, and expression, discover such an extraordinary seriousness and gravity, and such deep impressions made upon his spirit, as greatly affected the auditory, and even struck an awe upon them.

Read his reflection upon it in his diary:----" Me-
" thought I saw much of God in the carrying on of
" the work of this day. O, how good is the Lord, he is
" good, and doth good; the remembrance of it I shall
" never lose: to him be glory. I made many promises
" of diligence, faithfulness, &c. but I lay no stress at
" all on them, but on God's promise to me, that he
" will be with his ministers always to the end of the
" world. Amen, Lord, so be it. Make good thy word
" unto thy servant, wherein thou hast caused me to
" put my trust." And in another place, " I did this day
" receive as much honour and work as ever I shall
" be able to know what to do with: Lord Jesus, pro-
" portion supplies accordingly." Two scriptures he desired might be written in his heart, 2 Cor. vi. 4, 5, &c. and 2 Chron. xxix. 11.

Two years after, upon occasion of his being present at an ordination at Whitchurch, he thus writes: " This
" day my ordination-covenants were in a special man-
" ner renewed, as to diligence in reading, prayer, me-
" ditation, faithfulness in preaching, admonition, cate-
" chizing, sacraments, zeal against error and profane-
" ness, care to preserve and promote the unity and
" purity of the church, notwithstanding opposition and
" persecution, tho' to death. Lord, thou hast filled my
" hands with work, fill my heart with wisdom and
          " grace,

"grace, that I may difcharge my duty to thy glory, "and my own falvation of thofe that hear me." Amen.

Let us now fee how he applied himfelf to his work at Worthenbury. The fphere was too narrow for fuch a burning and fhining light: there were but forty-one communicants in that parifh when he firft fet up the ordinance of the Lord's Supper, and they were never doubled: yet he had fuch low thoughts of himfelf, that he not only never fought for a larger fphere, but would never hearken to any overtures of that kind made to him: and withal, he had fuch high thoughts of his work, and the worth of fouls, that he laid out himfelf with as much diligence and vigour here, as if he had had the over-fight of the greateft and moft confiderable parifh in the country.

The greateft part of the parifh were poor tenants, and labouring hufbandmen; but the fouls of fuch (he ufed to fay) are as precious as the fouls of the rich, and to be looked after accordingly. His prayer for them was, " Lord, defpife not the day of fmall things " in this place, where there is fome willingnefs, but " much weaknefs." And thus he writes upon the Judge's fettling a handfome maintenance upon him: " Lord, thou knoweft, I feek not theirs, but them: give me the fouls."—

He was in labours more abundant to win fouls: befides preaching, he expounded the fcriptures in order, catechized and explained the catechifm. At firft he took into the number of his catechumens fome that were adult, who (he found) wanted inftruction; and when he had taken what pains he thought needful with them, he difmifsed them from further attendance, with commendation of their proficiency, and counfel to hold faft the form of found words; to be watchful againft the fins of their age, and to apply themfelves to the ordinance of the Lord's fupper, and make ready for it; afterwards he catechized none above feventeen or eighteen years of age.

He set up a monthly lecture there of two sermons, one he himself preached, and the other his friend Mr Ambrose Lewis of Wrexham, for some years. He also kept up a monthly conference in private from house to house, in which he met with the more knowing and judicious of the parish; and they discoursed familiarly together of the things of God, to their mutual edification, according to the example of the apostles, who, tho' they had the liberty of public places, yet taught also from house to house, Acts v. 42. xx. 20. That which induced him to set and keep up this exercise as long as he durst (which was till August 1660,) was, that by this means he came better to understand the state of his flock, and so knew the better how to preach to them, and pray for them, and they to pray one for another. If they were in doubt about any thing relating to their souls, that was an opportunity of getting satisfaction. It was likewise a means of increasing knowledge, and love, and other graces; and thus it abounded to a good account.

He was very industrious in visiting the sick, instructing them, and praying with them; and in this he would say, he aimed at the good, not only of those that were sick, but also of their friends and relations that were about them.

He preached funeral sermons for all that were buried there, rich or poor, old or young, or little children; for he looked upon it as an opportunity of doing good: he called it, setting in the plough of the word, when providence had softened and prepared the ground. He never took any money for that or any other ministerial performance, besides his stated salary, for which he thought himself obliged to do his whole duty to them as a minister.

When he first set up the ordinance of the Lord's supper there, he did it with very great solemnity. After he had endeavoured to instruct them in his publick preaching, touching the nature of that ordinance, he discoursed personally with all that gave up their

names

The Life of Mr. Philip Henry. 43

names to the Lord in it, touching their knowledge, experience, and converfation, obliged them to obferve the law of Chrift, touching brotherly admonition in cafe of fcandal; and gave notice to the congregation who they were that were admitted; adding this: " concerning thefe, and myfelf, I have two things to " fay; 1. As to what is paft, we have finned: if we " fhould fay, we have not, we fhould deceive ourfelves, " and the truth were not in us; and yet this with- " al we can fay, and have faid it, fome of us with tears, " we are grieved that we have finned. 2. For time to " come we are refolved by God's grace to walk in " new obedience; and yet feeing we are not angels, " but men and women, compaffed about with infir- " mities and temptations, it is poffible we may fall; " but if we do, it is our declared refolution to fubmit " to admonition and cenfure, according to the rule of " the gofpel." And all along he took care fo to manage his admiffions to that ordinance, as that the weak might not be difcouraged, and yet the ordinance might not be profaned. He would tell thofe whom he was neceffitated to debar from the ordinance for ignorance, that he would undertake, if they were but truly willing, they might in a week's time, by the bleffing of God upon their diligent ufe of means, reading, prayer, and conference, get fuch a competent meafure of knowledge, as to be able to difcern the Lord's body. And thofe that had been fcandalous, if they would but come in and declare their repentance, and refolutions of new obedience, they fhould no longer be excluded.

To give a fpecimen of his lively adminiftrations of that ordinance, let me tranfcribe the notes of his exhortation at the firft facrament that ever he adminiftred, Nov. 27. 1659. I fuppofe they are but the hints of what he enlarged more upon, for he had always a great fluency upon fuch occafions:

" Dearly beloved in our Lord and Saviour Jefus
" Chrift, we are met together this day about the moft
" folemn weighty fervice under heaven; we are come

" to a feast, where the feast-maker is God the Father,
" the provision God the Son, whose flesh is meat in-
" deed, and whose blood is drink indeed; the guests
" a company of poor sinners, unworthy such an hon-
" our; the crumbs under the table were too good for
" us, and yet we are admitted to taste of the provision
" upon the table; and that which makes the feast is
" *hearty welcome*. God the Father bids you welcome;
" and ten thousand welcomes this day, to the flesh and
" blood of his Son: think you hear him saying it to
" you, O believing souls, Cant. v. 1. Eat, O friends;
" drink, yea, drink abundantly, O beloved. The end
" of this feast is to keep in remembrance the death of
" Christ, and our deliverance by it, and thereby to
" convey spiritual nourishment and refreshment to our
" souls. But withal, give me leave to ask you one
" question, What appetite have you to this feast? Are
" you come hungring and thirsting? such as have the
" promise, they shall be filled. He filleth the hungry
" with good things, but the rich are sent empty away:
" a honey-comb to a full soul is no honey-comb.---
" Canst thou say as Christ said? With desire I have de-
" sired to eat this. In this ordinance here's Christ and
" all his benefits exhibited to thee. Art thou weak?
" here's bread to strengthen thee. Art thou sad? here's
" wine to comfort thee. What is it thou standest in
" need of? A pardon? here it is sealed in blood, take
" it by faith, as I offer it to you in the name of the
" Lord Jesus. Though thy sins have been as scarlet,
" they shall be as wool, if thou be willing and obe-
" dient. It may be, here are some that have been drunk-
" ards, swearers, scoffers at goodliness, sabbath-
" breakers, and what not? and God hath put it into
" your hearts to humble yourselves, to mourn for and
" turn from all your abominations; O come hither,
" here's forgiveness for thee. What else is it thou
" wantest? O (saith the poor soul) I would have more
" of the spirit of grace, more power against sin, espe-
" cially my own iniquity: why, here it is for thee,
"   " from

" from the fullnefs that is in Jefus Chrift we receive,
" and grace for grace, John i. 16. We may fay as
" David did, Pfalm cviii. 7, 8. God hath fpoken in
" his holinefs; and then, Gilead is mine, and Manaffeh
" mine: fo God hath fpoken in his word fealed in his
" facrament, and then Chrift is mine, pardon is mine,
" grace is mine, comfort mine, glory mine; here I
" have his bond to fhew for it. This is to thofe a-
" mong you that have engaged their hearts to ap-
" proach unto God this day.

" But if there be any come hither with a falfe, un-
" believing, filthy, hard heart, I do warn you ferioufly,
" and with authority, in the name of Jefus Chrift,
" prefume not to come any nearer to this facred ordi-
" nance: you that live in the practice of any fin, or
" the omiffion of any duty againft your knowledge
" and confcience; you that have any malice or grudge
" to any of your neighbours, leave your gift, and go
" your ways; be reconciled to God, be reconciled to
" your brother, and then come.——Better fhame
" thyfelf for coming fo near, than damn thyfelf by
" coming nearer: I teftify to thofe, who fay they fhall
" have peace, though they go on ftill in their trefpaf-
" fes, that there's poifon in the bread; take it and
" eat it at your own peril: there's poifon in the cup
" too, you drink your own damnation: I wafh my
" hands from the guilt of your blood, look you to it.
" On the other hand, you poor penitent fouls that are.
" loft in yourfelves, here's a Chrift to fave you; come,
" O come, ye that are weary and heavy laden, &c."

It may not be amifs to tranfcribe alfo fome hints of preparation for the adminiftring of the ordinance of baptifm, which I find under his hand at his firft fetting out in the miniftry, as follows:

" It is a real manifeftation of the goodnefs and love
" of God to believers, that he hath not only taken
" them into covenant with himfelf, but their feed alfo;
" faying, I will be thy God, and the God of thy feed.
" Tho' to be born of fuch doth not neceffarily entitle
                                            " infants

" infants to the spiritual mercies of the covenant, for
" grace doth not run in a blood: we see the contrary
" many times, even godly parents have wicked chil-
" dren; Abraham had his Ishmael, and Isaac his Esau,
" yet questionless it doth entitle them to the external
" privileges of the covenant. The like figure unto
" Noah's ark, even baptism doth also now save us:
" Noah and all that were his, entered into the ark,
" though we have cause to doubt whether they all en-
" tered into heaven. While our Lord Jesus was here
" upon the earth, they brought little children to him,
" and he laid his hands on them, and blessed them;
" and said moreover, Suffer little children to come
" unto me, and forbid them not, (there are many at
" this day that forbid little children to come to Christ;)
" he adds the reason, For of such is the kingdom of
" heaven. Whether it be meant of the visible church,
" often so called in the gospel, or of the state of glory
" in another world; either way it affords an argu-
" ment for proof of infant baptism. When either pa-
" rent is in covenant with God, their children also are
" in covenant with him; and being in covenant, they
" have an undoubted right and title to this ordinance
" of baptism, which is the seal of the covenant. So
" that in the administration of this ordinance, this day,
" according to the institution of Jesus Christ, we look
" upon you, the father of this child, as a person
" in covenant with God: how far you have dealt un-
" faithfully in the covenant, is known to God and
" your own conscience; but this we know, the vows
" of God are upon you; and let every one that na-
" meth the name of Christ depart from iniquity. But
" before we baptize your child, I am to acquaint you
" in a few words what we expect from you.

" *Quest.* 1. Do you avouch God in Jesus Christ
" this day to be your God?—See to it that this be
" done in truth and with a perfect heart: you may
" tell us you do so, and you may deceive us, but God
" is not mocked. *Q.* 2. And is it your desire, that
                                                " your

The Life of Mr Philip Henry. 47

" your children alfo may be received into covenant
" with the Lord, and that the Lord's broad-feal of
" baptifm may be fet to it? Q. 3. And do you pro-
" mife, in the prefence of God, and of this congrega-
" tion, that you will do your endeavour towards the
" training of it up in the way of godlinefs, that as it
" is by you through mercy that it lives the life of na-
" ture, fo it may by you alfo, through the fame mer-
" cy, live the life of grace : elfe I muft tell you, if
" you be wanting herein, there will be a fad appear-
" ance one day, when you fhall meet together before
" the judgement-feat of Chrift, and this folemn en-
" gagement of yours will be brought in to witnefs a-
" gainft you."

Thefe were but the firft inftances of his fkilfulnefs, in difperifing the myfteries of the kingdom of God. He declined the private adminiftration of the Lord's fupper to fick perfons, as judging it not confonant to the rule and intention of the ordinance. He very rarely, if ever, baptized in private; but would have children brought to the folemn affembly upon the Lord's day, that the parent's engagement might have the more witneffes to it, and the child the more prayers put up for it, and that the congregation might be edified. And yet he would fay, there was fome inconvenience in it too, unlefs people would agree to put off the feafting part of the folemnity to fome other time, which he very much perfwaded his friends to; and obferved, that Abraham made a great feaft the fame day that Ifaac was weaned, (Gen. xxi. 8.) not the fame day that he was circumcifed.

His carriage towards the people of his parifh was very exemplary, condefcending to the meaneft, and converfing familiarly with them; bearing with the infirmities of the weak, and becoming all things to all men. He was exceeding tender of giving offence, or occafion of grief to any body, minding himfelf in his diary upon fuch occafions, that the wifdom that is from above, is " pure, and peaceable, and gentle, &c."

Yet

Yet he plainly and faithfully reproved what he faw a-
mifs in any, and would not fuffer fin upon them; mourning alfo for that which he could not mend. There
were fome untractable people in the parifh, who fometimes caufed grief to him, and exercifed his boldnefs
and zeal in reproving. Once hearing of a merry meeting at an ale-houfe on a Saturday night, he went himfelf and broke it up, and fcattered them. At another
time, he publickly witneffed againft a frolick of fome
vain people, that on a Saturday night came to the
church with a fiddler before them, and dreffed it up
with flowers and garlands, making it (as he told them)
more like a play-houfe; and was this their preparation
for the Lord's day, and the duties of it? &c. He minded them of Eccl. xi. 9. " Rejoice, O young man, in
" thy youth, but know thou"—

Many out of the neighbouring parifhes attended u-
pon his miniftry, and fome came from far, though
fometimes he fignified his diflike of their fo doing, fo
far was he from glorying in it. But they who had fpiritual fenfes exercifed to difcern things that differ, would
attend upon that miniftry which they found to be moft
edifying.

He was about eight years from firft to laft, labouring in the word and doctrine at Worthenbury, and his
labour was not altogether in vain: he faw in many of
the travel of his to the rejoycing of his heart, but with
this particular difpenfation (which I have heard him
fometimes fpeak of) that moft, or all of thofe in that
parifh, whom he was (through grace) inftrumental of
good to, died before he left the parifh, or quickly after; fo that within a few years after his removal thence,
there were very few of the vifible fruits of his miniftry
there; and a new generation fprung up there, who
knew not Jofeph. Yet the opportunity he found there
was of doing the more good, by having thofe that
were his charge near about him, made him all his days
bear his teftimony to parifh order, where it may be
had upon good terms, as much more eligible, and

more

more likely to anfwer the end, than the congregational way of gathering churches from places far diftant, which could not ordinarily meet to worfhip God together. From his experience here (though he would fay we muft do what we can, when we cannot do what we would) he often wifhed and prayed for the opening of a door, by which to return to that order again.

He had not been long at Worthenbury, but he began to be taken notice of by the neighbouring minifters, as likely to be a confiderable man. Though his extraordinary modefty and humility (which even in his youth he was remarkable for) made him to fit down with filence " in the loweft room, and to fay as Elihu, " Days fhall fpeak ;" yet his eminent gifts and graces could not long be hid, the ointment of the right hand will betray itfelf; and a perfon of his merits could not but meet with thofe quickly, who faid, " Friend, go up " higher;" and fo that fcripture was fulfilled, Luke xiv. 10. He was often called upon to preach the weekday lectures, which were fet up plentifully, and diligently attended upon in thofe parts, and his labours were generally very acceptable and fuccefsful. The *vox populi* faftened upon him the epithet of Heavenly Henry, by which title he was commonly known all the country over, and his advice was fought for by many neighbouring minifters and chriftians, for he was one of thofe that found favour and good underftanding in the fight of God and man. He was noted at his firft fetting out (as I have been told by one who was then intimately acquainted with him, and with his character and converfation) for three things, 1. Great piety and devotion, and a mighty favour of godlinefs in all his converfe. 2. Great induftry in the purfuit of ufeful knowledge: he was particularly obferved to be very inquifitive when he was among the aged and intelligent; hearing them, and afking them queftions : a good example to young men, efpecially young minifters. 3. Great felf-denial, felf-diffidence, and felf-abafement: this eminent humility put a luftre upon all his other graces. This character of him, minds me of a paffage I have fometimes heard him tell, as a check to the forwardnefs and confidence of young men, that once at a meeting of minifters, a queftion of moment was ftarted, to be debated among them : upon the firft propofal of it, a confident young man fhoots his bolt prefently, " Truly (faith he) I hold it fo." "You " hold, Sir, (faith a grave minifter,) it becomes you " to hold your peace."

Befides his frequent preaching of the lectures about him, he was a conftant and diligent attendant upon thofe within his reach, as a hearer ; and not only wrote the fermons he heard, but afterwards recorded in his diary what in each fermon reached his heart, affected him and did him good ; adding fome proper, pious ejaculations, which were the breathings of his heart, when he meditated upon, and prayed over the fermon.

What a wonderful degree of piety and humility doth it evidence, for one fo acquainted with the things of God, to write, " This I learnt out of fuch a fermon ;--- and, This was the truth I made up to myfelf out of fuch a fermon !" and indeed fomething out of every fermon. His diligent improvement of the word preached contributed (more than any one thing, as a means) to his great attainments in knowledge and grace. He would fay fometimes, that one great ufe of week-day lectures was, that it gave minifters an opportunity of hearing one another preach, by which they are likely to profit, when they hear not as mafters, but as fcholars ; not as cenfors, but as learners.

His great friend and companion, and fellow labourer in the work of the Lord, was the worthy Mr Richard Steel (minifter of Hanmers, one of the next parifhes to Worthenbury) whofe praife is in the churches of Chrift, for his excellent and ufeful treatifes, the Hufbandman's Calling ; an Antidote againft Diftractions, and feveral others. He was Mr Henry's *alter idem*, the man of his counfel ; with him he joined frequently at Hanmer, and elfewhere, in Chriftian conference,

ference, and in days of humiliation and prayer: befides, their meetings with other minifters at public lectures; after which it was ufual for them to fpend fome time among themfelves in fet difputations in Latin. This was the work that in thofe days was carried on among minifters who made it their bufinefs, as iron fharpens iron, to provoke one another to love and good works. What was done of this kind in Worcefterfhire, Mr Baxter tells us in his life.

In the beginning of thofe days he often laboured under bodily diftempers: it was feared that he was in a confumption; and fome blamed him for taking fo much pains in his minifterial work, fuggefting to him, Mafter, fpare thyfelf. One of his friends told him, he lighted up all his pound of candles together; and that he could not hold out long at that rate; and wifhed him to hufband his ftrength better. But he often reflected upon it with comfort afterwards, that he was not influenced by fuch fuggeftions. The more we do, the more we may do (he would fometimes fay) in the fervice of God. When his work was fometimes more than ordinary, and bore hard upon him, he thus appealed to God; " Thou knoweft, Lord, how well contented I am " to fpend and to be fpent in thy fervice; and if the out- " ward man decay, O let the inward man be renewed." Upon the returns of his indifpofition he expreffeth a great concern how to get fpiritual good by it; to come out of the furnace, and leave fome drofs behind; for it is a great lofs to lofe an affliction. He mentions it as that which he hoped did him good, that he was ready to look upon every return of diftemper as a fummons to the grave: thus he learned to die daily. " I find (faith he) my earthly tabernacle tottering, and " when it is taken down, I fhall have a building in hea- " ven, that fhall never fail. Bleffed be God the Father, " and my Lord Jefus Chrift and the good Spirit of grace. " Even fo, *Amen.*" This was both his ftrength and his fong, under his bodily infirmities.

While he was at Worthenbury he conftantly laid

by the tenth of his income for the poor, which he carefully and faithfully difpofed of, in the liberal things which he devifed, efpecially the teaching of poor children: and he would recommend it as a good rule to lay by for charity (in fome proportion, according as the circumftances are) and then it will be the eafier to lay out in charity; we fhall be the more apt to feek for opportunities of doing good, when we have money lying by us, of which we have faid, This is not our own, but the poor's. To encourage himfelf and others to works of charity, he would fay, " He is no fool who " parts with that which he cannot keep, when he is fure " to be recompenfed with that which he cannot lofe." And yet to prove alms to be righteoufnefs, and to exclude all boafting of them, he often ufed the words of David, " Of thine own, Lord, have we given thee."

In the year 1658, the minifters of that neighbourhood began to enlarge their correfpondence with the minifters of North-Wales; and feveral meetings they had at Ruthin and other places that year, for the fettling of a correfpondence, and the promoting of unity and love, and good underftanding among themfelves, by entering into an affociation, like thofe fome years before of Worcefterfhire and Cumberland, to which, as their pattern (thofe two having been publifhed) they did refer themfelves. They appointed particular affociations; and (notwithftanding the differences of apprehenfion that were among them; fome being in their judgments epifcopal, others congregational, and others claffical) they agreed to lay afide the thoughts of matters in variance, and to give to each other the righthand of fellowfhip; that with one fhoulder and with one confent, they might ftudy each in their places to promote the common interefts of Chrift's kingdom, and the common falvation of precious fouls. He obferved, that this year, after the death of Oliver Cromwell, there was generally throughout the nation a great change in the temper of God's people, and a mighty tendency towards peace and unity, as if they were by
confent

consent weary of their long clashings, which in his diary he expresseth his great rejoicing in, and his hopes that the time was at hand, when Judah should no longer vex Ephraim, nor Ephraim envy Judah, neither should they learn war any more. And though these hopes were soon disappointed by a change of the scene, yet he would often speak of the experience of that and the following year in those parts, as a specimen of what may yet be expected, (and therefore in faith prayed for) when the Spirit shall be poured out upon us from on high. But, alas! who shall live when God doth this? From this experience he likewise gathered this observation, " that it is not so much our difference of opinion
" that doth us the mischief, (for we may as soon expect
" all the clocks in the town to strike together, as to see
" all good people of a mind in every thing on this hea-
" ven,) but the mismanagement of that difference."

In the association of the ministers it was referred to Mr Henry to draw up that part of their agreement which concerned the worship of God, which task he performed to their satisfaction: his preface to what he drew up begins thus: " Though the main of our de-
" sires and endeavours be after unity in the greater
" things of God; yet we judge uniformity in the
" circumstances of worship a thing not to be al-
" together neglected by us; not only in regard of that
" influence which external visible order hath upon the
" beauty and comeliness of the churches of Christ,
" but also as it hath a direct tendency to the strength-
" ening of our hands in ministerial services, and
" withal to the removing of those prejudices which
" many people have conceived, even against religion
" and worship itself. We bless God from our very
" souls, for that whereunto we have already attained;
" and yet we hope some further thing may be done,
" in reference to our closer walking by the same rule,
" and minding the same things. The word of God
" is the rule which we desire and resolve to walk by
" in the administration of ordinances; and for those
" things

"things wherein the word is filent, we think we may
"and ought to have recourfe to Chriftian prudence,
"and the practice of the reformed churches, agreeing
"with the general rules of the word: and therefore
"we have had (as we think we ought) in our prefent
"agreement, a fpecial eye to the directory," &c.

Thefe agreements of theirs were the more likely to be for good, for that here (as in Worcefterfhire) when they were in agitation, the minifters fet apart a day of fafting and prayer among themfelves to bewail minifterial neglects, and to feek to God for direction and fuccefs in their minifterial work. They met fometimes for this purpofe at Mr Henry's houfe at Worthenbury.

One paffage may not improperly be inferted here, that once at a meeting of the minifters, being defired to fubfcribe a certificate concerning one whom he had not fufficient acquaintance with; he refufed, giving this reafon, that he preferred the peace of his confcience before the friendfhip of all the men in the world.

Sept. 29. 1658, the Lady Pulefton died. "She
"was (faith he) the beft friend I had on earth, but my
"Friend in heaven is ftill where he was, and he will
"never leave me nor forfake me." He preached her funeral fermon from Ifa. iii. laft, "Ceafe from man,
"whofe breath is in his noftrils." He hath noted this expreffion of her's not long before fhe died: "My
"foul leans to Jefus Chrift; lean to me, fweet Saviour." About this time, he writes, "A dark cloud is over
"my concernments in this family, but my defire is,
"that whatever becomes of me and my intereft, the
"intereft of Chrift may ftill be kept on foot in this
"place." *Amen*, fo be it. But he adds, foon after, that faying of Athanafius, which he was ufed often to quote and take comfort from; *Nubecula eft & cito pertranfibit.* It is a little cloud, and will foon blow over.

About a year after, Sept. 5. 1659, Judge Pulefton died, and all Mr Henry's intereft in Emeral family was buried in his grave. He preached the Judge's funeral fermon, from Neh. xiii. 14. "Wipe not out my
"good

" good deeds that I have done for the houſe of my
" God, and for the offices thereof:" the deſign of
which ſermon was not to applaud his deceaſed friend,
I find not a word in the ſermon to that purpoſe: but
he took occaſion from the inſtance of ſo great a benefactor to the miniſtry, as the judge was, to ſhew that
deeds done for the houſe of God, and the offices thereof, are good deeds: and to preſs people according as
their ability and opportunity was, to do ſuch deeds.
One paſſage I find in that ſermon which ought to be
recorded; that it had been for ſeveral years the practice of a worthy gentleman in the neighbouring county,
in renewing his leaſes, inſtead of making it a condition
that his tenants ſhould keep a hawk or a dog for him,
to oblige them that they ſhould keep a Bible in their
houſes for themſelves, and ſhould bring up their children to learn to read and to be catechized. This (ſaith
he) would be no charge to you, and it might oblige
them to that which otherwiſe they would neglect.
Some wiſhed (ſaith he, in his diary) that I had choſen
ſome other ſubject for that ſermon, but I approved myſelf to God; and if I pleaſe men, I am not the ſervant
of Chriſt.

What perſonal affronts he received from ſome of
the branches of that family at that time need not be
mentioned, but with what exemplary patience he bore
them ought not to be forgotten.

In March, 1658-9 he was very much ſolicited to
leave Worthenbury, and to accept of the vicarage of
Wrexham, which was a place that he had both a great
intereſt in, and a great kindneſs for, but he could not
ſee his call clear from Worthenbury, ſo he declined it.
The ſame year he had an offer made him of a conſi-
derable living near London; but he was not of them
that are given to change, nor did he conſult with fleſh
and blood, nor ſeek great things to himſelf.

That year he had ſome diſturbance from the quakers, who were ſet on by ſome others, who wiſhed ill to
his miniſtry: they challenged him to diſpute with them;
and

and that which he was to prove againſt them was, that the God he worſhipped was not an idol ; that John Baddely (a blackſmith in Malpas, and the ringleader of the quakers in that country) was not infallible, nor without ſin ; that baptiſm with water, and the Lord's ſupper, are goſpel-ordinances ; that the ſcriptures are the word of God, and that Jeſus Chriſt will come to judge the world at the laſt day : but he never had any public diſputes with them, nor ſo much diſturbance from them in public worſhip as ſome other miniſters had elſewhere about that time. He had ſome apprehenſions at that time, that God would make the quakers a ſcourge to this nation ; but had comfort in this aſſurance, that God would in due time vindicate his own honour, and the honour of his ordinances, and thoſe of them who will not repent, to give him glory, will be caſt into the fire.

One paſſage I cannot omit, becauſe it diſcovers what kind of ſpirit the quakers were of :—A debauched gentleman being in his revels at Malpas, drinking and ſwearing, was, after a ſort, reproved for it by Baddely the quaker, who was in company : Why (ſaith the gentleman) I'll aſk thee one queſtion, Whether is it better for me to follow drinking and ſwearing, or to go and hear Henry ? he anſwered, Of the two, rather follow thy drinking and ſwearing.

The Cheſhire riſing this year (in oppoſition to the irregular powers that then were uppermoſt) under Sir George Booth (afterwards Lord Delamere,) and that of North-Wales under Sir Thomas Middleton, could not but affect Worthenbury and the country thereabouts. Mr Henry's prayer for them in his diary, the day of their firſt appearing is, " Lord own them, if they " truly own thee." He notes, that Lambert's forces which came down to ſuppreſs them, did in that neighbourhood eſpouſe the quakers cauſe, and offer injury to ſome miniſters : and therefore (ſaith he) unleſs God intend the ruin of the nation by them, they cannot proſper : nor did they long, though in that expedition they

they had fuccefs. In their return, fome of Lambert's foldiers were at Worthenbury church, hearing Mr Henry upon a Lord's day; and one of them fat with his hat on, while they were finging pfalms, for which he publickly admonifhed him : and there being many anabaptifts among them, he hath recorded it as a good providence, that thofe queftions in the catechifm which are concerning baptifm came in courfe to be expounded that day. The firft rifing of the Chefhire forces was Aug. 1ft 1659, and the 19th following they were worfted and fcattered by Lambert's forces, near Northwich, a ftrange fpirit of fear being upon them, which quite took off their chariot-wheels. The country called it, not the Chefhire rifing, but the Chefhire race. Some blamed him that he did not give God thanks publickly for the defeat of Sir George Booth; to whom he anfwered with his ufual mildnefs, that his apprehenfions concerning that affair were not the fame with theirs. We are now (faith he) much in the dark, never more.

He preached the lecture at Chefter foon after, juft at the time when Mr Cook, an eminent minifter in Chefter, and feveral others, were carried prifoners to London, for their agency in the late attempt; and the city was threatned to have their charter taken away, &c. The text in courfe that day (for they preached over the latter part of that epiftle, if not the whole, at that lecture) happened to be Heb. xiii. 14. " We have here no continuing city," which he thought a word upon the wheels at that time. He notes in his diary, that when, after that, the army ruled, difturbed the Parliament, and carried all before them with a high hand, there were great grounds to fear fad times approaching; and his prayer is, " Lord, fit thy people for the fiery trial."

He was a hearty well-wifher to the return of the King, the fpring following, April 1660, and was much affected with the mercy of it. " While others rejoice " carnally (faith he) Lord, help thy people to rejoice fpi- " ritually, in our public national mercies." 'Twas upon
H that

that occasion that Mr Baxter preached his sermon of *right rejoicing*, on Luke x. 20.; but he and others soon saw cause to rejoice with trembling, and to sing both of mercy and judgment; for about that time he hath this melancholy remark, " Religion loses ground ex-
" ceedingly, and profaneness gets it; help, Lord!" how-
ever, he was very industrious to quiet the minds of some who were uneasy at that great revolution; and that scripture yielded him much satisfaction; John iii. 35. " The Father loveth the Son, and hath given all " things into his hands." If Christ be not only the head of the church, but head over all things to the church, we may be assured, that all things shall be made to work together for good to it. The text also which the Lord put into his heart to preach upon, on the day of publick thanksgiving for the king's restoration, was very comfortable to him, Prov. xxi. 1. " The king's heart is in the hand of the Lord." His sense of that great mercy of God to the nation, in the unbloody, peaceable, and legal settlement of King Char-
les II. upon the throne, was the same with that of mul-
titudes, besides both ministers and others that were of the quiet in the land, who yet not long after suffered very hard things under him. Soon after the return of the king, he notes how industrious some were to remove him from Worthenbury, on which he writes this as the breathing of his soul towards God; " Lord, if it
" please thee, fasten me here as a nail in a sure place;
" if otherwise, I will take nothing ill which thou dost
" with me:" and when prest by his friends more earnestly than before, to accept of some other place, " Lord, (saith
" he) mine eye is up unto thee, I am wholly at thy dis-
" posal, make my way plain before my face, because of
" mine enemies; my resolution is, to deny myself if thou
" callest me. Here (or any where 'tis no great matter
" where) I am."

There are two things further which I think it may be of use to give some account of in the close of this chapter. 1. Of the course of his ministry at Worthenbury,

bury, and, 2. Of the state of his soul, and the communion he had with God in those years.

As to the subjects he preached upon, he did not use to dwell long upon a text. Better one sermon upon many texts, (viz. many scriptures opened and applied,) than many sermons upon one text: to that purpose he would sometimes speak.

He used to preach in a fixed method, and linked his subjects in a sort of chain: he adapted his method and style to the capacity of his hearers, fetching his similitudes for illustration from those things which were familiar to them. He did not shoot the arrow of the word over their heads in high notions, or the flourishes of affected rhetorick, nor under their feet by blunt and homely expressions, as many do under pretence of plainness, but to their hearts in close and lively applications. His delivery was very graceful and agreeable, far from being either noisy and precipitate on the one hand, or dull and slow on the other. His doctrine did drop as the dew, and distil as the socking rain, and came with a charming pleasing power, such as many will bear witness to that have wondered at the gracious words which proceeded out of his mouth.

He wrote the notes of his sermons pretty large for the most part, and always very legible: but even when he had put his last hand to them, he commonly left many imperfect hints, which gave room for enlargements in preaching, wherein he had a great felicity. And he would often advise ministers not to tye themselves too strictly to their notes, but having well digested the matter before, to allow themselves a liberty of expression, such as a man's affections, if they be well raised, will be apt to furnish him with. But for this no certain rule can be given, there are diversities of gifts, and each to profit withal.

He kept his sermon-notes in very neat and exact order; sermons in course, according to the order of the subject; and occasional sermons according to the scripture-order of the texts; so that he could readily turn to any of them. And yet, though afterwards he was removed to a place far enough diftant from any of that auditory, yet (though fome have defired it) he feldom preached any of thofe hundreds of fermons which he had preached at Worthenbury, no not when he preached never fo privately, but to the laft he ftudied new fermons, and wrote them as elaborately as ever; for he thought a fermon beft preached when it was newly meditated: nay, if fometimes he had occafion to preach upon the fame text, yet he would make and write the fermons over; and he never offered that to God which coft him nothing.

When he went to Oxford, and preached there before the univerfity in Chrift-church, as he did feveral times, his labours were not only very acceptable, but fuccefsful too; particularly one fermon which he preached there, on Prov. xiv. 9. " Fools make a mock at fin:" for which fermon a young mafter of arts came to his chamber afterwards to return him thanks, and to acknowledge the good impreffions which divine grace, by that fermon, had made upon his foul, which he hoped he fhould never forget.

In his diary he frequently records the frame of his fpirit in ftudying and preaching. Sometimes bleffing God for fignal help vouchfafed, and owning him the Lord God of all his enlargements; at other times, complaining of great deadnefs and ftraitnefs, " It is a won-
" der (faith he) that I can fpeak of eternal things, with
" fo little fenfe of the reality of them. Lord, ftrengthen
" that which remains, which is ready to die." And he once writes thus upon a ftudying day; " I forgot
" explicitely and exprefsly when I began to crave help
" from God, and the chariot wheels drove according-
" ly. Lord, forgive my omiffions, and keep me in the
" way of duty."

As to the ftate of his foul in thefe years, it fhould feem, by his diary, that he was exercifed with fome doubts and fears concerning it. " I think (faith he)
" never did any poor creature pafs through fuch a
" mixture

"mixture of hope and fear, joy and sadness, assurance and doubting, down and up, as I have done these years past."—(The notice of this may be of use to poor drooping christians, that they may know their case is not singular; and that if God for a small moment hide his face from them, he deals with them no otherwise than as he useth sometimes to deal with the dearest of his servants.) It would affect one, to hear him that lived a life of communion with God, complaining of great straitness in prayer. "No life at all in the "duty, many wanderings: if my prayers were written "down, and my vain thoughts interlined, what inco- ", herent nonsense would there be! I am ashamed; "Lord, I am ashamed, O pity and pardon." To hear him suspecting the workings of pride of heart, when he gave an account to a friend, who inquired of him touching the success of his ministry, and that he should record this concern himself, with this ejaculation annexed, "The Lord pardon and subdue;" it was a sign that he kept a very watchful eye upon the motions of his own heart.

To hear him charging it upon himself, that he was present at such a duty in the midst of many distractions, not tasting sweetness in it, &c. When a fire is first kindled (saith he) there is a deal of smoke and smother, that afterwards wears away; so in young converts, much peevishness, frowardness, darkness; "so it hath "been with my soul, and so it is yet in a great mea- "sure. Lord, pity, and do not quench the smoking "flax; though as yet it do but smoke, let these sparks "be blown up into a flame."

"Great mercies, but poor returns; signal oppor- "tunities, but small improvements:" such are his complaints frequently concerning himself. And though few or none excelled him in profitable discourse, yet in that he often bewails his barrenness and unprofitableness. "Little good done or gotten such a day for want "of a heart; 'tis my sin and shame. O that I had "wings like a dove!"

Yet

Yet when he wanted a faith of affurance, he lived by a faith of adherence. "Such a day (faith he) a full " refignation was made of all my concernments, into " the hands of my heavenly Father, let him deal with " me as feemeth good in his eyes ; I am learning and " labouring to live by faith, Lord, help my unbelief. Another time he notes, that many perplexing fears being upon his fpirit, they were all filenced with that fweet word which was feafonably brought to his remembrance, "Fear none of thofe things which thou " fhalt fuffer."

He very frequently kept days of fafting and humiliation in fecret, which he calls his days of atonement. Sometimes he obferved thefe monthly, and fometimes only upon fpecial occafions ; but the memorandums in his diary (not only while he was at Worthenbury, but often after) fhew what fweet communion he had with God in thofe folemn duties, which no eye was witnefs to, but his who "fees in fecret, and will reward " openly. Remember, O my foul, fuch a day, as a " day of more than ordinary engagements entered in- " to, and ftrong refolutions taken up of clofer walking, " and more watchfulnefs: O my God, undertake for " me!" And upon another of thofe days of fecret prayer and humiliation, he notes, "if fowing in tears " be fo fweet, what then will the harveft be, when I " fhall reap in joy ? Blefs the Lord, O my foul, who " forgiveth all thine iniquities, and will in due time " heal all thy difeafes."

CHAP. IV.

His Marriage, Family, Family-Religion, and the Education of his Children.

HE removed from Emeral to the houfe in Worthenbury which the Judge had built for him in February 1658-9, and then had one of his fifters with him to keep his houfe. No fooner had he a tent, but God

God had an altar in it, and that a fmoaking altar. There he fet up repetition on Sabbath-evenings, and welcomed his neighbours to it.

His Chriſtian friends often, and fometimes his brethren in the miniſtry, kept days of faſting and prayer at his houſe. He uſed to tell people when they had built new houſes, they muſt dedicate them, (referring to Deut. xx. 5. and Pſal. xxx. ult.) that is, they muſt invite God to their houſes, and devote them to his ſervice.

Providence having thus brought him into a houſe of his own, ſoon after provided him a help-meet for him. After long agitation, and ſome difcouragement and oppoſition from the father, April 26th 1660 he married Katharine, the only daughter and heir of Mr Daniel Matthews of Broad-Oak, in the townſhip of Ifcoyd, in Flintſhire (but in the pariſh of Malpas, which is in Cheſhire, and about two miles diſtant from Whitchurch, a confiderable market town in Shropſhire.) Mr Matthews was a gentleman of a very competent eſtate; fuch a one as king James the Firſt uſed to ſay was the happieſt lot of all others, which ſet a man below the office of a juſtice of peace, and above that of a petty-conſtable. This was his only child: very fair and honourable overtures had been made for her difpoſal; but it pleaſed God ſo to order events, and to over-rule the ſpirits of thoſe concerned, that ſhe was reſerved to be a bleſſing to this good man, in things pertaining "both to life and godlineſs."

His purpoſe of marriage was publiſhed in the church three Lord's days before; a laudible practice, which he greatly approved, and perſwaded others to.

The day before his marriage he kept as a day of fecret prayer and faſting.

He uſed to ſay, thoſe who would have comfort in that change of their condition, muſt ſee to it, that they bring none of the guilt of the ſin of their ſingle ſtate with them into the married ſtate. And the preſence of Chriſt at a " wedding, will turn the water in-

" to

"to wine;" and he will come, if he be invited by prayer.

He took all occasions, while he lived, to exprefs his thankfulnefs to God for the great comfort he had in this relation. A day of mercy (fo he writes on his marriage day) never to be forgotten. God had given him one (as he writes afterwards) every way his help-er, in whom he had much comfort, and for whom he thanked God with all his heart. He writes in his diary, April 26th 1680, "This day we have been married " twenty years, in which time we have received of the " Lord more than twenty thoufand mercies; to God be " glory." Sometimes he writes " We have been fo long " married, and never reconciled;" that is, there never was any occafion for it. His ufual prayer for his friends in the married ftate was according to his own practice in that ftate; that they might be mutually ferviceable to each other's faith and holinefs, and jointly-ferviceable to God's honour and glory.

Her father, though he put fome hardfhips upon him in the terms, and had been fomewhat averfe to the match, yet by Mr Henry's great prudence, and God's good providence, he was influenced to give a free confent to it; and he himfelf, with his own hand, gave her in marriage. From this, as from other experiences, Mr Henry had learned to fay with affurance; " It is not " in vain to wait upon God, and to keep his way." Mr Matthews fettled part of his eftate before marriage upon them and theirs; he lived about feven years after; and when he died, the remainder of it came to them. This competent eftate, which the divine providence brought into his hand, was not only a comfortable fupport to him when he was turned out of his living, and when many faithful minifters of Chrift were reduced to great poverty and ftraits; but it enabled him like-wife, as he had opportunity, to preach the gofpel freely, which he did to his dying day; and not only fo, but to give for the relief of others that were in want, in which he fowed plentifully, to a very large proportion

of

of his income; and often bleffed God that he had wherewithal, remembering the words of the Lord, how he faid, " It is more blefled to give than to receive."

Such was his houfe, and fuch the vine which God gracioufly planted by the fide of his houfe. By her God gave him fix children, all born within lefs than eight years; the two eldeft fons, John and Matthew: the other four, daughters, Sarah, Katharine, Eleanor, and Ann. His eldeft fon John died of the meafles in the fixth year of his age, and the reft were in mercy continued to him.

The Lord having built him up into a family, he was careful and faithful in making good his folemn vow at his ordination, that " he and his houfe would ferve the " Lord." He would often fay, That we are really which we are relatively. It is not fo much what we are at church, as what we are in our families. Religion in the power of it will be family religion. In this his practice was very exemplary; he was one that walked before his houfe in a perfect way, with a perfect heart, and therein behav'd himfelf wifely. His conftant care and prudent endeavour was not only to put away iniquity far from his tabernacle, but that where he dwelt, the word of Chrift might dwell richly. If he might have no other church, yet he had a church in his houfe.

He made confcience of clofet-worfhip, and did abound in it, not making his family-worfhip to excufe for that. He hath this affecting note in his diary, upon the removing of his clofet but from one room in the houfe to another, This day (faith he) my new clofet was confecrated, if I may fo fay, with this prayer, " That " all the prayers that ever fhould be made in it, ac- " cording to the will of God, morning, evening, and " at noon-day, ordinary or extraordinary, might be " accepted of God, and obtain a gracious anfwer." Amen and amen. It was the caution and advice which he frequently gave to his children and friends. Be fure you look to your fecret duty, keep that up whatever you do; the foul cannot profper in the neglect of it.

He obferved, that apoftacy generally begins at the clofet-door. Secret prayer is firft neglected, and carelefly performed, then frequently omitted, and after a while wholly caft off; and then farewell God, and Chrift, and all religion.

He alfo advis'd that fecret duty be perform'd fecretly, which was the admonition he gave fometimes to thofe who caufed their voice to be hard on high in that duty.

Befides this, he and his wife conftantly prayed together morning and evening; and never if they were together at home or abroad was it intermitted; and from his own experience of the benefit of this practice, he would take all opportunities to recommend it to thofe in that relation, as conducing very much to the comfort of it, and to their furtherance in that, which he would often fay is the great duty of yoke-fellows; and that is, to all they can to help one another to heaven. He would fay, that this duty of hufbands and wives praying together, is intimated in that of the apoftle, 1 Pet. iii. 7. where they are exhorted to " live " as heirs together of the grace of life, that their prayers " (efpecially their prayers together) be not hindred;" that nothing may be done to hinder them from praying together, nor to hinder them in it, nor to fpoil the fuccefs of thofe prayers. This fanctifies the relation, and fetcheth in a bleffing upon it, makes the comforts of it the more fweet, and the cares and croffes of it the more eafy, and is an excellent means of preferving and increafing love in the relation. Many to whom he hath recommended the practice of this duty, have bleffed God for him, and for his advice concerning it. When he was abroad and lay with any of his friends he would mind them of his rule, That they who lye together muft pray together. In the performance of this part of his daily worfhip he he was ufually fhort, but often much affected.

Befides thefe he made confcience, and made a bufinefs of family-worfhip in all the parts of it; and in it he was uniform, fteady and conftant from the time

that

that he was firſt called to the charge of a family, to his dying day; and according to his own practice, he took all occaſions to preſs it upon others. His doctrine was from Joſh. xxiv. 15. was, That family worſhip is a family-duty. He would ſay ſometimes, If the worſhip of God be not in the houſe, write, "Lord have mercy on us," upon the door; for there is a plague, a curſe in it. It is the judgment of archbiſhop Tillotſon, in that excellent book which he publiſhed a little before-his death upon this ſubject; "That conſtant family-worſhip is ſo "neceſſary to keep alive a ſenſe of God and religion " in the minds of men, that he ſees not how any " family that neglects it can in reaſon be eſteemed a " family of chriſtians, or indeed to have any religion " at all." How earneſtly would Mr Henry reaſon with people ſometimes about this matter, and tell them what a bleſſing it would bring upon them and their houſes, and all that they had. He that makes his houſe a little church ſhall find, that God will make it a little ſanctuary. It may be of uſe to give a particular account of his practice in this matter, becauſe it was very exemplary. As to the time of it, his rule was, commonly the earlier the better, both morning and evening; in the morning before worldly buſineſs crowded in, "early will " I ſeek thee:" he that is the firſt would have the firſt; nor is it fit that the worſhip of God ſhould ſtand by and wait while the world's turn is ſerved. And early in the evening, before the children and ſervants began to be ſleepy; and therefore, if it might be, he would have prayer at night before ſupper, that the body might be the more fit to ſerve the ſoul in that ſervice of God. And indeed he did induſtriouſly contrive all the circumſtances of his family-worſhip, ſo as to make it moſt ſolemn and moſt likely to anſwer the end. He always made it the buſineſs of every day, and not (as too many make it) a by-buſineſs. This being his fixed principle, all other affairs muſt be ſure to give way to this. And he would tell thoſe who objected againſt family-worſhip, that they could not get time for it; that if they would

would but put on chriftian refolution at firft, they would not find the difficulty fo great as they imagined; but after a while, their other affairs would fall in eafily and naturally with this, efpecially where there is that wifdom which is profitable to direct; nay, they would find it to be a great preferver of order and decency in a family, and it would be like a hem to all their other bufinefs, to keep it from ravelling. He was very careful to have all his family prefent at family-worfhip; though fometimes, living in the country, he had a great houfehold; yet he would have not only his children and fojourners (if he had any) and domeftick fervants, but his work-men and day-labourers, and all that were employed for him, if they were within call to be prefent, to join with him in this fervice; and as it was an act of his charity many times to fet them to work for him, fo to that he added this act of piety, to fet them to work for God. And ufually when he paid his workmen their wages, he gave them fome good counfel about their fouls: yet if any that fhould come to family-worfhip were at a diftance, and muft be ftaid for long, he would rather want them, than put the duty much out of time; and would fometimes fay at night, "Better one away "than all fleepy."

The performances of his family-worfhip were the fame morning and evening. He obferved, that under the law, the morning and the evening lamb had the fame meat-offering and drink-offering, Exod. xxix. 38,—41. He always began with a fhort, but very folemn prayer, imploring the divine prefence and grace, affiftance and acceptance; particularly begging a bleffing upon the word to be read, in reference to which he often put up this petition; " That the fame fpirit " that indited the fcripture, would enable us to under- " ftand the fcripture, and to make up fomething to " ourfelves out of it that may do us good :" and efteeming the word of God as his neceffary food, he would fometimes pray in a morning, that " our fouls might " have a good meal out of it." he commonly concluded
even

even this short prayer, as he did also his blessings before and after meat, with a doxology, as Paul upon all occasions, " To Him be glory," &c. which is properly adoration, and is an essential part of prayer.

He next sung a psalm, and commonly he sung David's psalms in order, throughout; sometimes using the old translation, but generally Mr Barton's: and his usual way was to sing a whole psalm throughout, tho' perhaps a long one, and to sing quick; (yet with a good variety of proper and pleasant tunes) and that he might do so, usually the psalm was sung without reading the line betwixt (every one in the family having a book;) which he preferred much before the common way of singing, where it might conveniently be done, as more agreeable to the practice of the primitive church, and the reformed churches abroad; and by this means he thought the duty more likely to be perform'd " in the " spirit, and with the understanding;" the sense being not so broken, nor the affections interrupted, as in reading the line betwixt. He would say, that a scripture ground for singing psalms in families, might be taken from psalm cxviii. 15. " The voice of rejoicing and of " salvation, is in the tabernacles of the righteous;" and that it is a way to hold forth godliness (like Rahab's scarlet thread, Josh. ii. 17.) to such as pass by our windows.

He next read a portion of scripture, taking the Bible in order; he would sometimes blame those who only pray in their families, and do not read the scripture: in prayer we speak to God, by the word he speaks to us; and is there any reason (saith he) that we should speak all? in the tabernacle the priests were every day to burn incense, and to light the lamps; the former figuring the duty of prayer, the latter the duty of reading the word. Sometimes he would say, Those do well that pray morning and evening in their families; those do better, that pray and read the scriptures; but those do best of all that pray, and read, and sing psalms; and Christians should covet earnestly the best gifts.

He

He advifed the reading of the fcripture in order; for though one ftar in the firmament of the fcripture differ from another ftar in glory, yet wherever God hath a mouth to fpeak, we fhould have an ear to hear; and the diligent fearcher may find much excellent matter in thofe parts of fcripture, which we are fometimes tempted to think might have been fpar'd. How affectionately would he fometimes blefs God for every book, and chapter, and verfe, and line, in the Bible!

What he read in his family, he always expounded; and exhorted all minifters to do fo, as an excellent means of increafing their acquaintance with the fcripture. His expofitions were not fo much critical as plain, and practical, and ufeful; and fuch as tended to edification, and to anfwer the end for which the fcriptures were written, which is to make us wife to falvation. And herein he had a peculiar excellence, performing that daily exercife with fo much judgment, and at the fame time with fuch facility and clearnefs, as if every expofition had been premeditated; and very inftructive they were, as well as affecting to the auditors. His obfervations were many times very pretty and furprizing, and fuch as one fhall not ordinarily meet with. Commonly in his expofitions he reduced the matter of the chapter or pfalm read, to fome heads; not by a logical analyfis, which often minceth it too fmall and confounds the fenfe with the terms; but by fuch a diftribution as the matter did moft eafily and unforcedly fall into. He often mention'd that faying of Tertullian's, " I adore the fulnefs of the fcriptures;" and fometimes that, *Scriptura femper habit aliquid relegentibus.* When fometimes he had hit upon fome ufeful obfervation that was new to him, he would fay afterwards to thofe about him, " How often have I read this chapter, and " never before now took notice of fuch a thing in it!" he put his children, while they were with him, to write thefe expofitions; and when they were gone from him, the ftrangers that fojourned with him did the fame. What collections his children had, though but broken

and

and very imperfect hints; yet, when afterwards they were difpofed of in the world, were of good ufe to them and their families. Some expofitions of this nature, that is, plain and practical, and helping to raife the affections and guide the converfation by the word, he often wifhed were publifhed by fome good hand for the benefit of families: but fuch was his great modefty and felf-diffidence (though few more able for it) that he would never be perfwaded to attempt any thing of that kind himfelf. As an evidence how much his heart was upon it, to have the word of God read and underftood in families, take this paffage out of his laft will and teftament: " I give and bequeath to each of my four
" daughters, Mr Pool's Englifh annotations upon the
" Bible, in two volumes, of the laft and beft edition
" that fhall be to be had at the time of my deceafe,
" together with Mr Barton's laft and beft tranflation
" of the finging pfalms, one to each of them; requir-
" ing and requefting them to make daily ufe of the
" fame, for the inftruction, edification, and comfort of
" themfelves and their families." But 'tis time we proceed to the method of his family-worfhip.

The chapter or pfalm being read and expounded, he requir'd from his children fome account of what they could remember of it; and fometimes would difcourfe with them plainly and familiarly about it, that he might lead them into an acquaintance with it; and (if it might be) imprefs fomething of it upon their hearts.

He then pray'd, and always kneeling, which he looked upon as the fitteft and moft proper gefture for prayer; and he took care that his family fhould addrefs themfelves to the duty with the outward expreffions of reverence and compofednefs. He ufually fetch'd his matter and expreffions in prayer, from the chapter that was read, and the pfalm that was fung, which was often very affecting, and helped much to ftir up and excite praying graces. He fometimes obferved in thofe pfalms, where reference is had to the fcripture ftories, as pfalm lxxxiii. and many others, that thofe who are well acquainted

quainted with the scriptures, would not need to make use of the help of prescribed forms, which are very necessary for those that cannot do the duty without them, but are unbecoming those that can; as a go-cart is needful to a child, or crutches to one that is lame, but neither of them agreeable to one that needs them not: 'twas the comparison he commonly used in this matter. In family-prayer he was usually most full in giving thanks for family-mercies, confessing family-sins, and begging family-blessings. Very particular he would sometimes be in prayer for his family; if any were absent, they were sure to have an express petition put up for them. He us'd to observe concerning Job i. 5. that he offered burnt-offerings for his children, according to the number of them all, an offering for each child; and so would he sometimes in praying for his children, put up a petition for each child. He always observ'd at the annual return of the birth-day of each of his children, to bless God for his mercy to him and his wife in that child; the giving of it, the continuance of it, the comfort they had in it, &c. with some special request to God for that child. Every servant and sojourner, at their coming into his family and their going out (besides the daily remembrances of them) had a particular petition put up for them, according as their circumstances were. The strangers that were at any time within his gates, he was wont particularly to recommend to God in prayer, with much affection, and christian concern for them and their concernments. He was daily mindful of those that desired his prayers for them, and would say sometimes, It is a great comfort that God knows who we mean in prayer, though we do not name them. Particular providences concerning the country, as to health or sickness, good or bad weather, or the like, he commonly took notice of in prayer, as there was occasion; and would often beg of God to fit us for the next providence, whatever it might be: nor did he ever forget to pray for the peace of Jerusalem. He always concluded family-prayer, both

morning

morning and evening, with a solemn benediction, after the doxology; "the blessing of God Almighty, "the Father, the Son, and the Holy Ghost, be with "us," &c. Thus did he daily bless his houshold.

Immediately after the prayer was ended, his children together, with bended knee, ask'd blessing of him and their mother; that is, desired of them to pray to God to bless them: which blessing was given with great solemnity and affection; and if any of them were absent, they were remembered, "the Lord bless you "and your brother," or "you and your sister that is "absent."

This was his daily worship, which he never altered, (unless as is aftermentioned) nor ever omitted any part of, though he went from home ever so early, or returned ever so late, or had ever so much business for his servants to do. He would say that sometimes he saw cause to shorten them; but he would never omit any; for if an excuse be once admitted for an omission, it will be often returning. He was not willing (unless the necessity were urgent) that any should go from his house in a morning before family-worship; but upon such an occasion would mind his friends, that "Prayer "and provender never hinder a journey."

He managed his daily family-worship so as to make it a pleasure and not a task to his children and servants; for he was seldom long, and never tedious in the service; the variety of the duties made it the more pleasant; so that none who join'd with him had ever any reason to say, Behold what a weariness is it! Such an excellent faculty he had of rendering religion the most sweet and amiable employment in the world; and so careful was he (like *Jacob*) "to drive as the children "could go," not putting "new wine into old bottles." If some good people that mean well would do likewise, it might prevent many of those prejudices which young persons are apt to conceive against religion, when the services of it are made a toil, and a terror to them.

On Thurſday evenings (inſtead of reading) he catechized his children and ſervants in the Aſſembly's Catechiſm, with the proofs, or ſometimes in a little catechiſm, concerning the matter of prayer, publiſhed in the year 1674, and ſaid to be written by Dr Collins, which they learned for their help in the gift of prayer, and he explained it to them. Or elſe they read, and he examined them in ſome other uſeful book, as Mr Pool's Dialogues againſt the Papiſts, the Aſſembly's Confeſſion of Faith with the Scriptures, or the like.

On Saturday evenings, his children and ſervants gave him an account what they could remember of the chapters that had been expounded all the week before, in order, each a ſeveral part, helping one another's memories for the recollecting of it. This he called, " gathering up the fragments which remained, " that nothing might be loſt." He would ſay to them ſometimes as Chriſt to his diſciples, " Have ye under- " ſtood all theſe things?" If not, he took that occaſion to explain them more fully. This exerciſe (which he conſtantly kept up all along) was both delightful and profitable, and being managed by him with ſo much prudence and ſweetneſs, helped to inſtill into thoſe about him betimes, the knowledge and love of the holy ſcriptures.

When he had ſojourners in his family, who were able to bear a part in ſuch a ſervice, he had commonly, in the winter-time, ſet weekly conferences, on queſtions propoſed, for their mutual edification and comfort in the fear of God; the ſubſtance of what was ſaid, he himſelf took and kept an account of in writing.

But the Lord's day he called and counted the Queen of days, the Pearl of the week, and obſerved it accordingly. The fourth commandment intimates a ſpecial regard to be had to the Sabbath in families, " thou, " and thy ſon, and thy daughter," &c. it is " the Sab- " bath of the Lord in all your dwellings." In this therefore he was very exact, and abounded in the work of the Lord in his family on that day. Whatever were

the

the circumstances of his publick opportunities, (which varied, as we shall find afterwards) his family-religion on that day was the same : extraordinary sacrifices must never supersede the continual burnt-offering and his meat-offering, Numb. xxviii. 15. His common salutation of his family or friends, on the Lord's day in in the morning, was that of the primitive Christians; " the Lord is risen, he is risen indeed;" making it his chief business on that day, to celebrate the memory of Christ's resurrection ; and he would say sometimes, " Every Lord's day is a true Christian's Easter-day." He took care to have his family ready early on that day, and was larger in exposition and prayer on Sabbath-mornings than on other days. He would often remember, that under the law the daily sacrifice was doubled on Sabbath days, two lambs in the morning, and two in the evening. He had always a particular subject for his expositions on Sabbath-mornings ; the harmony of the Evangelists several times over, the Scripture prayers, Old Testament prophesies of Christ, " Christ the true treasure" (so he entitled that subject, " sought and found in the field of the Old Testament." He constantly sung a Psalm after dinner, and another after supper, on the Lord's days. And in the evening of the day his children and servants were catechized and examined in the sense and meaning of the the answers in the catechism ; that they might not say it (as he used to tell them) like a parrot, by rote. Then the day's Sermons were repeated, commonly by one of his Children, when they were grown up, and while they were with him ; and the family gave an account what they could remember of the word of the day, which he endeavoured to fasten upon them, as a nail in a sure place. In his prayers on the evening of the Sabbath, he was often more than ordinarily enlarged ; as one that found not only God's service perfect freedom, but his work its own wages, and a great reward; not only after keeping, but (as he used to observe from Psal. xix. 11.) in keeping God's commandments. A present reward of obedience in obedience. In that prayer he was usually very particular, in praying for his family and all that belong'd to it. It was a prayer he often put up, that we might have grace to carry it " as " a Minister, and a Minister's wife, and a Minister's " children, and a Minister's servants should carry it, " that the ministry might in nothing be blamed." He would sometimes be a particular intercessor for the towns and parishes adjacent : how have I heard him, when he hath been in the mount with God, in a Sabbath-evening-prayer, wrestle with the Lord for Chester, and Shrewsbury, and Nantwich, and Wrexham, and Whitchurch, &c. those nests of souls, wherein there are so many, that cannot discern between their right hand and their left in spiritual things, &c. He closed his Sabbath-work in his family with singing Psalm cxxxiv. and after it a solemn blessing of his family.

Thus was he prophet and priest in his own house ; and he was king there too, ruling in the fear of God, and not suffering sin upon any under his roof.

He had many years ago a man-servant that was once overtaken in drink abroad ; for which, the next morning at family-worship, he solemnly reproved him, admonished him, and prayed for him with a spirit of meekness, and soon after parted with him. But there were many that were his servants, who, by the blessing of God upon his endeavours, got those good impressions upon their souls which they retained ever after ; and blessed God with all their hearts that ever they came under his roof. Few went from his service till they were married, and went to families of their own; and some, after they had been married and had buried their yoke-fellows, returned to his service again, saying, " Master, it is good to be here."

He brought up his children in the fear of God, with a great deal of care and tenderness, and did by his practice, as well as upon all occasions in discourses, condemn the indiscretion of those parents who are partial in their affections to their children, making a difference

ference between them, which he observed did often prove of ill consequence in families; and lay a foundation of envy, contempt, and discord, which turns to their shame and ruin. His carriage towards his children was with great mildness and gentleness, as one who desir'd rather to be loved than feared by them. He was as careful not to provoke them to wrath, nor to discourage them, as he was to bring them up in the nurture and admonition of the Lord. He rul'd indeed, and kept up his authority, but it was with wisdom and love, and not with a high hand. He allowed his children a great degree of freedom with him, which gave him the opportunity of reasoning them, not frightning them, into that which is good. He did much towards the instruction of his children in the way of familiar discourse, acccording to that excellent directory for religious education, Deut. vi. 7. Thou shalt whet these things (so the word is, which he said noted frequent repetition of the same things) upon thy children, and shalt talk of them when thou sittest in thy house, &c, which made them love home, and delight in his company, and greatly endeared religion to them.

He did not burthen his childrens memories by imposing upon them the getting of chapters and psalms without book; but endeavoured to make the whole word of God familiar to them, (especially the scripture stories) and to bring them to understand it and love it, and then they would easily remember it. He used to observe from Psal. cxix. 93. " I will never forget " thy precepts, for with them thou hast quickned me;" that we are then likely to remember the word of God when it doth us good.

He taught all his children to write himself, and set them betimes to write sermons, and other things that might be of use to them. He taught his eldest daughter the Hebrew tongue when she was about six or seven years old, by an English Hebrew grammar, which he made on purpose for her; and she went so far in it, as to be able readily to read and construe a Hebrew psalm.

He

He drew up a short form of the baptismal covenant, for the use of his children; it was this:

"*I take God the Father to be my chiefest good, and highest end.*
I take God the Son to be my Prince and Saviour.
I take God the Holy Ghost to be my sanctifier, teacher, guide, and comforter.
I take the word of God to be my rule in all my actions,
And the people of God to be my people in all conditions.
I do likewise devote and dedicate unto the Lord, my whole self, all I am, all I have, and all I can do.
And this I do deliberately, sincerely, freely, and for ever."

This he taught his children, and they each of them solemnly repeated it every Lord's day in the evening, after they were catechized, he putting his Amen to it, and sometimes adding, " so say, and so do, and you " are made for ever."

He also took pains with them, to lead them into the understanding of it, and to perswade them to a free and cheerful consent to it. And when they grew up, he made them all write it over severally with their own hands, and very solemnly set their names to it, which he told them he would keep by him, and it should be produced as a testimony against them, in case they should afterwards depart from God, and turn from following after him.

He was careful to bring his children betimes (when they were about sixteen years of age) to the ordinance of the Lord's Supper, to take the covenant of God upon themselves, and to make their dedication to God their own act and deed; and a great deal of pains he took with them, to prepare them for that great ordinance, and so to transmit them into the state of adult church-membership: And he would often blame parents, who would think themselves undone if they had not their children baptized, and yet took no care when they grew up and made a profession of the Christian religion

religion, to perfwade them to the Lord's fupper. 'Tis true (he would fay) buds and bloffoms are not fruit, but they give hopes of fruit, and parents may and fhould take hold of the good beginnings of grace which they fee in their children, by thofe who bind them fo much the clofer to, and lead them fo much the fafter in the way that is called holy. By this folemn engagement the door which ftood half open before, and invited the thief, is fhut and bolted againft temptation. And to thofe who pleaded that they were not fit, he would fay, that the further they went into the world, the lefs fit they would be. *Qui non eft hodie cras minus aptus erit.* Not that children fhould be compell'd to it, nor thofe that are wilfully ignorant, untoward, and perverfe, admitted to it; but thofe children that are hopeful and well inclin'd to the things of God, and appear to be concern'd in other duties of religion, when they begin to put away childifh things, fhould be incited, and encouraged, and perfwaded to this, that the matter may be brought to an iffue. " Nay, but we " will ferve the Lord;" faft bind, faft find. Abundant thankfgivings have been rendered to God by many of his friends for his advice and affiftance herein.

In dealing with his children about their fpiritual ftate, he took hold of them very much by the handle of their infant-baptifm, and frequently inculcated that upon them, that they were born in God's houfe, and were betimes dedicated and given up to him, and therefore were oblig'd to be his fervants, Pfal. cxvi. 16. I am thy fervant, becaufe the fon of thy handmaid. This he was wont to illuftrate to them by the comparifon of taking a leafe of a fair eftate for a child in the cradle, and putting his life into it; the child then knows nothing of the matter, nor is he capable of confenting; however, then he is maintained out of it, and hath an intereft in it : and when he grows up and becomes able to chufe, and refufe for himfelf, if he go to his landlord, and claim the benefit of the leafe, and promife to pay the rent, and do the fervices, well and good,

good, he hath the benefit of it, if otherwife, it is at his peril. " Now, children, (would he fay) our great " Landlord was willing that your lives fhould be put " into the leafe of heaven and happinefs, and it was done " accordingly, by your baptifm, which is the feal of " the righteoufnefs that is by faith ; and by that it " was aſſur'd to you, that if you would pay the rent " and do the fervice, that is, live a life of faith and " repentance, and fincere obedience, you fhall never " be turn'd off the tenement ; but if now you diflike the " terms, and refufe to pay this rent (this chief rent, " fo he would call it, for its no rack) you forfeit the " leafe ; however, you cannot but fay, that you had a " kindnefs done you, to have your lives put into it." Thus did he frequently deal with his children, and even travel in birth again to fee Chrift formed in them, and from this topick he generally argued, and he would often fay, If infant baptifm were more improved, it would be lefs difputed.

He not only taught his children betimes to pray, (which he did efpecially by his own pattern, his method and expreffions in prayer being very eafy and plain) but when they were young he put them upon it, to pray together, and appointed them on Saturdays in the afternoon to fpend fome time together ; none but they and fuch of their age as might occafionally be with them, in reading good books, efpecially thofe for children, and in finging and praying ; and would fometimes tell them for their encouragement, that the God with whom we have to do underftands broken language. And if we do as well as we can in the fincerity of our hearts, we fhall not only be accepted, but taught to do better : " to him that hath fhall be given."

He fometimes fet his children, in their own reading of the Scriptures, to gather out fuch paſſages as they took moſt notice of, and thought moſt confiderable, and write them down : though this performance was very fmall, yet the endeavour was of good ufe. He alfo directed them to infert in a paper book, which each of them had for the purpofe, remarkable fayings, and ftories, which they met with in reading fuch other good books as he put into their hands.

He took a pleafure in relating to them the remarkable providences of God, both in his own time, and in the days of old, which he faid, parents were taught to do by that appointment, Exod. xii. 26, 27. Your children fhall afk you in time to come, What mean you by this fervice? and you fhall tell them fo and fo.

What his pious care was concerning his children, and with what a godly jealoufy he was jealous over them, take in one inftance :—when they had been for a week, or a fortnight, kindly entertained at B. (as they were often,) he thus writes in his diary upon their return home: " My care and fear is, left converfe with
" fuch fo far above them, though of the beft, fhould
" have influence upon them to lift them up, when I
" had rather they fhould be kept low." For as he did not himfelf, fo he was very folicitous to teach his children, not to mind high things; not to defire them, not to expect them in this world.

We fhall conclude this chapter with another paffage out of his diary, April 12. 1681. " This day four-
" teen years the Lord took my firft-born fon from me,
" the beginning of my ftrength, with a ftroke. In the
" remembrance whereof my heart melted this even-
" ing: I begg'd pardon for the Jonah that raifed the
" ftorm; I bleffed the Lord that hath fpar'd the reft,
" I begg'd mercy, mercy for every one of them, and
" abfolutely and unrefervedly devoted and dedicated
" them, myfelf, my whole felf, eftate, intereft, and life,
" to the will and fervice of that God from whom I
" received all. Father, hallowed be thy name. Thy
" kingdom come," &c.

I.

CHAP. V.

His ejectment from Worthenbury, his Nonconformity, his removes to Broad Oak, and the providences that were concerning him to the year 1672.

HAVING thus laid together the inftances of his family-religion, we muft now return to the hiftory of events that were concerning him, and are obliged to look back to the firft year after his marriage, which was the year that king Charles the fecond came in; a year of great changes and ftruggles in the land, which Mr Baxter in his life gives a full and clear and impartial idea of; by which it may eafily be guefs'd how it went with Mr Henry in his low and narrow fphere, whofe fentiments in thofe things were very much the fame with Mr Baxter's.

Many of his beft friends in Worthenbury parifh were lately removed by death; Emeral family, contrary to what it had been; and the fame fpirit which that year reviv'd all the nation over, was working violently in that country, viz. a fpirit of great enmity to fuch men as Mr Henry was. Worthenbury, upon the king's coming in, returned into its former relation to Bangor, and was look'd upon as a chappelry dependent upon that. Mr Robert Fogg had for many years held the fequeftred rectory of Bangor, which now Dr Henry Bridgman (fon to John bifhop of Chefter, and brother to the Lord Keeper Bridgman) return'd to the poffeffion of. By which Mr Henry was foon apprehenfive that his intereft at Worthenbury was fhaken, but thus he writes: " The will of the Lord be done. Lord, if
" my work be done here, provide fome other for this
" people that may be more fkilful, and more fuccefs-
" ful, and cut out work for me elfewhere; however,
" I will take nothing ill which God doth with me."

He labour'd what he could to make Dr Bridgman his friend, who gave him good words, and was very civil

vil to him, and affured him that he would never remove him till the law did. But he muft look on himfelf as the Doctor's curate, and depending upon his will, which kept him in continual expectation of a removal; however, he continued in his liberty there above a year, though in very fickle and precarious circumftances.

The grand queftion now on foot was, whether to conform or no. He us'd all means poffible to fatisfy himfelf concerning it, by reading and difcourfe (particularly at Oxford with Dr Fell, afterwards bifhop of Oxford) but in vain, his diffatisfaction remain'd; "however, (faith he) I dare not judge thofe that do conform, for who am I that I fhould judge my brother?" He hath noted, that being at Chefter, in difcourfe with the Dean and Chancellor and others, about this time, the great argument they ufed with him to perfwade him to conform was, that elfe he would lofe his preferment, and what (faid they) you are a young man, and are you wifer than the king and bifhops? But this is his reflection upon it afterwards, " God grant I " may never be left to confult with flefh and blood " in fuch matters."

In September 1660, Mr Fogg, and Mr Steel, and Mr Henry were prefented at Flint-affizes for not reading the common-prayer, though as yet it was not enjoin'd, but there were fome bufy people, that would out-run the law. They entered their appearance, and it fell; for foon after, the king's declaration, touching ecclefiaftical affairs, came out, which promifed liberty, and gave hopes of fettlement; but the fpring-affizes afterwards Mr Steel and Mr Henry were prefented again. On this he writes, " Be merciful to me, O God, for " man would fwallow me up. The Lord fhew me " what he would have me to do, for I am afraid of " nothing but fin."

It appears by the hints of his diary that he had melancholy apprehenfions at this time about public affairs, feeing and hearing of fo many faithful minifters difturb'd, filenced and enfnar'd; the ways of Sion mourning,

mourning, and the quiet in the land treated as the troublers of it; his foul wept in secret for it. And yet he join'd in the annual commemoration of the king's restoration, and preached on Mark xii. 17. " Render to Cæsar the things that are Cæsar's;" considering (saith he) that it was his right; also the sad posture of the civil government through usurpers, and the manner of his coming in, without bloodshed. This he would all his days speak of as a national mercy, but what he rejoiced in with a great deal of trembling for the Ark of God; and he would sometimes say, That " during those years between forty and sixty, though on civil accounts there were great disorders, and the foundations were out of course, yet in the matters of God's worship, things went well; there was freedom and reformation, and a face of godliness was upon the nation, though there were those that made but a mask of it. Ordinances were administred in power, and purity, and though there was much amiss, yet religion, at least in the profession of it, did prevail: This (saith he) we know very well, let men say what they will of those times.

In November, 1660, he took the oath of allegiance at Orton, before Sir Thomas Hanmer, and two other Justices, of which he hath left a memorandum in his diary, with this added, " God so help me, as I purpose " in my heart to do accordingly :" Nor could any more conscientiously observe that oath of God than he did, nor more sincerely promote the ends of it.

That year (according to an agreement with some of his brethren in the ministry, who hoped thereby to o- blige some people) he preached upon Christmas-day. The sabbath before, it happen'd that the 23d chapter of Leviticus (which treats entirely of the Jewish feasts, called there the feasts of the Lord) came in course to be expounded, which gave him occasion to distinguish of feasts into divine and ecclesiastical ; the divine feasts that the Jews had were those there appointed; their ecclesiastical feasts were those of Purim and of dedica-
cation :

cation: and in the application of it, he faid, "he knew no divine feaft we have under the gofpel but the Lord's day, intended for the commemoration of the whole mercy of our redemption. And the moft that could be faid for *Chriftmas* was, that it is an *ecclefiaftical* feaft; and it is queftionable with fome, whether church or ftate, though they might make a good day, Efth. ix. 19. could make a holy day: neverthelefs, forafmuch as we find our Lord Jefus (Job x. 22.) fo far complying with the church feaft of dedication, as to take occafion from the people's coming together, to preach to them, he purpofed to preach upon Chriftmas day, knowing it to be his duty, in feafon and out of feafon." He preached on 1 John iii. 8. "For this purpofe was "the Son of God manifefted, that he might deftroy "the works of the devil." And he minded his people that it is double difhonour to Jefus Chrift, to practife the works of the devil then when we keep a feaft in memory of his manifeftation.

His annuity from Emeral was now with-held becaufe he did not read the common prayer, (tho' as yet there was no law for reading of it) hereby he was difabled to do what he had been wont, for the help and relief of others; and this he has recorded as that which troubled him moft under that difappointment; but he bleffed God, that he had a heart to do good, even when his hand was empty.

When Emeral family was unkind to him, he reckoned it a great mercy, which he gave God thanks for, (who makes every creature to be that to us that it is) that Mr Broughton and his family (which is of confiderable figure in the parifh) continued their kindnefs and refpects to him, and their countenance of his miniftry, which he makes a grateful mention of, more than once in his diary.

Many attempts were made in the year 1661 to difturb and enfnare him, and it was ftill expected that he would have been hindred: " Methinks (faid he) " Sabbaths were never fo fweet as they are, now we
" are

"are kept at such uncertainties; now a day in thy
"courts is better than a thousand; such a day as this
"(faith he of a Sacrament-day that year) better than
"ten thousand: O that we might yet see many such
"days."

He was advis'd by Mr Ratcliff of Chester, and others of his friends, to enter an action against Mr P. for his annuity, and did so; but concerning the success of it (faith he) " I am not over solicitous; for tho' it be my due, (Luke x. 7.) yet it was not that which I preached for; and God knows I would much rather preach for nothing, than not at all; and besides, I know assuredly, if I should be cast, God would make it up to me some other way." After some proceedings, he not only mov'd, but solicited Mr P. to refer it; " ha-
" ving learned (faith he) that it is no disparagement,
" but an honour, for the party wrong'd to be first in
" seeking reconciliation; the Lord, (if it be his will)
" incline his heart to peace. I have now two great
" concerns upon the wheel, one in reference to my
" maintenance for time past; the other as to my con-
" tinuance for the future; the Lord be my friend in
" both; but of the two, rather in the latter. But ma-
" ny of greater gifts and grace than I are laid aside
" already, and when my turn comes I know not, the
" will of God be done: He can do his work with-
" out us."

The issue of this affair was, that there having been some disputes between Mr P. and Dr Bridgman, about the tithe of Worthenbury, wherein Mr P. had clearly the better claim to make, yet, by the mediation of Sir Tho. Hanmer, they came to this agreement, Sept. 11. 1661. that Dr Bridgman and his successors, parsons of Bangor, should have and receive all the tithe-corn and hay of Worthenbury, without the disturbance of the said Mr P. or his heirs (except the tithe-hay of Emeral Demesn) upon condition that Dr Bridgman should, before the first of November following, avoid and discharge the present minister, or curate, Philip Henry,

from

from the chapel of Worthenbury, and not hereafter at any time re-admit the said minister, Philip Henry, to officiate the said cure. This is the substance of the articles agreed upon between them, pursuant to which, Dr Bridgman soon after dismiss'd Mr Henry; and by a writing under his hand, which was published in the church of Worthenbury, by one of Mr Puleston's servants, October the 27th following, notice was given to the parish of that dismission. That day he preached his farewell sermon on Phil. i. 27. " only let your " conversation be as becomes the gospel of Christ." In which (as he saith in his diary) his desire and design was rather to profit than to affect; it matters not what becomes of me (whether I come unto you, or else be absent) but let your conversation be as becomes the gospel. His parting prayer for them was, " the " Lord, the God of the spirits of all flesh, set a man " over the congregation." Thus he ceased to preach to his people there, but he ceased not to love them, and pray for them; and could not but think there remained some dormant relation betwixt him and them.

As to the arrears of his annuity from Mr P. when he was displaced; after some time Mr P. was willing to give him 100*l*. which was a good deal less than what was due, upon condition that he would surrender his deed of annuity, and his lease of the house, which he for peace sake was willing to do, and so he lost all the benefit of judge Puleston's great kindness to him. This was not compleated till Sept. 1662. until which time he continued in the house at Worthenbury, but never preached so much as once in the church, tho' there were vacancies several times.

Mr R. Hilton was immediately put into the curacy of Worthenbury, by Dr Bridgman: Mr Henry went to hear him while he was at Worthenbury, and join'd in all the parts of the public worship, particularly attending upon the Sacrament of baptism; " not daring (saith he) to turn my back upon God's ordinance, while the essentials of it are retained, tho' corrupted circumstantially in the administration of it, which God amend." Once being allow'd the liberty of his gesture, he join'd in the Lord's Supper. He kept up his correspondence with Mr Hilton, and (as he saith in his diary) endeavour'd to possess him with right thoughts of his work, and advis'd him the best he could in the foul affairs of that people ; " which (saith he) he seemed to take well ; I am sure I meant it so, and the Lord make him faithful."

Immediately after he was removed and silenced at Worthenbury, he was solicited to preach at Bangor, and Dr Bridgman was willing to permit it, occasionally, and intimated to his curate there, that he should never hinder it; but Mr Henry declin'd it : though his silence was his great grief, yet such was his tenderness, that he was not willing so far to discourage Mr Hilton at Worthenbury, nor to draw so many of the people from him as would certainly have followed him to Bangor : " but (saith he) I cannot get my heart into such a spiritual frame on Sabbath-days now, as formerly ; which is both my sin and my affliction. Lord, quicken me with quickening grace."

When the king came in first, and shewed so good a temper, as many thought, some of his friends were very earnest with him to revive his acquaintance and interest at court, which it was thought he might easily do. 'Twas reported in the country, that the Duke of York had enquired after him ; but he heeded not the report, nor would he be perswaded to make any addresses that way : " for (saith he) my friends do not know so well as I the strength of temptation, and my own inability to deal with it." *Qui bene latuit, bene vixit* ; Lord, lead me not into temptation.

He was greatly affected with the temptations and afflictions of many faithful Ministers of Christ at this time, by the pressing of conformity ; and kept many private days of fasting and prayer in his own house at Worthenbury, seeking to turn away the wrath of God from the Land. He greatly pitied some, who by the urgency

urgency of friends, and the fear of want, were overperfwaded to put a force upon themfelves in their conformity. The Lord keep me (faith he) in the critical time.

He preached fometimes occafionally in divers neighbouring places, till Bartholomew-day, 1662; " the day (faith he) which our fins have made one of the faddeft days to England fince the death of Edward the VI. but even this for good," though we know not how nor which way. He was invited to preach at Bangor on the black Bartholomew-day, and prepared a fermon on John vii. 37. " In the laft day, that " great day of the feaft," &c. but was prevented from preaching it, and was loth to ftrive againft fo ftrong a ftream.

As to his non-conformity, which fome of his worft enemies have faid was his only fault, it may not be amifs here to give fome account of it.

1. His reafons for his non-conformity were very confiderable. 'Twas no rafh act, but deliberate and well weigh'd in the balances of the fanctuary. He could by no means fubmit to be re-ordain'd; fo well fatisfied was he in his call to the miniftry, and his folemn ordination to it, by the laying on of the hands of the prefbytery, which God had gracioufly own'd him in, that he durft not do that which looked like a renunciation of it, as null and finful, and would be at leaft a tacit invalidating and condemning of all his adminiftrations. Nor could he truly fay, that he thought himfelf moved by the Holy Ghoft to take upon him the office of a Deacon. He was the more confirmed in this objection, becaufe the then Bifhop of Chefter, Dr Hall, (in whofe diocefe he was) befides all that was required by law, exacted from thofe that came to him to be re-ordained, a fubfcription to this form :---" Ego
" A. B. prætenfas meas ordinationis literas, a quibuf-
" dam prefbyteris olim obtentas jam penitus renuncio,
" & dimitto pro vanis; humiliter fupplicans quatenus
" Rev. in Chrifto Pater, & Dominus Georgius permiffione

"missione divina Cestr. Episc. me ad sacrum diacona- tus ordinem juxta morem & ritus Ecclesiæ Angli- canæ dignaretur admittere." This of re-ordination was the first and great bar to his conformity, and which he mostly insisted on. He would sometimes say, that for a Presbyter to be ordain'd a Deacon, is at best, "suscipere gradum Simeonis."

Besides this, he was not at all satisfied to give his unfeigned assent and consent, to all and every thing contained in the book of Common-Prayer, &c. for he thought that thereby he should receive the book itself, and every part thereof, rubrics and all, both as true and good; whereas there was several things which he could not think to be so. The exceptions which the ministers made against the liturgy, at the Savoy con- ference, he thought very considerable; and could by no means submit to, much less approve of, the impo- sition of the ceremonies: He often said, that when Christ came to free us from the yoke of one ceremo- nial law, he did not leave it in the power of any man, or company of men, in the world, to lay another up- on our necks. Kneeling at the Lord's Supper he was. much dissatisfied about; and it was for many years his great grief, and which in his diary he doth often most pathetically lament; that by it he was debarred from partaking of that ordinance, in the solemn af- sembly: for, to submit to that imposition, he thought, whatever it was to others, (whom he was far from judging) would be sin to him. He never took the covenant, nor ever expressed any fondness for it; and yet he could not think, and therefore durst not de- clare that (however unlawfully impos'd,) it was in it- self an unlawful oath, and that no person that took it was under the obligation of it: For sometimes "quod fieri non debuit factum valet." In short, it cannot be wondered at, that he was a non-conformist, when the terms of conformity were so industriously contriv- ed to keep out of the church such men as he; which is manifest by the full account which Mr Baxter hath

left

left to posterity of that affair; and it is a paſſage worth noticing here, which Dr Bates, in his funeral ſermon on Mr Baxter, relates; that when the Lord Chamberlain, Mancheſter, told the king, (while the act of uniformity was under debate) that he was afraid that the terms were ſo hard, that many of the miniſters would not comply with them; Biſhop Sheldon being preſent, replied, I am afraid they will. And it is well known how many of the moſt ſober, pious, and laborious miniſters, in all parts of the nation, conformiſts as well non-conformiſts did diſlike thoſe impoſitions.

He thought it a mercy (ſince it muſt be ſo) that the caſe of non-conformity was made ſo clear as it was, abundantly to ſatisfy him in his ſilence and ſufferings. I have heard that Mr Anthony Burges, who heſitated before, when he read the act, bleſſed God that the matter was put out of doubt. And yet to make ſure work, the printing and publiſhing of the new book of Common-Prayer was ſo deferred, that few of the miniſters, except thoſe in London, could poſſibly get a ſight of it, much leſs duly confider of it before the time prefixed; which Mr Steel took notice of in his farewell-ſermon at Hanmer, Aug. 17. 1662, That he was ſilenced and turned out, for not declaring his unfeigned aſſent and conſent to a book which he never ſaw nor could ſee.

One thing which he comforted himſelf with in his non-conformity was, that as to matters of doubtful diſputation touching church-government, ceremonies, and the like, he was unſworn, either on the one ſide or the other, and ſo was free from thoſe ſnares and bands in which ſo many find themſelves both tied up from what they would do, and entangled that they knew not what to do. He was one of thoſe that fear'd an oath, Eccl. x. 2. and would often ſay, Oaths are edg'd tools, and not to be played with. One paſſage I find in his papers, which confirmed him in this ſatisfaction; 'tis a letter from no leſs a clergyman than Dr F. of Whitchurch to one of his pariſhioners, who deſired him to give way that his child might be baptised by another without the cross and godfathers, if he would not do it so himself; both which he refused: 'Twas in the year 1672-3. "For my part, (saith the Doctor) " I freely profess my thoughts, that the strict urging " of indifferent ceremonies, hath done more harm than " good; and possibly (had all men been left to their " liberty therein) there might have been much more " unity, and not much less uniformity. But what " power have I to dispense with myself, being now " under the obligation of a law and an oath?" And he concludes, "I am much grieved at the unhappy con- " dition of myself, and other ministers, who must ei- " ther lose their parishioners love, if they do not com- " ply with them, or else break their solemn obliga- " tions to please them."

This he would say was the mischief of impositions, which ever were, and ever will be bones of contention. When he was at Worthenbury, though in the Lord's Supper he used the gesture of sitting himself, yet he administered it without scruple to some who chose rather to kneel; and he thought that minister's hands should not, in such things be tied up; but that he ought in his place, (though he suffered for it,) to witness against the making of those things the indispensable terms of communion, which Jesus Christ hath not made to be so. " Where the Spirit of the " Lord, and the spirit of the gospel is, there is liber- " ty."

Such as these were the reasons of his non-conformity, which, as long as he lived, he was more and more confirm'd in.

2. His moderation in his non-conformity was very exemplary and eminent, and had a great influence upon many, to keep them from running into an uncharitable and schismatical separation; which, upon all occasions, he bore his testimony against, and was very industrious to stem the tide of. In church-government, that which he desired and wished for, was Archbishop Usher's

Usher's reduction of Episcopacy. He thought it lawful to join in the common-prayer in public assemblies, and practised accordingly, and endeavoured to satisfy others concerning it. The spirit he was of, was such as made him much afraid of extremes, and solicitous for nothing more than to maintain and keep Christian love and charity among professors: We shall meet with several instances of this, in the progress of his story, and therefore wave it here. I have been told of an aged minister of his acquaintance, who being asked upon his death-bed, What his thoughts were of his non-conformity? replied, He was well satisfied in it, and should not have conformed so far as he did, (viz. to join in the liturgy,) if it had not been for Mr Henry. Thus was his moderation known unto all men.

But to proceed in his story :---at Michaelmas 1662, he quite left Worthenbury, and came with his family to Broad-Oak, just nine years from his first coming into the country. Being cast by divine Providence into this new place and state of life, his care and prayer was, that he might have grace and wisdom to manage it to the glory of God, which (saith he) is my chief end. Within three weeks after his coming hither, his second son was born, which we mention for the sake of the remark he has upon it :----" We have no reason (saith he) to call him *Benoni*, I wish we had none to call him *Ichabod*." And on the day of his family-thanksgiving for that mercy, he writes, " We have
" reason to rejoice with trembling, for it goes ill with
" the church and people of God, and reason to fear
" worse, because of our sins, and our enemies wrath."

At the latter end of this year he hath in his diary this note : " It is observed of many who have con-
" formed of late, and fallen from what they formerly
" professed, that, since their so doing, from unblam-
" able, orderly, pious men, they are become exceed-
" ing dissolute and profane, and instanceth in some.
" What need have we every day to pray, Lord, lead
" us not into temptation."

For

For several years after he came to live at Broad-Oak, he went constantly on the Lord's day to the public worship, with his family, at Whitewell-chapel, (which is hard by) if there were any supply there, as sometimes there was from Malpas; and if none, then to Tylstock, (where Mr Zachary Thomas continued for about half a year, and the place was a little sanctuary,) and when that string fail'd, usually to Whitchurch; and did not preach for a great while, unless occasionally, when he visited his friends, or to his own family on Lord's days, when the weather hindred them from going abroad. He comforted himself, that sometime in going in public, he had opportunity of instructing and exhorting those that were in company with him, by the way, according as he saw they had need; and in this his lips fed many, and his tongue was as choice silver; and he acted according to that rule which he often laid down to himself and others, That when we cannot do what we would, we must do what we can, and the Lord will accept us in it. He made the best of the sermons he heard in public. It is a mercy (saith he) we have bread, though it be not as it hath been, of the finest of the wheat. Those are froward children who throw away the meat they have, if it be wholesome, because they have not what they would have. When he met with preaching that was weak, his note is, That's a poor sermon indeed, out of which no good lesson may be learned. He had often occasion to remember that verse of Mr Herbert's,

" The worst speaks something good, if all want sense,
" God takes the text, and preacheth patience."

Nay, and once he saith, he could not avoid thinking of Eli's sons, who made the sacrifices of the Lord to be abhorred: yet he went to bear his testimony to public ordinances; " For still (saith he) the Lord loves " the gates of Zion more than all the dwellings of " Jacob," and so do I. Such then were his sentiments of things, expecting that God would yet open

a door

a door of return to former public liberty, which he much defired and prayed for, and in hopes of that, was backward to fall into the ftated exercife of his miniftry otherwife, (as were all the fober non-conformifts generally in thofe parts,) but it was his grief and burthen, that he had not an opportunity of doing more for God. He had fcarce one talent of opportunity, but that one he was very diligent and faithful in the improvement of. When he vifited his friends, how did he lay out himfelf to do them good ? Being afked once, (where he made a vifit,) to expound and pray, which his friends returned him thanks for ; he thus writes upon it, " They cannot thank me fo much for " my pains, but I thank them more, and my Lord " God efpecially, for the opportunity." Read his conflict with himfelf at this time : " I own myfelf a mi- " nifter of Chrift, yet do nothing as a minifter ; what " will excufe me ! Is it enough for me to fay, Behold, " I ftand in the market-place, and no man hath hired " me ?" And he comforts himfelf with this appeal, " Lord, thou knoweft what will I have to thy work, " public or private, if I had a call and opportunity ;" and fhall this willing mind be accepted ? Surely this is a melancholy confideration, and lays a great deal of blame fomewhere, that fuch a man as Mr Henry, fo well qualified with gifts and graces for minifterial work, and in the prime of his time for ufefulnefs ; fo found and orthodox, fo humble and modeft, fo quiet and peaceable, fo pious and blamelefs, fhould be fo induftrioufly thruft out of the vineyard, as a ufelefs and unprofitable fervant, and laid afide as a defpifed broken veffel, and a veffel in which there was no pleafure. This is a lamentation, and fhall be for a lamentation ; efpecially fince it was not his cafe alone, but the lot of fo many hundreds of the fame character.

In thefe circumftances of filence and reftraint, he took comfort himfelf, and adminiftered comfort to others from that Scripture, Ifa. xvi. 4. " Let my out- " cafts dwell with thee, Moab." God's people may

be

be an out-cast people, cast out of men's love, their synagogues, their country; but God will own his people when men cast them out; they are out-casts, but they are his, and somewhere or other he will provide a dwelling for them. There were many worthy, able ministers, thereabouts turn'd out, both from work and subsistence, that had not such comfortable support for the life that now is, as Mr Henry had, for whom he was most affectionately concerned, and to whom he shewed much kindness. There were computed, within a few miles round him, so many ministers turned out to the wide world, stript of all their maintenance, and exposed to continual hardships, as with their wives and children, (having most of them numerous families,) made up above a hundred, that lived upon Providence; and though often reduced to wants and straits, yet were not forsaken, but were enabled to rejoice in the Lord, and to joy in the God of their salvation notwithstanding: to whom the promise was fulfilled, Psal. xxxvii. 3. " So shalt thou dwell in the " land, and verily thou shalt be fed." The world was told long since, by the conformists plea, that the worthy Mr Lawrence, (Mr Henry's intimate friend) when he was turned out of Baschurch, and (if he would have consulted with flesh and blood) having (as was said of one of the martyrs) eleven good arguments against suffering, viz. a wife and ten children, was asked how he meant to maintain them all, and cheerfully replied, they must all live on the vi. of Matthew, " Take no thought for your life," &c. and he often sung with his family Psal. xxxvii. 16. And Mr Henry hath noted concerning him in his diary, some time after he was turn'd out, that he bore witness to the love and care of our heavenly Father, providing for him and his in his present condition, beyond expectation.

One observation Mr Henry made not long before he died, when he had been young and now was old, that though many of the ejected ministers were brought very

very low, had many children, were greatly harraffed by perfecution, and their friends generally poor and unable to fupport them; yet in all his acquaintance he never knew, nor could remember to have heard, of any non-conformift minifter in prifon for debt.

In October 1663, Mr Steel and Mr Henry, and fome other of their friends, were taken up and brought prifoners to Hanmer, under pretence of fome plot faid to be on foot againft the Government; and there they were kept under confinement fome days, on which he writes, " It is fweet being in any condition with a clear confcience: The fting of death is fin, and fo of imprifonment alfo. 'Tis the firft time I was ever a prifoner, but perhaps may not be the laft. We felt no hardfhip, but we know not what we may." They were, foon after, examined by the deputy lieutenants, charged with they knew not what, and fo difmiffed, finding verbal fecurity to be forthcoming upon twenty-four hours notice whenever they fhould be called for. Mr Henry returned to his tabernacle with thankfgivings to God, and a hearty prayer for his enemies, that God would forgive them. The very next day after they were releafed, a great man in the country, at whofe inftigation they were brought into that trouble, died (as was faid) of a drunken furfeit. So that a man fhall fay, " Verily there is a God that judgeth " in the earth."

In the beginning of the year 1665, when the act for a royal aid to his Majefty of two millions and a half came out, the commiffioners for Flintfhire were pleafed to nominate Mr. Henry fub-collector of the faid tax for the townfhip of Ifcoyd, and Mr Steel for the townfhip of Hanmer. They intended thereby to put an affront and difparagement upon their miniftry, and to fhew that they looked upon them but as lay-men; his note upon it is, " It is not a fin which they put us upon, but it is a crofs, and a crofs in our way, and therefore to be taken up and borne with patience. When I had better work to do, I was wanting in my duty about it, it, and now this is put upon me, the Lord is righteous." He procured the gathering of it by others, only took account of it, and faw it duly done ; and deferved (as he faid he hop'd he fhould) that infcription mentioned in Suetonius, To the memory of an honeft Publican.

In September the fame year he was again, by warrant from the deputy lieutenants, fetched prifoner to Hanmer, as was alfo Mr Steel and others. He was examined about private meetings : fome fuch (but private indeed) he own'd he had been prefent at of late in Shropfhire, but the occafion was extraordinary; the plague was at that time raging in London, and he, and feveral of his friends, having near relations there, thought it time to feek the Lord for them, and this was imputed to him as his crime. He was likewife charged with adminiftring the Lord's Supper, which he denied, having never adminiftred it fince he was difabled by the act of Uniformity. After fome days confinement, feeing they could prove nothing upon him, he was difcharged upon recognizance of 20l. with two fureties to be forthcoming upon notice, and to live peaceably. But (faith he) our reftraint was not ftrict, for we had liberty of prayer and conference together, to our mutual edification : Thus, " out of the " eater came forth meat, and out of the ftrong, fweet- " nefs;" and we found honey in the carcafe of the lion. It was but a little before this that Mr Steel, fetting out for London, was, by a warrant from the juftices, under colour of the report of a plot, ftopped and fearched, and finding nothing to accufe him of, they feized his almanack, in which he kept his diary for that year; and it not being written very legibly, they made what malicious readings and comments they pleafed upon it, to his great wrong and reproach; though, to all fober and fenfible people, it difcovered him to be a man that kept a ftrict watch over his own heart, and was a a great hufband of his time, and many faid they got good by it, and fhould love him the better for it, Pfal. xxxvii. 5, 6. This event made Mr Henry fomewhat

more

more cautious and sparing in the records of his diary, when he saw how evil men dig up mischief.

At Lady-day, 1666, the five-mile act commenced, by which all non-conformist ministers were forbidden, upon pain of six months imprisonment, to come or be within five miles of any corporation, or of any place where they had been ministers, unless they would take an oath; of which Mr Baxter saith, 'twas credibly reported, that the Earl of Southampton, then Lord high treasurer of England, said, No honest man could take it. Mr Baxter, in his Life, hath set down at large, his reasons against taking this Oxford-oath, as it was called, part ii. p. 396, &c. part iii. p. 4, &c. Mr Henry set his down in short, 'Twas an oath, not at any time to endeavour any alteration of the government in the church or state. He had already taken an oath of allegiance to the King, and he looked upon this to amount to an oath of allegiance to the bishops, which he was not free to take. Thus he writes, March 22, 1665-6:

" This day methoughts it was made more clear to
" me than ever, by the hand of my God upon me, and
" I note it down, that I may remember it. (1.) That
" the government of the church of Christ ought to
" be managed by the ministers of Christ." It appears, Heb. xiii. 7. that they are to rule us that speak to us the word of God. " (2.) That, under prelacy,
" ministers have not the management of church-go-
" vernment, not in the least, being only the publish-
" ers of the prelates decrees, as in excommunication
" and absolution, which decrees sometimes are given
" forth by lay-chancellors. (3.) That therefore
" prelacy is an usurpation in the church of God, u-
" pon the crown and dignity of Jesus Christ, and u-
" pon the gospel-rights of his servants the ministers.
" And therefore, (4.) I ought not to subscribe to it,
" nor to swear not to endeavour, in all lawful ways,
" the alteration of it, viz. by praying and perswading,
" where there is opportunity. But, (5.) That I may

safely

"safely venture to suffer in the refusal of such an oath, committing my soul, life, estate, liberty, all to Him who judgeth righteously."

And on March 25, the day when that act took place, he thus writes: "A sad day among poor ministers up and down this nation; who, by this act of restraint, are forced to remove from among their friends, acquaintance, and relations, and to sojourn among strangers, as it were in Mesech and in the tents of Kedar. But there is a God who tells their wandrings, and will put their tears, and the tears of their wives and children into his bottle; are they not in his book? The Lord be a little sanctuary to them, and a place of refuge from the storm, and from the tempest; and pity those places from which they are ejected, and come and dwell where they may not."

He wished their removes might not be figurative of evil to these nations, as Ezekiel's were, Ezek. xii. 1, 2, 3. This severe dispensation forced Mr Steel and his family from Hanmer, and so he lost the comfort of his neighbourhood; but withal it drew Mr Laurence from Buschurch to Whitchurch parish, where he continued till he was driven thence too.

Mr Henry's house at Broad-Oak was but four computed miles from the utmost limits of Worthenbury parish, but he got it measured, and accounting 1760 yards to a mile (according to the Statute 35 Eliz. cap. 6.) it was found to be just five miles and threescore yards, which one would think, might have been his security: but there were those near him who were ready to stretch such laws to the utmost rigor, under pretence of construing them in favour of the King, and therefore would have it be understood of computed miles. This obliged him for some time to leave his family, and to sojourn among his friends, to whom he endeavoured, where-ever he came, to impart some spiritual gift. At last he ventured home; presuming, among other things, that the warrant by which he was made collector of the royal aid, while that continued, would secure him,

according

according to a proviso in the last clause of the act, which, when the gentlemen perceived, they discharged him from that office before he had served out the time.

He was much affected with it, that the burning of London happened so soon after the non-conformists were banished out of it. He thought it was in mercy to them that they were removed before that desolating judgment came, but that it spoke aloud to our governors, " Let my people go, that they may serve " me; and if ye will not, behold thus and thus will I " do unto you." This was the Lord's voice crying in the city.

In the beginning of the year 1667, he removed with his family to Whitchurch, and dwelt there above a year, except that for one quarter of a year, about harvest, he returned again to Broad-Oak. His remove to Whitchurch was partly to quiet his adversaries, who were ready to quarrel with him upon the five-mile act, and partly for the benefit of the school there for his children.

There, in April following, he buried his eldest son, not quite six years old, a child of extraordinary pregnancy and forwardness in learning, and of a very towardly disposition: his character of this child is,

. *Præterque aetatem nil puerile fuit.*

This child, before he was seized with the sickness whereof he died, was much affected with some verses, which he met with in Mr White's Power of Godliness, said to be found in the pocket of a hopeful young man, who died before he was twenty-four years old. Of his own accord he got them without book, and would be often rehearsing them, they were these:

> Not twice twelve years (he might say
> Not half twelve years) full told, a wearied breath
> I have exchanged for a happy death.
> Short was my life; the longer is my rest,
> God takes them soonest whom he loveth best.

He

He that is born to-day, and dies to-morrow,
Lofes fome hours of joy, but months of forrow;
Other difeafes often come to grieve us,
Death ftrikes but once, and that ftroke doth relieve us.

This was a great affliction to the tender parents: Mr Henry writes upon it in the reflection,

Quicquid amas cupias non placuiffe nimis.

Many years after, he faid, he thought he did apply to himfelf at that time, but too fenfibly, that fcripture, Lam. iii. 1. "I am the man that hath feen affliction." And he would fay to his friends upon fuch occafions, " Lofers think they may have leave to fpeak, but they " muft have a care what they fay, left, fpeaking amifs " to God's difhonour, they make work for repentance, " and fhed tears that muft be wept over again." He obferved concerning this child, that he had always been very patient under rebukes, "The remembrance of which (faith he) teacheth me now how to carry it under the rebukes of my heavenly Father." His prayer under this providence was, "Shew me, Lord, fhew me wherefore thou contendeft with me; have I over-boafted, over-lov'd, over-priz'd?" A Lord's day intervening between the death and burial of the child, " I attended (faith he) on publick ordinances, though fad in fpirit, as Job, who, after all the evil tidings that were brought him, whereof death of children was the laft and heavieft, yet fell down and worfhipped." And he would often fay upon fuch occafions, that weeping muft not hinder fowing. Upon the interment of the child, he writes, "My dear child, now mine no longer, was laid in the cold earth; not loft, but fown to be raifed again a glorious body, and I fhall go to him, but he fhall not return to me." A few days after, his dear friend Mr Lawrence (then living in Whitchurch parifh) buried a daughter, that was grown up and very hopeful, and gave good evidence of a work of grace wrought upon her foul: How willing (faith he) may parents be to part with fuch when the Lord calls; they
are

are not *amiſſi* but *praemiſſi*. And he hath this further remark, " The Lord hath made his poor servants, that have been often companions in his work, now companions in tribulation, the very same tribulation; me for my sin, him for his trial."

While he liv'd at Whitchurch, he attended constantly upon the publick ministry, and there (as ever) he was careful to come to the beginning of the service, which he attended upon with reverence and devotion; standing all the time, even while the chapters were read. In the evening of the Lord's day, he spent some time in instructing his family, to which a few of his friends and neighbours in the town would sometimes come in; and it was a little gleam of opportunity, but very short, for (as he notes) " He was offended at it, who should rather have rejoiced, if by any means the work might be carried on in his people's souls."

He observes in his diary this year, how zealous people had generally been for the observation of Lent a while ago, and how cold they are towards it now. The same he notes of processions in ascension-week; for (faith he) what hath no good foundation will not hold up long; but in that which is duty, and of God, it is good to be zealously affected always.

In this year (I think) was the first time that he administred the Lord's Supper (very privately to be sure) after he was silenced by the act of uniformity, and he did not do it without mature deliberation. A fear of separation kept him from it so long; what induced him to it at last, I find thus under his own hand: " I am a minister of Christ, and as such I am obliged, *Virtute officii*, by all means to endeavour the good of souls. Now here's a company of serious Christians, whose lot is cast to live in a parish where there is one set over them who preacheth the truth; and they come to hear him, and join with him in other parts of worship; only as to the Lord's Supper; they scruple the lawfulness of the gesture of kneeling; and he tells them, his hands are tied, and he cannot administer it unto them any

other

other way; wherefore they come to me, and tell me, they earneftly long for that ordinance; and there is a competent number of them, and opportunity to partake; and how dare I deny this requeſt of theirs, without betraying my miniſterial truſt, and incurring the guilt of a grievous omiſſion."

In February 1667-8, Mr Laurence and he were invited by fome of their friends to Betley in Staffordſhire, and (there being fome little public connivance at that time) with the confent of all concerned, they adventured to preach in the church, one in the morning, and the other in the afternoon of the Lord's day, very peaceably and profitably. This action of theirs was prefently after reported in the Houſe of Commons by a member of Parliament, with theſe additions, that they tore the common-prayer book, trampled the furplice under their feet, pull'd the miniſter of the place out of the pulpit, &c. Reports which there was not the leaſt colour for. But that, with fome other fuch like falfe ſtories, produced an addrefs of the Houfe of Commons to the King, to iſſue out a proclamation, fòr the putting of the laws in execution againſt papiſts and nonconformiſts, which was iſſued out accordingly; though the King, at the opening of that feſſion, a little before, had declared his defire, that fome courfe might be taken to compofe the minds of his proteſtant fubjects in matters of religion; which had raifed the expectations of fome, that there would be fpeedy enlargement; but Mr Henry had noted upon it, " We cannot expect too little from man, nor too much from GOD."

And here it may be very pertinent to obferve, how induſtrious Mr Henry was at this time, when he and his friends fuffered fuch hard things from the government, to preferve and promote a good affection to the government notwithſtanding. It was commonly charged at that time upon the non-conformiſts in general, efpecially from the pulpits, that they were all a factious and turbulent people, and, as was faid of old, Ezra iv. 16, " hurtful to Kings and provinces;" that their

meetings

meetings were for the fowing of fedition and difcontents, and the like; and there is fome reafon to think, that one thing intended by the hardfhips put upon them was to drive them to this. There is a way of making a wife man mad. But how peaceably they carried themfelves, is manifeft to God, and in the confciences of many. For an inftance of it, it will not be amifs to give fome account of a fermon which Mr Henry preached in fome very private meetings, fuch as were called feditious conventicles, in the year 1669, when it was a day of treading down, and of perplexity; it was on that text, Pfal. xxxv. 20. " Againft them that " are quiet in the land;" whence (not to curry favour with rulers, for whatever the fermon was, the very preaching of it, had it been known, muft have been feverely punifhed, but purely out of confcience towards God) he taught his friends this doctrine, " That it is the character of the people of God, that " they are a quiet people in the land." " This quietnefs " he defcribed to be an orderly, peaceable fubjection " to governors and government in the Lord. We muft " maintain a reverent efteem of them, and of their " authority, in oppofition to defpifing dominion, 2 " Pet. ii. 10.; we muft be meek under fevere com-
" mands, and burthenfome impofitions, not murmur-
" ing and complaining, as the Ifraelites againft Mofes
" and Aaron; but take them up as our crofs in our
" way, and bear them as we do foul weather. We
" muft not fpeak evil of dignities, Jude, ver. 8.; nor
" revile the gods, Exod. xxii. 28. Paul checked him-
" felf for this, Acts xxiii. 5. I did not confider it, if
" I had, I would not have faid fo. We muft not tra-
" duce their government as Abfalom did David's, 2
" Sam. xv. 3. Great care is to be taken, how we fpeak
" of the faults of any, efpecially of rulers, Eccl. x.
" 20.---The people of God do make the word of God
" their rule, and by that they are taught, (1.) that
" magiftracy is God's ordinance, and magiftrates
" God's minifters; that by Him kings reign, and the

"powers that be are ordained of him. (2.) That they, as well as others, are to have their dues, honour, and fear, and tribute. (3.) That their lawful commands are to be obey'd, and that readily and chearfully, Titus iii. 1. (4.) That the penalties inflicted for not obeying unlawful commands are patiently to be undergone. This is the rule, and as many as walk according to this rule, peace shall be upon them, and there can be no danger of their unpeaceablenefs. They are taught to pray for kings and all in authority, 1 Tim. ii. 1, 2.; and God forbid we should do otherwife: yea, tho' they perfecute, Jer. xxix. 7.; peaceable prayers befpeak a peaceable people, Pfal. cix. 4. If fome profeffing religion have been unquiet, their unquietnefs hath given the lye to their profeffion, Jude, ver. 8, 11, 12. Quietnefs is our badge, Col. iii. 12.; 'twill be our ftrength, Ifa. xxx. 7, 15.; our rejoicing in the day of evil, Jer. xviii. 18.; it is pleafing to God, 1 Tim. ii. 2, 3.; it may work upon others, 1 Peter ii. 12, 13. The means he prefcribed for the keeping of us quiet, were to get our hearts fill'd with the knowledge and belief of thefe two things, 1. That the kingdom of Chrift is not of this world, John xviii. 36.; many have thought otherwife, and it hath made them unquiet. 2. That the wrath of man worketh not the righteoufnefs of God, James i. 20.; he needs not our fin to bring to pafs his own counfel. We muft mortify unquietnefs in the caufes of it, James iv. 1.; we muft always remember the oath of God, Eccl. viii. 2.; the oath of allegiance is an oath of quietnefs: and we muft beware of the company and converfe of thofe that are unquiet, Prov. xxii. 24, 25. Tho' deceitful matters be devis'd, yet we muft be quiet ftill; nay, be fo much the more quiet."

I have been this large in gathering thefe hints out of that fermon, (which he took all occafions in other fermons to inculcate, as all his brethren likewife did) that if poffible it may be a conviction to the prefent generation;

neration; or however, may be a witnefs in time to come, that the non-conformift minifters were not enemies to Cæfar, nor troublers of the land; nor their meetings any way tending to the difturbance of the publick peace, but purely defign'd to help to repair the decays of Chriftian piety.

All that knew Mr Henry, knew very well that his practice all his days was confonant to thefe his fettled principles.

In May, 1668, he return'd again with his family from Whitchurch to Broad-Oak, which, through the good hand of his God upon him, continued his fettled home, without any remove from it, till he was removed to his long home above twenty-eight years after.

The edge of the five-mile act began now a little to rebate, at leaft in that country; and he was defirous to be more ufeful to the neighbours, among whom God had given him an eftate, than he could be at a diftance from them by relieving the poor, employing the labourers, and efpecially inftructing the ignorant, and helping as many as he could to heaven. He made that fcripture his ftanding rule, and wrote it in the beginning of his book of accounts, Prov. iii. 9, 10. " Honour the Lord with thy fubftance, &c." And having fet apart a day of fecret prayer and humiliation, to beg of God a wife and underftanding heart, and to drop a tear (as he expreffeth it) over the fins of his predeceffors, formerly in that eftate, he laid out himfelf very much in doing good. He was very ferviceable upon all accounts in the neighbourhood, and tho' it took up a great deal of his time, and hindred him from his beloved ftudies, yet it might be faid of him, as the Bifhop of Salisbury faith of Archbifhop Tillotfon, in his fermon at his funeral, that he " chofe rather to " live to the good of others than to himfelf; and " thought, that to do an act of charity, or even of " tendernefs and kindnefs, was of more value both in " itfelf, and in the fight of God, than to purfue the
" pompous

" pompous parts of learning, how much foever his
" own genius might lead him to it."

He was very ufeful in the common concernments of the townfhip and country, in which he was a very prudent counfellor; it was indeed a narrow fphere of activity, but fuch as it was) to him as to Job xxix. 21, 22. " Men gave ear and waited, and kept filence at his counfel; after his words they fpake not again;" and many of the neighbours who refpected him not as a minifter, yet lov'd and honour'd him as a knowing, prudent, and humble neighbour. In the concernments of private families, he was very far from bufying himfelf, and further from feeking himfelf, but he was very much bufied, advifing many about their affairs, and the difpofal of themfelves and their children, arbitrating and compofing differences among relations and neighbours, in which he had an excellent faculty, and often good fuccefs, inheriting the bleffing entail'd upon the peace-makers. References have fometimes been made to him by rule of court, at the affizes, with confent of parties. He was very affable and eafy of accefs, and admirably patient in hearing every one's complaint, which he would anfwer with fo much prudence and mildnefs, and give fuch apt advice, that many a time to confult with him, was to afk counfel at Abel, and fo to end the matter. He obferved in almoft all quarrels that happened, that there was a fault, on both fides; and that generally they were almoft in the fault that were moft forward and clamorous in their complaints. One making her moan to him of a bad hufband fhe had, that in this, and 'tother inftance was unkind; and (Sir,) faith fhe, after a long complaint which he patiently heard, What would you have me to do now? "Why truly (faith he) I would
" have you go home and be a better wife to him,
" and then you'll find that he will be a better hufband
" to you."

Labouring to perfuade one to forgive an injury that had been done him; he urged this, Are you not a Chriftian?

Chriſtian? and follow'd that argument ſo cloſe, that at laſt he prevailed.

He was very induſtrious, and oft ſuccefsful, in perſuading people to recede from their right, for peace ſake; and he would for that purpoſe tell them Luther's ſtory of the two goats, that met upon a narrow bridge over a deep water; they could not go back, they durſt not fight; after a ſhort parley, one of them lay down, and let the other go over him, and no harm done. He would likewiſe relate ſometimes a remarkable ſtory, worthy to be here inſerted, concerning a good friend of his, Mr T. Y. of Whitchurch, who in his youth was greatly wrong'd by an unjuſt uncle of his, being an orphan; his portion, which was 200 *l*. was put into the hands of that uncle; who, when he grew up, ſhuffled with him, and would give him but 40 *l*. inſtead of his 200 *l*. and he had no way of recovering his right but by law; but before he would engage in that, he was willing to adviſe with his miniſter, who was the famous Dr Twiſs of Newberry: the counſel he gave him (all things conſidered) was for peace ſake, and for the preventing of ſin and ſnares, and trouble, to take the 40 *l*. rather than contend; and, Thomas, (ſaith the Doctor) if thou doſt ſo, aſſure thyſelf, that God will make it up to thee and thine, ſome other way, and they that defraud thee will be the loſers by it at laſt. He did ſo, and it pleaſed God ſo to bleſs that little which he began the world with, that when he died in a good old age, he left his ſon poſſeſs'd of ſome hundreds a year, and he that wrong'd him fell into decay.

Many very pious worthy families in the country ſaid of Mr Henry, that they had no friend like minded, who did naturally care for their ſtate, and ſo affectionately ſympathize with them, and in whom their hearts could ſafely truſt.

He was alſo very charitable to the poor, and was full of almſdeeds, which *he did* (as it is ſaid of Tabitha, Acts chapter ix. 36.) not which he ſaid he would do, or which he put others on to do, but
which

which he did himself, difperfing abroad, and giving to the poor, feeking and rejoicing in opportunities of that kind: and whenever he gave an alms for the body, he ufually gave with it a fpiritual alms, fome good word of counfel, reproof, inftruction, or comfort, as there was occafion, and in accommodating thefe to the perfons he fpoke to, he had a great dexterity.

He was very forward to lend money freely, to any of his poor neighbours that had occafion, and would fometimes fay, that in many cafes there was more charity in lending than in giving, becaufe it obliged the borrower both to honefty and induftry. When one of his neighbours, to whom he had lent three pound, fail'd, fo that he was never likely to fee a farthing of it, he writes thus upon it, " notwithftanding this, yet ftill I judge it my duty to lend," Luke xi. 35. Tho' what is lent in charity be not repaid, yet it is not loft. When thofe that had borrowed money of him paid him again, he ufually gave them back fome part, to encourage honefty. He judged the taking of moderate intereft for money lawful, where the borrower was in a way of gaining by it : but he would advife his friends that had money, rather to difpofe of it otherways, if they could.

It muft not be forgotten, how punctual and exact he was in all his accounts with tenants, workmen, &c. being always careful to keep fuch things in black and white (as he us'd to fay) which is the fureft way to prevent miftakes, and a man's wronging either himfelf or his neighbour ; fuch was his prudence, and fuch his patience and peaceablenefs, that of all the time he was at Broad-Oak, he never fued any, nor ever was fued, but was inftrumental to prevent many a vexatious law-fuit among his neighbours. He ufed to fay, There are four rules to be duly obferved in going to law; (1.) We muft not go to law for trifles, as he did who faid, he would rather fpend a hundred pound in law than lofe a pennyworth of his right, Matt. v. 39, 40, 41. (2.) We muft not be rafh and hafty in it, but try

try all other means poffible to compofe differences, wherein he that yields moft, as Abraham did to Lot, is the better man, and there is nothing loft by it in the end, 1 Cor. vi. 1, 2. (3.) We muft fee that it be without malice or defire of revenge. If the undoing of our brother, be the end of our going to law, as it is with many, 'tis certainly evil, and it fpeeds accordingly. (4.) It muft be with a difpofition to peace, whenever it may be had, and an ear open to all overtures of that kind. The two mottos proper for the great guns are applicable to this, *Ratio ultima Regum* and *Sic quaerimus Pacem*.

Four rules he fometimes gave to be obferved in our converfe with men :

> Have communion with few,
> Be familiar with one;
> Deal juftly with all,
> Speak evil of none.

He was noted for an extraordinary neat hufband about his houfe and ground, which he would often fay, he could not endure to fee like the field of the flothful, and the vineyard of the man void of underftanding. And it was ftrange, how eafily one that had been bred up utterly a ftranger to fuch things; yet when God fo ordered his lot, acquainted himfelf with, and accommodated himfelf to the affairs of the country, making it the diverfion of his vacant hours, to over-fee his gardens and fields ; when he better underftood that known epode of Horace, " Beatus ille " qui procul negotiis," than he did when in his youth he made an ingenious tranflation of it. His care of this kind was an act of charity to poor labourers whom he employed ; and it was a good example to his neighbours, as well as for the comfort of his family. His converfe likewife with thefe things was excellently improved, for fpiritual purpofes, by occafional meditations, hints of which there are often in his diary, as thofe that converfed with him had many in difcourfe :

Inftances

Inftances of this were eafy, but endlefs to give. He ufed to fay, that therefore many of the fcripture parables and fimilitudes are taken from the common actions of this life, that when our hands are employed about them, our hearts may the more eafily pafs through them to divine and heavenly things. I have heard him often blame thofe, whofe irregular zeal in the profeffion of religion, makes them to neglect their worldly bufinefs, and let the houfe drop through; the affairs of which the good man will order with difcretion; and he would tell fometimes of a religious woman, whofe fault it was, how fhe was convinced of it, by means of an intelligent godly neighbour; who coming into the houfe, and finding the good woman, far in the day, in her clofet, and the houfe fadly neglected, children not tended, fervants not minded; " What, faith he, is there no fear of God in this houfe?" which much ftartled and affected the good woman, that over-heard him. He would often fay, " Every thing is beautiful in its feafon;" and that it is the wifdom of the prudent, fo to order the duties of their general callings as Chriftians, and thofe of their particular callings in the world, as that they may not clafh or interfere: I have heard it obferved from Eccl. vii. 16. That there may be over-doing in well-doing.

I cannot omit one little paffage in his diary, becaufe it may be inftructive: When he was once defired to be bound for one that had upon a particular occafion been bound for him, he writes, Solomon faith " He " that hateth furetifhip is fure; but he faith alfo, he " that hath friends muft fhew himfelf friendly." But he always cautioned thofe that became fureties, not to be bound for any more than they knew themfelves able to pay, nor for more than they would be willing to pay, if the principal fail.

His houfe at Broad Oak was by the road fide, which, though it had its inconveniences, yet (he would fay) pleafed him well, becaufe it gave his friends an opportunity of calling on him the oftner, and gave him an

opportunity

opportunity of being kind to ſtrangers, and ſuch as were any way diſtreſſed upon the road, to whom he was, upon all occaſions, cheerfully ready; fully anſwering the apoſtle's character of a biſhop, that he muſt be of good behaviour, decent, affable, and obliging and given to hoſpitality, 1 Tim. iii. 2.; like Abraham, fitting at his tent-door, in queſt of opportunities to do good. If he met with any poor near his houſe, and gave them alms in money, yet he would bid them go to his door beſides, for relief there. He was very tender and compaſſionate towards poor ſtrangers and travellers, though his charity and candor were often impoſed upon by cheats and pretenders, whom he was not apt to be ſuſpicious of; but would ſay in the moſt favourable ſenſe, Thou knoweſt not the heart of a ſtranger. If any aſked his charity, whoſe repreſentation of their caſe he did not like, or who he thought did amiſs to take that courſe, he would firſt give them an alms, and then mildly reprove them; and labour to convince them that they were out of the way of duty, and that they could not expect that God ſhould bleſs them in it; and would not chide them, but reaſon with them: And he would ſay, if he ſhould tell them of their faults, and not give them an alms, the reproof would look only like an excuſe to deny his charity, and would be rejected accordingly.

In a word, his greateſt care about the things of this world was, how to do good with what he had, and to deviſe liberal things; deſiring to make no other acceſſion to his eſtate, but only that bleſſing which attends beneficence. He did firmly believe (and it ſhould ſeem few do) that what is given to the poor is lent to the Lord, who will pay it again in kind or kindneſs; and that religion and piety is ſurely the beſt friend to outward proſperity, and he found it ſo; for it pleaſed God abundantly to bleſs his habitation, and to make a hedge about him, and about all that he had round about: and tho' he did not delight himſelf in the abundance of wealth; yet, which is far better, he delighted himself in the abundance of peace, Psal. xxxvii. 11. All that he had and did observably prospered; so that the country oftentimes took notice of it, and called his family, a family which the Lord had blessed. And his comforts of this kind were (as he used to pray they might be) oil to the wheels of his obedience, and in the use of these things he served the Lord his God with joyfulness and gladness of heart, yet still mindful of and grieved for the affliction of Joseph. He would say sometimes, when he was in the midst of the comforts of this life, as that good man :---All this, and heaven too! surely then we serve a good Master. Thus did the Lord bless him, and make him a blessing; and this abundant grace through the thanksgiving of many, redounded to the glory of God.

Having given this general account of his circumstances at Broad-Oak, we shall now go on with his story, especially as to the exercise of his ministry there, and thereabouts; for that was the thing in which he was, and to which he chiefly gave himself. After this settlement at Broad-Oak, whenever there was preaching at Whitewell Chapel (as usually there was two Lord's days in the month) he constantly attended there with his family, was usually with the first, and reverently joined in the public service; he diligently wrote the sermons; always staid if the ordinance of baptism was administred, but not if there were a wedding, for he thought that a solemnity not proper for the Lord's day. He often din'd the minister that preach'd; after dinner he sung a psalm, repeated the morning sermon, and pray'd; and then attended in like manner in the afternoon. In the evening he preach'd to his own family; and perhaps two or three of his neighbours would drop in to him. On those Lord's days when there was no preaching at the Chapel, he spent the whole day at home, and many an excellent sermon he preach'd, when there were present only four besides his own family (and perhaps not so many) according to the limitation of the conventicle act. In these narrow private circumstances he preached over the former part of the Assembly's Catechism, from divers texts; he also preached over psalm cxvi. besides many particular occasional subjects.

What a grief of heart it was to him, to be thus put under a bushel, and confin'd to such a narrow sphere of usefulness, read in his own words, which I shall transcribe out of an elegy he made (to give vent to his thoughts) upon the death of his worthy friend Mr Geo. Mainwaring, sometime minister of Malpas, (who was silenced by the act of uniformity, and died Mar. 14. 1669-70.) wherein he thus bewails (feelingly enough) the like restraints and confinements of his friend:

> *His later years he sadly spent,*
> *Wrapt up in silence and restraint.*
> *A burthen such as none do know,*
> *But they that do it undergo,*
> *To have a fire shut up and pent*
> *Within the bowels, and no vent ;*
> *To have gorg'd Breasts, and by a law,*
> *Those that fain would, forbidden to draw.*
> *But his dumb Sabbaths here, did prove*
> *Loud crying Sabbaths in heav'n above.*
> *His tears, when he might sow no more,*
> *Wat'ring what he had sown before.*

Soon after his settlement at Broad Oak, he took a young scholar into the house with him; partly to teach his son, and partly to be a companion to himself to converse with him, and to receive help and instruction from him; and for many years he was seldom without one or other such; who before their going to the University, or in the intervals of their attendance there, would be in his family, fitting under his shadow. One of the first he had with him, in the year 1668, (and after) was Mr William Turner, born in the neighbourhood; afterwards of Edmund Hall in Oxford, now vicar of Walberton in Sussex, to whom the world is beholden

holden for that elaborate hiftory of all religions which he publifhed in the year 1695, and from whom is earneftly expected the performance of that noble and ufeful project for the record of providences. Betwixt Mr Henry and him there was a moft entire and affectionate friendfhip; and notwithftanding that diftance of place, and conftant and endearing correfpondence, kept up as long as Mr Henry liv'd.

It was obferv'd that feveral young men who had fojourn'd with him, and were very hopeful and likely to be ferviceable to their generations, dy'd foon after their removal from him, (I could inftance fix or feven,) as if God had fent them to him to be prepared for another world, before they were call'd for out of this; yet never any dy'd while they were with him.

He had fo great a kindnefs for the univerfity, and valu'd fo much the mighty advantages of improvement there, that he advis'd all his friends who defign'd their children for fcholars, to fend them thither, for many years after the change, though he always counted upon their conformity. But long experience altered his mind herein, and he chofe rather to keep his own fon at home with him, and to give him what help he could there, in his education, than venture him into the fnares and temptations of the univerfity.

It was alfo foon after this fettlement of his at Broad-Oak, that he contracted an intimate friendfhip with that learned, and pious, and judicious gentleman Mr Hunt of Boreatton, (the fon of colonel Hunt of Salop) and with his excellent lady Frances, daughter of the right honourable the lord Paget. The acquaintance then begun betwixt Mr Henry and that worthy family continued to his dying day, about thirty years. One Lord's day in a quarter he commonly fpent with them, befides other interviews; and it was a conftant rejoicing to him to fee religion and the power of godlinefs uppermoft, in fuch a family as that, when not many mighty, not many noble are called; and the branches of it branches of righteoufnefs, the planting of the Lord.

Lord. Divers of the honourable relations of that family contracted a very great respect for him, particularly the present lord Paget, his Majesty's Ambassador at the Ottoman court, and Sir Henry Ashurst, whom we shall have occasion afterwards to make mention of.

In the time of trouble and distress, by the conventicle act, in 1670, he kept private and stirr'd little abroad, as loth to offend those that were in power, and judging it prudence to gather in his sails, when the storm was violent: He then observ'd, as that which he was troubled at; " That there was a great deal of
" precious time lost among professors, when they came
" together, in discoursing of their adventures to meet,
" and their escapes, which he feared tended more to
" set up self, than to give glory to God." Also in telling how they got together, and such a one preached, but little enquiring what spiritual benefit and advantage was reaped by it; and that we are apt to make the circumstances of our religious services, more the matter of our discourse, than the substance of them.

We shall close this chapter with two remarks out of his diary, in the year 1671, which will shew what manner of spirit he was of, and what were his sentiments of things at that time. One is this, " All ac-
" knowledge that there is at this day a number of so-
" ber, peaceable men, both ministers and others, a-
" mong dissenters, but who either saith or doth any
" thing to oblige them? who desireth or endeavour-
" eth to open the door to let in such? nay, do they
" not rather provoke them to run into the same ex-
" travagancies with others by making no difference,
" but laying load on them as if they were as bad as
" the worst." 'Tis true, that about this time the lord keeper Bridgman and bishop Wilkins, and the lord Chief Justice Hale, were making some overtures towards an accommodation with them; but it is as true, that those overtures did but the more exasperated their adversaries, (who were ready to account such moderate

ate men the worſt enemies the church of England had,) and the event was, greater acts of feverity.

Another is this, " If all that hath been ſaid and " written to prove that prelacy is antichriſtian, and " that it is unlawful to join in the common-prayer, " had been effectually to perſwade biſhops to ſtudy " and do the duty of church-rulers, in preaching and " feeding the flock, according to the word, and to " perſwade people to be ſerious inward, and ſpiritual " the in uſe of forms, it had been better with the " church of God in England, than it now is." Conſonant to the ſpirit of this remark, was that which he took all occaſions to mention as his ſettled principle : " In thoſe things wherein all the people of God are " agreed, I will ſpend my zeal; and wherein they " differ I will endeavour to walk according to the " light that God hath given me, and charitably be-" lieve that others do ſo too."

CHAP. VI.

His liberty by the indulgence in the year 1672, and thenceforwards to the year 1681.

NOTWITHSTANDING the ſevere act againſt conventicles, in the year 1670, yet the non-conformiſts in London ventur'd to ſet up meetings in 1671, and were conniv'd at; but in the country there was little liberty taken till the King's declaration of March 15, 1671-2, gave countenance and encouragement to it. What were the ſecret ſprings which produced that declaration time diſcovered ; however, it was to the poor diſſenters as life from the dead, and gave them ſome reviving in their bondage; God graciouſly ordering it ſo, that the ſpirit he had made might not fail before him. But ſo precarious a liberty was it, that it ſhould never be ſaid, thoſe people were hard to be pleaſed, who were ſo well pleaſed with that, and thanked ed God, who put such a thing into the King's heart. The tenor of that declaration was this: "In consideration of the inefficacy of rigor, tried for divers years, and to invite strangers into the kingdom, ratifying the establishment in the church of England, it suspends penal laws against all non-conformists and recusants, promiseth to licence separate places for meetings, limiting papists only to private houses."

On this Mr Henry writes, "It is a thing diversly
" resented, as mens interests lead them; the conform-
" ists displeased, the presbyterians glad, the indepen-
" dents very glad, the papists triumph. The danger
" is (saith he) lest the allowing of separate places help
" to overthrow our parish-order, which God hath
" own'd, and to beget divisions and animosities among
" us, which no honest heart but would rather should
" be healed. We are put hereby (saith he) into a
" dilemma, either to turn independents in practice,
" or to strike in with the conformists, or to sit down
" in former silence and sufferings (and silence he ac-
" counted one of the greatest sufferings) till the Lord
" shall open a more effectual door." That which (he saith) he then heartily wished for, was, "That those who
" were in place, would admit the sober non-conform-
" ists to preach sometimes occasionally in their pul-
" pits; by which means he thought prejudices would
" in time wear off on both sides, and they might mu-
" tually strengthen each other's hands against the
" common enemy the papists, who he foresaw would
" fish best in troubled waters." This he would chuse much rather than to keep a separate meeting: but it could not be had; no, not so much as leave to preach in Whitewell-chapel when it was vacant, as it often was, though 'twere three long miles from the parish-church. He found that some people, the more they are courted, the more coy they are; however, the overtures he made to this purpose, and the slow steps he took towards the setting up of a distinct congregation, yielded him satisfaction afterwards in the reflection,

tion, when he could fay, we would have been united, and they would not.

'Twas feveral weeks after the declaration came out, that he received a licenfe to preach, as Paul did, in his own houfe, and elfewhere, no man forbidding him. This was procur'd for him by fome of his friends in London, without his privity, and came to him altogether unexpected. The ufe he made of it was, that at his own houfe, what he did before to his own family, and in private, the doors being fhut for fear, he now did more publicly; threw his doors open, and welcomed his neighbours to him, to partake of his fpiritual things. Only one fermon in the evening of the Lord's day, when there was preaching at Whitewell-chapel, where he ftill continued his attendance with his family and friends as ufual ; but when there was not, he fpent the whole day, at public time, in the fervices of the day, expofition of the fcriptures read, and preaching, with prayer and praife. This he did gratis, receiving nothing for his labours, either at home or abroad, but the fatisfaction of doing good to fouls (which was his meat and drink) with the trouble and charge of giving entertainment to many of his friends, which he did with much chearfulnefs; and he would fay, he fometimes thought that the bread did even multiply in the breaking; and he found that God did abundantly blefs his provifion, with that blefling, which, as he ufed to fay, will make a little to go a great way. He was wont to obferve, for the encouragement of fuch as had meetings in their houfes, (which fometimes drew upon them inconveniences) that the ark is a gueft that always pays well for its entertainment. And he noted, that when Chrift had borrowed Peter's boat to preach a fermon out of it, he prefently repaid him for the loan, with a great draught of fifhes, Luke v. 3, 4.

Many thoughts of heart he had concerning this ufe he made of the liberty, not knowing what would be in the end hereof; but after ferious confideration, and many prayers, he faw his way very plain before him, and

and addressed himself with all diligence, to the improvement of this gale of opportunity. Some had dismal apprehensions of the issue of it; and that there would be an after-reckoning: but (saith he) let us mind our duty, and let God alone to order events, which are his work, not ours.

It was a word upon the wheels, which he preached at that time for his own encouragement, and the encouragement of his friends, from that scripture, Eccl. xi. 4. " He that observes the wind shall not sow, and " he that regardeth the clouds shall not reap." Those that are minded either to do good, or get good, must not be frighted with seeming difficulties and discouragements. Our work is to sow and reap, to do good and get good; and let us mind that, and let who will mind the winds and clouds. " A lion in the way, a lion in " the streets;" a very unlikely place (he would say) for lions to be in; and yet that serves the sluggard for an excuse.

While this liberty lasted, he was in labours more abundant; many lectures he preached abroad in Shropshire, Cheshire, and Denbighshire, laying out himself exceedingly for the good of souls, spending and being spent in the work of the Lord. And of that neighbourhood and of that time it was said, that "this and " that man was born again, then and there;" and many there were who asked the way to Zion with their faces thitherwards, and were (not proselyted to a party, but) savingly brought home to Jesus Christ. I mean this; such as had been vain and worldly, and careless, and mindless of God and another world, became sober and serious, and concern'd about their souls, and a future state. This was the conversion of souls, aimed at, and laboured after, and through grace not altogether in vain. Whatever lectures were set up in the country round, 'twas still desired that Mr Henry would begin them (which was thought no small encouragement to those who were to carry them on) and very happy he was, both in the choice and management of his subjects

at such opportunities, seeking to find out acceptable words. Take one specimen of his address, when he began a lecture with a sermon on Heb. xii. 15. "I as-
"sure you (saith he) and God is my witness, I am
"not come to preach, either sedition against the peace
"of the state, or schism against the peace of the church,
"by persuading you to this or that opinion or party;
"but as a minister of Christ, that hath received mer-
"cy from the Lord, to desire to be faithful, my er-
"rand is to exhort you to all possible seriousness, in
"the great business of your eternal salvation, accord-
"ing to my text, which, if the Lord will make as pro-
"fitable to you, as it is material and of weight in it-
"self, neither you nor I shall have cause to repent our
"coming hither, and our being here to-day; looking
"diligently. lest any of you fail of the grace of God.
"Ir it were the last sermon I were to preach, I did not
"know how to take my aim better to do you good."

In doing of this work, he often said, that he looked upon himself but as an assistant to the parish ministers, in promoting the common interests of Christ's kingdom, and the common salvation of precious souls, by the explication and application of those great truths wherein we are all agreed. And he would compare the case to that in Hezekiah's time, when the Levites helped the Priests to kill the sacrifice, which was something of an irregularity; but the exigence of affairs called for it, the priests being too few, and some of them not so careful as they should have been, to sanctify themselves, 2 Chr. xxix. 34.; and wherever he preached, he usually pray'd for the parish minister, and for a blessing upon his ministry. He hath often said how well pleas'd he was, when, after he had preached a lecture at Oswestry, he went to visit the minister of the place, Mr Edwards, a worthy good man, and told him, he had been sowing a handful of seed among his people, and had this answer, "That's well, the Lord pros-
"per your seed and mine too, there's need enough of
"us both." And another worthy conformist that
came

came privately to hear him, but was reprimanded for it by his fuperiors, told him afterwards with tears, that his heart was with him.

His heart was wonderfully enlarged in his work at this time, the fields were white unto the harveft; and he was bufy, and God did remarkably own him, fetting many feals to his miniftry, which much confirmed him in what he did. He hath this obfervable paffage in his diary, about this time, which he recorded for his after benefit (and the example of it may be inftructive) " Remember, that if trouble fhould come hereaf-
" ter, for what we do now in the ufe of prefent liberty,
" I neither fhrink from it, nor fink under it; for I do
" therein approve myfelf to God, and to my own con-
" fcience, in truth and uprightnefs; and the Lord
" whom I ferve, can, and will certainly both bear me
" out, and bring me off with comfort in the end. I
" fay, Remember, and forget it not, this 24th day of
" March, 1672-3."

'Twas at the beginning of this liberty that the Society at Broad Oak did commence; made up (befides their neighbourhood) of fome out of Whitchurch, and Whitchurch parifh, that had been Mr Porter's people, fome out of Hanmer parifh, that had been Mr Steel's, and fome out of the parifhes of Wem, Prees, and Ellifmere; perfons generally of very moderate and fober principles, quiet and peaceable lives, and hearty wellwifhers to the King and Government; and not rigid or,fchifmatical in their feparation, but willing to attend (though fometimes with difficulty and hazard) upon thofe adminiftrations which they found moft lively and edifying, and moft helpful to them, in the great bufinefs of working out their falvation. To this Society he would never call himfelf a paftor, nor was he willing that they fhould call him fo; but a helper, and a minifter of Chrift for their good. He would fay, " That
" he look'd upon his family only as his charge, and
" his preaching to others was but accidental, whom if
" they came, he could no more turn away than he
" could

" could a poor hungry man, that should come to his
" door for an alms. And being a minister of Jesus
" Christ, he thought himself bound to preach the gos-
" pel as he had opportunity."

Usually once a month he administred the ordinance of the Lord's supper. Some of his opportunities of that kind he sets a particular remark upon, as sweet sealing days, on which he found it good to draw near to God.

When about the year's end there was a general expectation of the cancelling of the indulgence, he hath this note upon a precious sabbath and sacrament day, as he calls it, " Perhaps this may be the last; Father, thy
" will be done: it is good for us to be at such uncer-
" tainties; for now we receive our liberty from our
" Father fresh every day, which is best and sweetest
" of all."

On the 3d of March, 1676-7, being Saturday night, the Town of Wem in Shropshire (about six miles from him) was burnt down; the church, market-house, and about one hundred and twenty-six dwelling houses, and one man, in little more than an hour's time, the wind being exceeding violent; at which time Mr Henry was very helpful to his friends there, both for their support under, and their improvement of this sad providence. It was but about half a year before, that a threatning fire had broke out in that town, but did little hurt; some serious people there, presently after, celebrated a thanksgiving for their deliverance, in which Mr Henry imparted to them a spiritual gift (Oct. 3. 1676.) from Zech. iii. 2. " Is not this a brand plucked out of the
" fire?" in the close of that sermon, pressing them from the consideration of that remarkable deliverance, to personal reformation and amendment of life: that those who had been proud, covetous, passionate, liars, swearers, drunkards, sabbath-breakers, would be so no more; and urging Ezra. ix. 13, 14. he added, " If this provi-
" dence have not this effect upon you, you may in
" reason expect another fire: for when God judgeth,
" he

" he will overcome;" and minded them of Lev. xxvi. where 'tis so often threatned against those who walk contrary to God, that he would punish them yet seven times more. The remembrance of this could not but be affecting, when, in so short a time after, the whole town was laid in ruins. The first time he went thither after that calamity, a neighbouring justice having notice of it, sent to forbid him to preach, to his own grief as well as to the grief of many others, who came expecting. But (saith he in his diary) there was a visible sermon before us, the ruins preaching that sin is an evil thing, and God a terrible God. However, a few days after, he got an opportunity of preaching to them a word in season, which some will not forget, from Hos. vi. 1. " Come, and let us return unto the Lord, " for he hath torn---And at the return of the year, when the town was in the rebuilding, he gave them another very suitable sermon, from Prov. iii. 33. " The " curse of the Lord is in the house of the wicked, but " he blesseth the habitation of the just." " Though it " be rising again (saith he in his diary) out of its ashes, " yet the burning of it should not be forgotten, especi-" ally not the sin that kindled it." He oft prayed for them, that the fire might be a refining fire.

In the years 1677, 1678, and 1679, in the course of his ministry at Broad Oak he preached over the Ten Commandments, and largely opened from other texts of scripture the duties required, and sins forbidden, in each commandment. For tho' none delighted more than he in preaching Christ and gospel grace; yet he knew that Christ came not to destroy the law and the prophets, but to fulfil; and that, though through grace we are not under the law, as a covenant; yet we are under it as a rule, under the law to Christ. He was very large and particular in pressing second table duties, as essential to Christianity. " We have known " those (saith he) that have called preaching on such " subjects good moral preaching; but let them call it " as they will, I am sure it is necessary and as much
" now

"now as ever." How earneftly would he prefs upon the people the neceffity of righteoufnefs and honefty, in their whole converfations. "A good Chriftian (he "ufed to fay) will be a good hufband, and a good fa- "ther, and a good mafter, and a good fubject, and a "good neighbour, and fo in other relations." How often would he urge to this purpofe, that it is the will and command of the great God, the character of all the citizens of Zion, the beauty and ornament of our Chriftian profeffion; and the fureft way to thrive and profper in the world. "Honefty is the beft policy." He would fay, that thefe are things in which the children of this world are competent judges. They that know not what belongs to faith, and repentance, and prayer, yet know what belongs to the making of an honeft bargain: they are alfo parties concerned, and oftentimes are themfelves careful in thefe things; and therefore thofe who profefs religion fhould walk very circumfpectly, that the name of God and his doctrine be not blafphemed, nor religion wounded through their fides. Thus he preached, and his conftant practice was a comment upon it. One thing I remember he was more than ordinarily enlarged in the preffing of, which was upon the ninth commandment, to fpeak evil of no man, from Tit. iii. 2. If we can fay no good of perfons, we muft fay nothing of them. He gave it as a rule, "Never to fpeak of any ones faults to others, till we "have firft fpoken of them to the offender himfelf." He was himfelf an eminent example of this rule. Some that have converfed much with him, have faid, that they never heard him fpeak evil of any body; nor could he bear to hear any fpoken evil of, but often drove away a backbiting tongue with an angry countenance. He was known to be as faithful a patron of offenders before others, as he was a faithful reprover of them to themfelves.

Whenever he preached of moral duties, he would always have fomething of Chrift in his fermon; either his life, as the great pattern of the duty, or his love,

as

as the great motive to it; of his merit, as making atonement for the neglect of it.

In the year 1680 he preached over the doctrines of faith and repentance, from several texts of scripture. He used to say, that he had been told concerning the famous Mr Dod, that some called him in scorn, Faith and Repentance; because he insisted so much upon those two, in all his preaching. But (saith he) " if this be " to be vile, I will be yet more vile;" for faith and repentance are all in all in christianity.

Concerning repentance he hath sometimes said, " If " I were to die in the pulpit, I would defire to die " preaching repentance; as if I die out of the pulpit, " I would defire to die practifing repentance." And he had often this saying concerning repentance; " He " that repents every day, for the sins of every day, " when he comes to die, will have the sins but of one " day to repent of. Even reckonings make long " friends."

That year, and 1681, he preached over the duties of hearing the word and prayer; of the former, from the parable of the four sorts of ground; of the latter, from Luke xi. 1. &c. when he preached over the Lord's prayer, in above thirty excellent and elaborate discourses. He looked upon the Lord's prayer, to be not only a directory or pattern for prayer, but (according to the advice of the assembly of divines) proper to be used as a form; and accordingly he often used it both in public and in his family. And as he thought 'twas an error on the one hand, to lay so much stress upon it as some do, who think no solemn prayer accepted, nor any solemn ordinance or administration of worship compleat without it, and so repeat it five or six times, and perhaps oftener, at one meeting; so he thought it an error on the other hand not to use it at all; since it is a prayer, a compendious comprehensive prayer, and may be of use to us, at least as other scripture prayers; but he thought it a much greater error to be angry at those that do use it, to judge and censure them, and for

no other reason to conceive prejudices against them and their ministry. " A great strait (saith he) poor mini-
" sters are in, when some will not hear them, if they
" do not use the Lord's prayer, and others will not
" hear them if they do: what is to be done in this case?
" we must walk according to the light we have, and
" approve ourselves to God, either in using or not us-
" ing it, and wait for the day when God will mend
" the matter, which I hope he will do in his own due
" time."

He was in the close of his exposition of the Lord's prayer, when a dark cloud was brought upon his assemblies, and he was necessitated to contract his sails.

CHAP. VII.

The Rebukes he lay under at Broad Oak, betwixt the years 1680, and 1687.

IN the beginning of the year 1681 in April and May, the country was greatly afflicted and threatned by an extreme drought; there was no rain for several weeks, the grass failed; corn that was sown languished, and much that was intended to be sown, could not; the like had not been known for many years: 'twas generally apprehended that a dearth would ensue, especially in that country, which is for the most part dry. And now it was time to seek the Lord, and (according to his own appointment,) to " ask of him rain in " the season thereof:" several serious thinking people being together at the funeral of that worthy minister of Jesus Christ, Mr Malden; it was there said, how requisite it was that there should be some time set apart on purpose for fasting and prayer, in a solemn assembly upon this occasion. Thomas Millington of Weston in Hodnet parish in Shropshire, desired it might be at his house; and Tuesday June 14. was the day pitched upon. The connivance of authority was presumed upon,

upon, becaufe no difturbance of meetings was heard of at London, or any where elfe. Mr Henry was defired to come and give his affiftance at that day's work. He afked upon what terms they ftood with their neighbouring juftices, and it was anfwered, Well enough. The drought continuing in extremity, fome that had not ufed to come to fuch meetings, yet came thither upon the apprehenfion they had of the threatning judgment which the country was under. Mr Edward Bury of Bolas (well known by feveral ufeful books he hath publifhed) prayed, Mr Henry prayed and preached on Pfal. lxvi. 18. " If I regard iniquity in my heart, " the Lord will not hear me;" whence his doctrine was, That iniquity regarded in the heart will certainly fpoil the fuccefs of prayer. When he was in the midft of his fermon clofely applying this truth Sir T. V. of Hodnet, and Mr M. of Ightfield, two juftices of the peace for Shropfhire, with feveral others of their retinue, came fuddenly upon them, difturbed them, fet guards upon the houfe-door, and came in themfelves, feverely rally'd all they knew reflected upon the late Honourable Houfe of Commons, and the vote they paffed concerning the prefent unreafonablenefs of putting the laws in execution againft Proteftant diffenters, as if in fo voting they had acted beyond their fphere, as they who did who took away the life of King Charles I. They diverted themfelves with very abufive and unbecoming talk; fwearing, and curfing, and reviling bitterly. Being told the occafion of the meeting was to feek to turn away the anger of God from us in the prefent drought: 'twas anfwered, " Such meetings as thefe were the caufe of God's anger."---- While they were thus entertaining themfelves, their clerks took the names of thofe that were prefent, in all, about one hundred and fifty, and fo difmiffed them for the prefent. Mr Henry hath noted, in the account he kept of this event, that the Juftices came to this good work from the ale-houfe upon Prees-Heath, about two miles off; to which, and the bowling-green adjoining,

adjoining, they, with other juftices, gentlemen, and clergymen, of the neighbourhood, had, long before, obliged themfelves to come every Tuefday, during the fummer time, under the penalty of twelve pence a time if they were abfent; and there to fpend the day in drinking and bowling; which is thought to be as direct a violation of the law of the land, viz. the ftatute of 33 Henry VIII. cap. 9. for debarring unlawful games, which was never yet repealed, as the meeting was of the ftatute of 22d Car. II. and as much more to the difhonour of God, and the fcandal of the Chriftian profeffion; as curfing, and fwearing, and drunkennefs, is worfe than praying and finging pfalms, and hearing the word of God It is fuppofed that the Juftices knew of the meeting before, and might have prevented it by the leaft intimation; but they were willing to take the opportunity of making fport to themfelves, and trouble to their neighbours. After the feat done, they returned back to the alehoufe, and made themfelves and their companions merry with calling over the names they had taken, making their reflections as they faw caufe; and recounting the particulars of the exploit. There was one of the company, whofe wife happened to be prefent at the meeting, and her name taken among the reft; with which upbraiding him, he anfwered, that fhe had been better employed than he was, and if Mr Henry might be admitted to preach in a church, he would go a great many miles to hear him. For which words he was forthwith expelled their company, and never more to fhew his face again at that bowling-green; to which he replied, If they had fo ordered long ago, it had been a great deal the better for him and his family. Two days after, they met again at Hodnet, where, upon the oath of two witneffes, who, as was fuppofed, were fent on purpofe to inform, they figned and fealed two records of conviction. By one record they convicted the mafter of the houfe, and fined him L.20, and L.5 more as conftable of the town that year, and with him

all

The Life of Mr PHILIP HENRY.

all the perfons prefent whofe names they had taken, and fined them five fhillings a-piece, and iffued out warrants accordingly. By another record they convicted the two minifters, Mr Bury and Mr Henry.---- The act makes it only punifhable to preach or teach in any fuch conventicle; and yet they fined Mr Bury L.20, though he only prayed, and did not fpeak one word in the way either of preaching or teaching, not fo much as " let us pray ;" however, they faid, praying was teaching, and right or wrong he muft be fined; though his great piety, peaceablenefs, and ufefulnefs, befides his deep poverty, one would think might have pleaded for him, againft fo palpable a piece of injuftice. They took L.7 off from him, and laid it upon others, as they faw caufe; and for the remaining L. 13, he being utterly unable to pay it, they took from him, by diftrefs, the bed which he lay upon, with blanket and rug; alfo another feather-bed, nineteen pair of fheets, moft of them new; of which he could not prevail to have fo much as one pair returned for him to lye in; alfo books to the value of L. 5, befides brafs and pewter. And though he was at this time perfectly innocent of that heinous crime of preaching and teaching, with which he was charged, (for fo the record runs again and again, concerning Mr Henry and Mr Bury, *Quod ad tunc & ibidem precaverunt, prædicaverunt & docuerunt.*) Yet he had no way to right himfelf, but by appealing to the Juftices themfelves in Quarter Seffions, who would be fure to affirm their own decree, (as the Juftices in Montgomeryfhire had done not long before, in a like cafe,) efpecially when it was to recover to themfelves treble cofts. So the good man fat down with his lofs, and " took joyfully the fpoiling of his goods; knowing in himfelf, that he had in heaven a better, and a more enduring fubftance."

But Mr Henry being the greateft criminal, and having done the moft mifchief, muft needs be animadverted upon accordingly, and therefore he was fined L.40,

the pretence of which was this:----In the year 1679, Oct. 15, Mr Kynaston of Oatly, a Justice of Peace in Shropshire, meeting him and some others coming, as he supposed, from a conventicle, he was pleas'd to record their conviction, upon the notorious evidence and circumstance of the fact. The record was filed at Salop the next sessions after; but no notice was ever sent of it, either to Mr Henry or the Justices of Flintshire; nor any prosecution upon it, against any of the parties charged, (the reason of which, Mr Henry, in a narrative he wrote of this affair, supposeth to be not only the then favourable posture of public affairs towards dissenters, but also the particular prudence and lenity of Mr Kynaston,) so that having never smarted for this, he could not be supposed to be deterred from the like offence; nor if he were wronged in that first conviction, had he ever any opportunity of making his appeal. However, the Justices being resolved he should have *summum jus*, thought that first record sufficient to give denomination to a second offence, and so he came to be fined double. This conviction (according to the direction of the act,) they certified to the next adjoining Justices of Flintshire, who had all along carried themselves with great temper and moderation towards Mr Henry, and had never given him any disturbance; though if they had been so minded, they had not wanted opportunities; but they were now necessitated to execute the sentences of the Shropshire Justices.----
'Twas much pressed upon him to pay the fine, which might prevent his own loss, and the Justices' trouble. But he was not willing to do it; partly, because he would give no encouragement to such prosecutions, nor voluntarily reward the informers for that which he thought they should rather be punished for; and partly because he thought himself wronged in the doubling of the fine. Whereupon his goods were distrained upon, and carried away; in the doing of which many passages occurred which might be worth the noting, but that the repetition of them would perhaps

haps grate and give offence to some. Let it therefore suffice (waving the circumstances) to remember only that their warrant not giving them authority to break open doors, nor their watchfulness getting them an opportunity to enter the house, they carried away about thirty-three cart load of goods without doors, corn cut upon the ground, hay, coals, &c. This made a great noise in the country, and raised the indignation of many against the decrees which prescribed this grievousness; while Mr Henry bore it with his usual evenness and serenity of mind, not at all moved or disturbed by it. He did not boast of his sufferings, or make any great matter of them; but would often say, " Alas! this is nothing to what others suffer, nor " to what we ourselves may suffer before we die."---And yet he rejoiced and blessed God that it was not for debt, or for evil-doing, that his goods were carried away. " And (saith he) while it is for well-doing that " we suffer, they cannot harm us." Thus he writes in his diary upon it, " How oft have we said that chan-" ges are at the door; but blessed be God there is no " sting in this." He frequently expressed the assurance he had, that whatever damage he sustained, God is able to make it up again. And (as he used to say,) " Though we may be losers for Christ, yet we shall not " be losers by him in the end." He had often said, " That his preaching was likely to do the most good, " when it was sealed to by suffering; and if this be the " time, (saith he) welcome the will of God; even this " also shall turn to the furtherance of the gospel of " Christ:" *Bene agere & male pati vere Christianum est.*

Soon after this was the assizes for Flintshire held at Mold, where Sir George Jeffries, afterwards Lord Chancellor, then Chief Justice of Chester, sat Judge. He did not, in private conversation, seem to applaud what was done in this matter, so as was expected; whether out of a private pique against some that were active in it, or for what other reason, is not known; but

but it was said, he pleasantly asked some of the gentlemen, By what new law they pressed carts, as they passed upon their occasions along the road, to carry away goods distrained for a conventicle? It was also said, that he spoke with some respect of Mr Henry; saying, he knew him and his character well, and that he was a great friend of his mother's, Mrs Jeffries of Acton near Wrexham, (a very pious, good woman,) and that sometimes, at his mother's request, Mr Henry had examined him in his learning, when he was a school-boy, and had commended his proficiency. And it was much wondered at by many, that, of all the times Sir George Jeffries went to that circuit, (though 'tis well enough known what was his temper, and what the temper of that time,) yet he never sought any occasion against Mr Henry, nor took the occasions that were offered, nor countenanced any trouble intended him, though he was the only non-conformist in Flintshire. One passage, I remember, not improper to be mentioned;----there had been an agreement among some ministers, (I think it began in the west of England, where Mr Allen was) to spend some time, either in secret or in their families, or both, between six and eight o'clock every Monday morning, in prayer, for the church of God, and for the land and nation, more fully and particularly than at other times, and to make that their special errand at the throne of grace; and to engage as many of their praying friends as they could, to the observance of it. This had been communicated to Mr Henry by some of his friends at London, and he punctually observed it in his own practice, I believe, for many years. He also mentioned it to some of his acquaintance, who did in like manner observe it. It happened that one in Denbighshire, to whom he had communicated it, was so well pleased with it, that he wrote a letter of it to a friend of his at a distance; which letter happened into hands that perverted it, and made information upon it, against the writer and receiver of the letter, who were

bound

bound over to the affizes, and great fufpicions Sir Geo. Jeffries had, that it was a branch of the Prefbyterian plot, and rallied the parties accufed feverely. It appeared, either by the letter, or by the confeffion of the parties, that they received the project from Mr Henry, which (it was greatly feared) would bring him into trouble ; but Sir George, to the admiration of many, let it fall, and never enquired further into it. It feems there are fome men, whofe ways fo pleafe the Lord, that he makes even their enemies to be at peace with them; and there is nothing loft by trufting in God.

Mr Henry, at the next affizes after he was diftrained upon, was prefented by one of the high conftables, 1. For keeping a conventicle at his houfe; and, 2. For faying, That the law for fuppreffing conventicles ought not to be obeyed, and that there was never a tittle of the word of God in it. As to this latter prefentment, 'twas altogether falfe. He had, indeed, in difcourfe with the high conftable, when he infifted fo much upon the law, which required him to be fo rigorous in the profecution, objected, That all human laws were not to be obeyed, merely becaufe they were laws. But as to any fuch reflections upon the law he fuffered by, he was far from it, and had prudence enough to keep filence at that time ; for it was an evil time when fo many were made offenders for a word. But thefe prefentments met with fo little countenance from Judge Jeffries, that Mr Henry only entered his appearance in the Prothonotary's office, and they were no more heard of; wherein he acknowledged the hand of God, who turneth the hearts of the children of men as the rivulets of-water.

As to what was taken from him by the diftrefs, they who took it made what markets they pleafed of it, paid thofe they employed, and what the remainder was is not known for certainty ; but it was faid, that the following fummer, about L 27 was paid to Sir T.V. of which, (and the reft that was levied in other places,
. which

which amounted to a confiderable fum,) it was credibly reported, (and I have not heard it contradicted,) that neither the king nor the poor had their fhare, (which by the act is to be two-thirds) nor the informers all theirs either; but people faid, the Gentlemen had occafion for it all. But as they that had it were never the richer for it, fo he that loft it would often fay, that he found that God did fo abundantly blefs the remainder to him, that he was never the poorer; which he would mention for the encouragement of his friends, not to baulk duty (as he ufed to exprefs it) for fear of fuffering.

In the fame year, 1681, happened a public difcourfe at Ofweftry, betwixt the then bifhop of St Afaph, (Dr William Lloyd, now bifhop of Coventry and Litchfield) and fome non-conformift minifters, of which Mr Henry was one.

The ftory, in fhort, is as followeth:---That learned bifhop, at his firft coming to the diocefe of St Afaph, in his zeal for the eftablifhed church, fet himfelf with vigour to reduce diffenters to it; and that he might do it with the cords of a man, he refolved, before he took any other methods, to reafon the matter with them, and to endeavour their conviction by difcourfe, in which he had a very great facility, both by his learning and temper. If there were any that declined difcourfing with him, he improved that againft them very much; urging, (as he wrote afterwards to Mr Henry,) " That no man can pretend confcience
" for not coming when he is required, to give an ac-
" count of his religion to them that have authority
" to demand it, by the laws under which he lives, and
" to hear from their mouths what can be faid for the
" eftablifhed religion. Thefe are things from which
" confcience is fo far from exempting, that the great
" rule of confcience requires it, as an indifpenfible
" duty; that we fhould always be ready to give
" an account of the hope that is in us; and that we
" fhould hear them that are in Mofes' chair, &c. and
" there-

The Life of Mr Philip Henry.

" therefore thofe who refufed this, he would confider
" as men governed, not by confcience, but obftinacy."

He publickly difcourfed with the Quakers at Lanvillin in Montgomeryfhire; their champion was Dr Lloyd a phyfician: one of the moft confiderable nonconformift minifters in his diocefe was Mr James Owen of Ofweftry, then very young, but well known fince by his learned book, which he calls, A Plea for Scripture Ordination; proving ordination by prefbyters, without diocefan bifhops, to be valid, (publifhed in the year 1694.) a point of controverfy which he was then obliged in his own defence to fearch into. Several difcourfes the bifhop had with him in private; at laft his lordfhip was pleafed to appoint him, to give him the meeting in the town-hall of Ofweftry, on Tuefday, Sept. 27, 1681; there to give account by what right he excrcifed the miniftry, not having epifcopal ordination. He directed him alfo to procure what other minifters he could to affift him, for he would be glad to hear what any of them had to fay for themfelves. The notice was very fhort, not above four or five days: fome whofe affiftance was defired, apprehended it might do more hurt than good, and might be prejudicial to their own liberty, and therefore declin'd it. It was not agreeable to Mr Henry's mild and modeft temper, to appear in fuch circumftances; but he was loath to defert his friend Mr Owen, and fo with much importunity he was prevailed with to come to Ofweftry, at the time appointed; and there came no other but he and Mr Jonathan Roberts of Denbighfhire, in the diocefe of Bangor, a plain man, of great integrity, and a very good fcholar. The bifhop came according to appointment, and brought with him for his affiftant the famous Mr Henry Dodwell: Mr Henry, who was utterly a ftranger to the bifhop, preffed hard to have had the difcourfe in private, before a felect number, but it would not be granted. He alfo defired his lordfhip that it might not be expected from him, being of another diocefe, to concern himself in the discourse, but only as a hearer: " Nay, Mr Henry, (said the bishop) it is not the concern of my diocese alone, but it is the common cause of religion, and therefore I expect you should interest yourself in it more than as a hearer." His lordship was pleased to promise, that nothing that should be said by way of argument should be any way turned to the prejudice of the disputants, nor advantage taken of it to give them trouble. There were present divers of the clergy and gentry of the country, with the magistrates of the town and a great number of people, which, if it could have been avoided, was not easy to Mr Henry, who never loved any thing that made a noise; herein like his Master, who did not strive nor cry. The discourse began about two o'clock in the afternoon, and continued till between seven and eight at night: much was said *pro* and *con*, touching the identity of bishops and presbyters, the bishoping and unbishoping of Timothy and Titus, the validity of presbyterian ordination, &c. 'Twas managed with a great deal of liberty, and not under the strict laws of disputation, which made it hard to give any tolerable account of the particulars of it. The arguments on both sides, may better be fetched from the books written on the subject, than from such a discourse. The bishop managed his part of the conference with a great deal of gravity, calmness, and evenness of spirit, and therein gave an excellent pattern to all that are in such stations. Mr Henry's remark upon this business in his diary is this, " That whereas many reports went abroad far and near concerning it, every one passing their judgment upon the result of it as they stood affected; for my own part (saith he) upon reflection, I find I have great reason to be ashamed of my manifold infirmities and imperfections; and yet do bless God, that seeing I could manage it no better, to do the truth more service, there was not more said and done to its disservice; to God be glory." But there were others, who said that Mr Henry was an

instrument

instrument of glorifying God, and serving the church in that affair, almost as much as in any thing that ever he did, except the preaching of the gospel. And some who were adversaries to the cause he pleaded, though they were not convinced by his arguments, yet by his great meeknefs and humility, and that truly Christian spirit, which appeared fo evidently in the whole management, were brought to have a better opinion of him, and the way in which he walked.

The conference broke off a little abruptly; the bishop and Mr Henry being somewhat close at an argument, in the recapitulation of what had been discoursed of; Mr Jonathan Roberts whispered to Mr Henry, " Pray let my lord have the last word;" which a justice of peace upon the bench over-hearing; presently replied, " You say my lord shall have the
" last word, but he shall not, for I will : we thank
" God we have the sword of power in our own hands,
" and by the grace of God we will keep it, and it
" shall not rust, and I hope every lawful magistrate
" will do as I do : and look to yourfelves, Gentlemen,
" by the grace of God I'll root you out of the coun-
" try." To which a forward man in the crowd said,
" *Amen*, throw them down stairs." This the bishop heard with silence, but the Mayor of the town took order for their safety.

Two days after this difcourfe, the bishop wrote a very obliging letter to Mr Henry, to fignify to him how very much he was pleased with the good temper and spirit that he found in him at Ofweftry, and that he looked upon him as one that intended well, but laboured under prejudices; and to defire further acquaintance and converfation with him; particularly that he would come to him ftraitway to Wrexham; and about three months after, he fent for him again to Chefter ; in both which interviews a great deal of difcourfe, with much freedom, passed between them in private, in which they feemed to vie nothing more than candor and obligingnefs, shewing to each other all meeknefs. I remember the bifhop was pleafed to fhew him his plan for the government of his diocefe, and the method he intended to take in church cenfures, which Mr Henry very well approved of; but pleafantly told his lordfhip, he hoped he would take care that Juvenal's verfe fhould not be again verified,

Dat veniam Corvis, vexat cenfura Columbas. (Sat. ii.)

which the bifhop fmil'd at, and told him he would take care it fhould not. His lordfhip obferving his true catholick charity and moderation, told him, that if he were in his diocefe, he did not queftion but that he fhould find out fome way to make him ufeful. But all his reafonings could not fatisfy Mr Henry's confcience of the lawfulnefs of being re-ordain'd and conforming. The bifhop for fome years after, when he came that way, towards London, either call'd on Mr Henry at his houfe, or fent for him to him at Whitchurch, and ftill with all outward expreffions of friendfhip.

The trouble which Mr Henry was in, about the meeting at Wefton, obliged him for a while to keep his fabbaths at home fomewhat private; but in the year 1682 he took a greater liberty, and many flocked to him on Lord's days, through the kind connivance of the neighbouring magiftrates: but in the year 1683, when the meetings were generally fuppreft throughout the kingdom, he was again neceffitated to contract his fails, and confine his labours more to his own family, and his friends that vifited him. He continued his attendance at Whitewell-chapel, as ufual; and when he was abridged of his liberty, he often bleffed God for his quietnefs. Once when one of the curates preached a bitter fermon againft the diffenters, on a Lord's day morning; fome wondered that Mr Henry would go again in the afternoon, for the fecond part; " But (faith he) if he do not know his duty, I " know mine; and I blefs God I can find honey in a " carcafe."

In this time of treading down, and of perplexity, he stirred little abroad, being forced (as he used to express it) to " throw the plough under the hedge ;" but he preached constantly at home without disturbance; and often comforted himself with this, " When we can-
" not do what we would, if we do what we can,
" God will accept of us : when we cannot keep open
" shop, we must drive a secret trade." And he would say, " There is a mean, if we could hit it, between
" fool-hardiness and faint-heartedness." While he had some opportunity of being useful at home, he was afraid lest he should prejudice that by venturing abroad. One of his friends in London earnestly soliciting him to make a visit thither in this time of restraint in the country, he thus wrote to him ; " I should be glad
" once more to kiss my native soil, though it were but
" with a kiss of valediction ; but my indisposedness to
" travel, and the small prospect there is of doing good
" to countervail the pains, are my prevailing argu-
" ments against it. I am here ('tis true) buried alive,
" but I am quiet in my grave, and have no mind to
" be a walking ghost. We rejoice, and desire to be
" thankful, that God hath given us a home, and con-
" tinued it to us, when so many, better than we, have
" not where to lay their head, having no certain
" dwelling-place :" ('twas at the time of the dispersion of the French protestants.) " Why they exiles,
" and not we ? they strangers in a strange land, and
" not we ? We must not say, we will die in our nests;
" lest God say, nay : nor we will multiply our days
" as that bird, the Phœnix, (referring to Job xxix. 18.)
" lest God say, This night, &c. Our times and all
" our ways are at his dispose, absolutely and universal-
" ly, and it is very well they are so."

At the time of the Duke of Monmouth's descent, and the insurrection in the West, in the year 1685, Mr Henry, as many others, (pursuant to a general order of the Lord Lieutenant, for securing all suspected persons; and particularly all nonconformist ministers,)
was

was taken up by a warrant from the deputy Lieutenants, and sent under a guard to Chester Castle, where he was about three weeks a close prisoner: he was lodged with some gentlemen and ministers that were fetched thither out of Lancashire, who were all strangers to him; but he had great comfort in the acquaintance and society of many of them.

He often spake of this imprisonment, not as matter of complaint, but of thanksgiving, and blessed God he was in nothing uneasy all the while. In a sermon to his family, the day after he came home, he largely and affectionately recounted the mercies of that providence: as for instance, "That his imprisonment was
"for no cause: 'tis guilt that makes a prison. That
"it was his security in a dangerous time. That he
"had good company in his sufferings, who prayed
"together, and read the Scriptures together, and dis-
"coursed to their mutual edification. That he had
"health there; not sick, and in prison; that he was
"visited and prayed for by his friends. That he was
"very chearful and easy in his spirit, many a time a-
"sleep and quiet, when his adversaries were disturbed
"and unquiet. That his enlargement was speedy and
"unsought for, and that it gave occasion to the magis-
"trates who committed him, to give it under their
"hands, that they had nothing in particular to lay to
"his charge; and especially that it was without a
"snare, which was the thing he feared more than any
"thing else."

It was a surprise to some that visited him in his imprisonment, and were big with the expectations of the Duke of Monmouth's success, to hear him say, " I
"would not have you to flatter yourselves with such
"hopes, for God will not do his work for us in these
"nations, by that man; but our deliverance and sal-
"vation will arise some other way."

It must not be forgotten how ready he was, nay, how studious and industrious to serve and oblige such as had been any way instruments of trouble to him,
as

as far as it lay in his power, and he had any opportunity to do it; fo well had he learned that great leffon of forgiving and loving enemies; of this it were eafy to give inftances.

When a gentleman who had fometimes been an inftrument of trouble to him, had occafion to make ufe of his help to give him fome light into a caufe he had to be tried, Mr Henry was very ready to ferve him in it; and though he might have declined it, and it was fomewhat againft his own intereft too, yet he appeared a witnefs for him, which fo won upon the gentleman, that he was afterwards more friendly to him. Mentioning in his diary the death of another gentleman in Shropfhire; he notes, that he was one that had been his profeffed enemy; " but (faith he) God knows I " have often prayed for him."

Some have wondered to fee how courteoufly and friendly he would fpeak to fuch as had been any way injurious to him, when he met with them, being as induftrious to difcover his forgiving of wrongs, as fome are to difcover their refentments of them. It was faid of Archbifhop Cranmer, that the way to have him ones friend, was to do him a difkindnefs; and I am fure it might be faid of Mr Henry, that doing him a difkindnefs would not make him ones enemy. This minds me of an exemplary paffage concerning his worthy friend Mr Edward Lawrence, once going with fome of his fons, by the houfe of a gentleman that had been injurious to him, he gave a charge to his fons to this purpofe, that they fhould never think or fpeak amifs of that gentleman, for the fake of any thing he had done againft him; but whenever they went by his houfe, fhould lift up their hearts in prayer to God for him and his family. And who is he that will harm thofe, who are thus followers of him that is good, in his goodnefs? It is almoft the only temporal promife in the New Teftament, which is made to the meek, Mat. v. 5. That they fhall inherit the earth; the meaning whereof Dr Hammond in his practical catechifm, takes to be especially this, that in the ordinary dispensations of God's Providence, the most mild and quiet people are most free from disturbance. Those only have every man's hand against them, that have theirs against every man.

CHAP. VIII.

The last Nine years of his Life in liberty and enlargement at Broad-Oak, from the year 1687.

IT was in the latter end of the year 1685, when the stream run so very strong against the dissenters, that Mr Henry being in discourse with a very great man of the church of England, mentioned K. Charles's indulgence in 1672, as that which gave rise to his stated preaching in a separate assembly; and added, If the present king James should in like manner give me leave, I would do the same again: to which that great man replied, "Never expect any such thing from him: " for take my word for it, he hates you nonconfor- " mists in his heart." " Truly (said Mr Henry) I " believe it, and I think he doth not love you of the " church of England neither." It was then little thought that the same Right Reverend person who said so to him, should have the honour, as he had soon after, to be one of the seven bishops committed to the Tower by king James; as it was also far from any ones expectation, that the same king James should so quickly give liberty to the nonconformists: but we live in a world, wherein we are to think nothing strange, nor be surprised at any turn of the wheel of nature, as 'tis called, James iii. 6.

The measures then taken by king James's Court and Council were soon laid open, not only to view, but to contempt, being in a short time, by the overruling Providence of God, broken and defeated: however, the indulgence granted to dissenters in April 1687,

1687, muſt needs be a reviving to thoſe who for ſo many years had lain buried in ſilence and feſtraint; nor can any, who will allow themſelves the liberty of ſuppoſing the caſe their own, wonder that they ſhould rejoice in it, though the deſign of it being manifeſt, they could not chuſe but rejoice with trembling. Mr Henry's ſentiments of it were, " whatever mens ends " are in it, I believe God's end in it is to do us good."

There were many that ſaid, Surely the diſſenters will not embrace the liberty which is intended only for a ſnare to them. Mr Henry read and conſidered the letter of advice to the diſſenters at that juncture; but concluded, " Duty is ours, and events are God's." He remembred the experience he had had of the like in king Charles's time, and that did good and no hurt; and why might not this do ſo too? " All power is " for edification, not for deſtruction." Did Jeremiah fit ſtill in the court of the priſon, becauſe he had his diſcharge from the king of Babylon? Nay, did not Paul, when he was perſecuted by his countrymen, for preaching the goſpel, appeal to Cæſar, and find more kindneſs at Rome than he did at Jeruſalem? In ſhort, the principle of his converſation in the world being not fleſhly wiſdom, or policy, but the grace of God, and particularly the grace of ſimplicity and godly ſincerity, he was willing to make the beſt of that which was, and to hope the beſt of the deſign and iſſue of it. Doubtleſs it was intended to introduce popery; but it is certain, that nothing could arm people againſt popery more effectually than the plain and powerful preaching of the goſpel; and thus they who granted that liberty, were out-ſhot in their own bow, which manifeſtly appeared in the event and iſſue. And as they did good ſervice to the Proteſtant Religion among ſcholars, who wrote ſo many learned books againſt popery at that time, for which we return them our beſt thanks; ſo they did no leſs ſervice among the common people (who are the ſtrength and body of the nation) that preached ſo many good ſermons to arm their hearers againſt that ſtrong deluſion, which Mr Henry (as the reſt of the nonconformiſts generally did) took all occaſions to do. How often would he commend his hearers (as Dr Holland, Divinity profeſſor in Oxford, was wont to do) " to the love of God, and the " hatred of Popery."

Beſides his preaching profeſſedly to diſcover the errors and corruptions of the church of Rome (which he would have taken occaſion to do more fully, had he ſeen thoſe he preached to in any immediate danger of the infection) there could not be a more effectual antidote againſt popery, than the inſtructing and confirming of people in the truth, as it is in Jeſus; and advancing the knowledge of and a value and veneration for the Holy Scriptures; to which, how much Mr Henry in his place did contribute, all that knew him will bear record. He uſed to obſerve, that the fall of Babylon followed upon the free and open preaching of the everlaſting gofpel, Rev. xiv. 6, 7. He apprehended this liberty likely to be of very ſhort continuance, and to end in trouble; and becauſe he could not ſee now his not uſing of it would help to prevent the trouble; but he did ſee, that his vigorous improvement of it would help to prepare for the trouble, he ſet himſelf, with all diligence, to make the beſt uſe he could of this gleam, both at home and abroad, on Sabbath-days and week-days, to his power; yea, and beyond his power.

The great ſubject of debate at this time in the nation, was, concerning the repeal of penal laws and teſts. Mr Henry's thoughts were, as to the penal laws, that if thoſe againſt the diſſenters were all repealed, he would rejoice in it, and be very thankful both to God and man; for he would ſometimes ſay, without reflection upon any, he could not but look upon them as a national ſin; and as for thoſe againſt the Papiſts, if our law-givers ſee cauſe to repeal them in a regular way, I will endeavour (faith he) to make the beſt of it, and to ſay, " The will of the Lord be done."

When

When king James came his progrefs into that country, in September 1687, to court the complements of the people, Mr Henry joined with feveral others, in and about Whitchurch, Nantwich, and Wem, in an addrefs to him, which was prefented when he lay at Whitchurch; the purport of which was, not to facrifice their lives and fortunes to him and to his intereft, but only to return him thanks for the liberty they had, with a premife to demean themfelves quietly in the ufe of it.

Some time after, Commiffioners were fent abroad into the country, to enquire after the trouble that diffenters had fuftained by the penal laws; and how the money that was levied upon them was difpofed of, little of it being found paid into the Exchequer: they fent to Mr Henry to have an account from him of his fufferings; he returned anfwer by letter, that he had indeed been fined fome years before, for a conventicle, and diftrained upon, and his goods carried away; which all the country knew, and to which he referred himfelf. But being required to give a particular account of it upon oath; though he faid he could be glad to fee fuch inftruments of trouble legally removed; yet he declined giving any further information concerning it; having (as he wrote to the Commiffioners) " long fince, from his heart, forgiven all the agents, " inftruments and occafions of it; and having purpof- " ed never to fay any thing more of it."

It was on Tuefday, June 14, 1681, that he was difturbed at Wefton in Shropfhire, when he was preaching on Pfal. lxvi. 18. and on Tuefday, June 14, 1687, that day fix years he preached there again without difturbance, finifhing what he was then prevented from delivering, concerning prayer, and going on to ver. 19, 20. " But verily God hath heard me----bleffed be " God"----concerning the duty of thankfgiving. This feventh year of their filence and reftraint, proved, through God's wonderful good providence, the year of releafe.

T 2

In

In May, 1688, a new commiſſion of the peace came down for the county of Flint, in which (by whoſe intereſt or procurement was not known) Mr Henry was nominated a Juſtice of Peace for that county. It was no ſmall ſurpriſe to him, to receive a letter from the Clerk of the Peace, directed to Philip Henry, Eſq. acquainting him with it, and appointing him when and whither, to come to be ſworn. To which he returned anſwer, that he was very ſenſible of his unworthineſs of the honour, and his unfitneſs for the office which he was nominated to, and therefore deſired to be excuſed, and he was ſo, and did what he could that it might not be ſpoken of in the country. There were ſome, who upon this occaſion unhappily remembered, that a few years before, a reverend clergyman in Shropſhire told Mr Henry to his face, that he had done more miſchief in the country, than any man that ever came into it; and that he himſelf hoped ſhortly to be in the commiſſion of peace, and then he would rid the country of him. But alas he was quite diſappointed. Thus honour is like the ſhadow, which flies from thoſe that purſue it, and follows thoſe that flee from it.

For two years after this liberty began, Mr Henry ſtill continued his attendance, as uſual, at Whitewellchapel, whenever there was preaching there; and he preached at his own houſe only when there was no ſupply there, and in the evening of thoſe days when there was. For doing thus he was greatly clamoured againſt, by ſome of the rigid ſeparatiſts, and called a diſſembler, and one that halted between two, and the like. Thus (as he notes in his diary) one ſide told him he was the author of all the miſchief in the country, in drawing people from the church; and the other ſide told him, he was the author of all the miſchief, in drawing people to the church: and " which of " thoſe (faith he) ſhall I ſeek to pleaſe: Lord, neither, " but thyſelf alone, and my own conſcience, and " while I can do that, I have enough."

In

In a fermon at Whitewell-chapel, one Lord's day in the afternoon, where he and his family, and many of his congregation were attending, much was faid with fome keen reflections, to prove the diffenters fchifmaticks, and in a damnable ftate: when he came immediately after to preach at his own houfe, before he began his fermon, he expreffed himfelf to this purpofe; " Perhaps fome of you may expect now that I fhould " fay fomething in anfwer to what we have heard, by " which we have been fo feverely charged; but truly- " I have fomething elfe to do;" and fo, without any further notice taken of it, went on to preach Jefus Chrift and him crucified.

It was not without fome fear and trembling that Mr Henry received the tidings of the Prince of Orange's landing, in November 1688, as being fomewhat in the dark concerning the clearnefs of his call, and dreading what might be the confequence of it. He ufed to fay, " Give peace in our time, O Lord," was a prayer that he would heartily fet his Amen to. But when fecret things were brought to light, and a regular courfe was taken to fill the vacant throne with fuch a King and fuch a Queen, none rejoiced in it more heartily than he did. He celebrated the national thankfgiving for that great deliverance, with an excellent fermon on that text, Rom. viii. 31. " What " fhall we then fay to thefe things? If God be for us, " who can be againft us?"

Soon after that happy fettlement, there were overtures made towards a comprehenfion of the moderate diffenters, with the church of England; which Mr Henry moft earneftly defired, and wifhed for, if it could be had upon any terms lefs than finning againft his confcience; for never was any more averfe to that which looked like a feparation than he was, if he could poffibly have helped it, *falva confcientia.* His prayers were conftant, and his endeavours, as he had opportunity, that there might be fome healing methods found out and agreed upon. But it is well known what was

the

the *v. x cleri* at that time, viz. That forafmuch as the oaths, fubfcriptions, and ceremonies were impofed only to keep out fuch men, they would never confent to their removal, for the letting them in again. *Nolumus leges angliæ mutari*, was a faying perverted to this purpofe: and the fixed principle was, Better a fchifm without the church, than a faction within it, &c. This was at that time publifhed and owned, as the fenfe of the clergy in convocation; which temper and refolve, fo contrary to that which might have been expected, upon that happy and glorious revolution, did a little alter his fentiments in that matter, and he faw himfelf perfectly driven from them. Defpairing therefore to fee an accommodation, he fet himfelf the more vigoroufly to improve the prefent liberty. In June 1689, the act of indulgence paffed, which not only tolerated, but allowed the diffenters' meetings, and took them under the protection of the government.

Soon after which, though he never in the leaft changed his judgement, as to the lawfulnefs of joining in the common-prayer, but was ftill ready to do it occafionally, yet the minifters that preached at Whitewell-chapel, being often uncertain in their coming, which kept his meeting at Broad-Oak at like uncertainties, to the frequent difappointment of many of his hearers that came from far; he was at laft prevailed with to preach at public time every Lord's day, which he continued to do while he lived, much to his own fatisfaction, and the fatisfaction of his friends. An eminent minifter in Lancafhire, who did in like manner alter his practice about that time, gave this for a reafon, " That he had been for twenty-feven years ftriv-
" ing to pleafe a generation of men, who after all
" would not be pleafed, and therefore he would no
" longer endeavour it as he had done."

It may be of ufe to give fome account how he managed his minifterial work in the latter part of his time, wherein he had as fignal tokens of the prefence of God with him, as ever; enabling him ftill to bring forth
fruit

fruit in old age, and to renew his youth like the eagles. Though what he did he ftill did gratis, and would do fo, yet he was not willing to have any conftant affiftant, nor had he any; fo much was he in his element, when he was about his Mafter's work: 'twas his meat and drink to do it.

1. As to his conftant Sabbath work, he was uniform and abundant in it. He began his morning family worfhip, on Lord's days, at eight o'clock, when he read and expounded pretty largely, fung a pfalm and prayed; and many ftrove to come time enough to join with him in that fervice. He began in public juft at nine o'clock Winter and Summer. His meeting-place was an out-building of his own, near adjoining to his houfe, fitted up very decently and conveniently for the purpofe. He began with prayer, then he fung Pfal. c. without reading the line; next he read and expounded a chapter in the Old Teftament in the morning, and in the New Teftament in the afternoon. He looked upon the public reading of the fcriptures in religious affemblies to be an ordinance of God, and that it tended very much to the edification of people by that ordinance, to have what is read expounded to them. The bare reading of the word, he ufed to compare to the throwing of a net into the water; but the expounding of it, is like the fpreading out of that net, which makes it the more likely to catch fifh; efpecially as he managed it with practical profitable obfervations. Some that have heard him read a chapter with this thought, how will he make fuch a chapter as this ufeful to us? have been furprized with fuch pertinent, ufeful inftructions, as they have owned to be as much for their edification as any fermon. And commonly when he had expounded a chapter, he would defire them when they came home to read it over, and recollect fome of thofe things that had been fpoken to them out of it,

In his expounding of the Old Teftament, he induftrioufly fought for fomething in it concerning Chrift,

who

who is the true treasure hid in the field, the true manna hid in the dew of the Old Testament. Take one instance; the last Sabbath that ever he spent with his children at Chester, in the public morning worship, he read and expounded the last chapter of the book of Job: after he had gone through the chapter, and observed what he thought fit out of it, he expressed himself to this purpose: " When I have read a chapter
" in the Old Testament, I use to enquire what there
" is in it that points at Christ, or is any way appli-
" cable to Christ; here is in this chapter a great deal
" of Job; but is there nothing of Christ here? Yes;
" you have heard of the patience of Job, and have
" in him seen the end of the Lord. This in Job is
" applicable to Christ, that after he had patiently
" gone through his sufferings, he was appointed an
" intercessor for his unkind friends, ver. 8." ' Go to
' my servant Job, and my servant Job shall pray for you,
' for him will I accept.' " If any one hath an errand
" to God, let him go to Jesus Christ, and put it into
" his hand, for there is no acceptance to be hoped
" for with God, but by him, who is his beloved Son;
" not only with whom he is well pleased, but in whom
" viz. with us in him: he hath made us accepted in
" the beloved."

After the exposition of the chapter he sung a psalm, and commonly chose a psalm suitable to the chapter he had expounded; and would briefly tell his hearers how they might sing that psalm with understanding, and what affections of soul should be working towards God in the singing of it: his hints of that kind were of great use, and contributed much to the right performance of that service; he often said, " The more
" singing of psalms there is in our families and con-
" gregations on Sabbath days, the more like they are
" to heaven, and the more there is in them of the
" everlasting Sabbath." He would say sometimes, he loved to sing whole psalms, rather than pieces of psalms.

After

After the fermon in the morning, he fung the cxvii. Pfalm, without reading the line.

He intermitted at noon about an hour and a half, and on facrament days not near fo long, in which time he took fome little refreshment in his ftudy, making no folemn dinner; yet many of his friends did partake of his carnal, as well as of his fpiritual things, as thofe did that followed Chrift, of whom he was careful they fhould not faint by the way. The morning fermon was repeated, by a ready writer, to thofe that ftaid in the meeting-place, as many did, and when that was done, he began the afternoon's exercife; in which he not only read and expounded a chapter, but catechifed the children, and expounded the catechifm briefly before fermon. Thus did he go from ftrength to ftrength, and from duty to duty, on Sabbath-days; running the ways of God's commandments with an enlarged heart. And the variety, and vivacity of his public fervices, made them exceeding pleafant to all that join'd with him, who never had caufe to complain of his being tedious. He ufed to fay, " Every minute " of Sabbath-time is precious, and none of it to be " loft;" and that he fcarce thought the Lord's day well fpent, if he were not weary in body at night; wearied with his work, but not weary of it, as he ufed to diftinguifh. He would fay fometimes to thofe about him, when he had gone through the duties of a Sabbath; " Well, if this be not the way to Heaven, " I do not know what is." In prefling people to number their days, he would efpecially exhort them to number their Sabbath-days, how many they have been, and how ill they have been fpent; how few 'tis like they may be that they may be fpent better: and to help in the account, he would fay, that " for every " twenty years of our lives, we enjoy above a thou- " fand Sabbaths," which muft all be accounted for in the day of reckoning.

As to his conftant preaching, it was very fubftantial and elaborate, and greatly to edification. He ufed to fay, say, he could not starch in his preaching; that is, he would not; as knowing where the language and expression is stiff, and forced, and fine (as they call it) it doth not reach the greatest part of the hearers. When he grew old he would say, sure he might now take a greater liberty to talk (as he called it) in the pulpit; that is, to speak familiarly to people; yet to the last he abated not in his preparations for the pulpit, nor ever delivered any thing raw and undigested; much less any thing unbecoming the gravity and seriousness of the work. If his preaching were talking, it were talking to the purpose. His sermons were not common place, but even when his subjects were the most plain and trite, yet his management of them was usually peculiar and surprising. In those years, as formerly, he kept for the most part in a method for subjects, and was very seldom above one Sabbath upon a text. And his constant practice was, as it had been before, when he concluded a subject that he had been a good while upon, he spent one Sabbath in a brief rehearsal of the marrow and substance of the many sermons he preached upon it; which he called the clenching of the nail, that it might be as a nail in a sure place. So very industrious was he, and no less ingenious in his endeavours, that his hearers might be " able, after " his decease, to have these things always in remem- " brance, 2 Pet. i. 15. and it is hoped, that by the blessing of God, the effect did not altogether disappoint his expectation. In the latter times of his ministry, he would often contrive the heads of his sermons to begin with the same letter, or rather two and two of a letter; but he did not at all seem to affect or force it; only if it fell in naturally and easily he thought it a good help to memory, and of use, especially to the younger sort. And he would say, the chief reason why he did it was, because 'tis frequently observed in the scripture, particularly the book of Psalms. And though it be not a fashionable ornament of discourse, if it be a scripture ornament, that is sufficient to recommend it, it, at least to justify it against the imputation of childishness; (Mr Porter of Whitchurch very much used it, so did Mr Malden.) But the excellency of his sermons lay chiefly in the enlargements, which were always very solid, grave, and judicious; but in expressing and marshalling his heads, he often condescended below his own judgment, to help his hearers' memories. Some of his subjects (when he had finished them) he made some short memorandums of in verse, a distich or two of each Sabbath's work, and gave them out in writing, among the young ones of his congregation, many of whom wrote them, and learned them, and profited by them.

It might be of use (especially to those who had the happiness of sitting under his ministry) to give some account of the method of his Sabbath subjects, during the last eight or nine years of his ministry; and it was designed, till 'twas found 'twould swell this narrative into too great a bulk.

2. As to the administration of the sacraments, those mysteries of God, which ministers are the stewards of.

As to the sacrament of baptism, he had never (that I know of) baptized any children (except his own) from the time he was turned out in 1662, till this last liberty came, though often desired to do it:—such was the tender regard he had to the established church; but now he revived the administration of that ordinance in his congregation. The occasion was this; one of the parish-ministers preaching at Whitewell-chapel, Mr Henry and his family, and many of his friends being present, was earnestly cautioning people not to go to conventicles, and used this as an argument against it, "That they were baptized into the church of England." Mr Henry's catholic charity could not well digest this monopolizing of the great ordinance of baptism, and thought it time to bear his testimony against such narrow principles, which he ever expressed his dislike of in all parties and persuasions. Accordingly he took the next opportunity that offered itself, itfelf, publickly to baptize a child, and defired the congregation to bear witnefs, " That he did not baptize " that child into the church of England, nor into the " church of Scotland, nor into the church of the dif- " fenters, nor into the church at Broad-Oak, but in- " to the vifible catholic church of Jefus Chrift." After this he baptized very many, and always publickly, though being in the country they were commonly carried a good way. The public adminiftration of baptifm he not only judged moft agreeable to the nature and end of the ordinance, but found to be very profitable and edifying to the congregation; for he always took that occafion, not only to explain the nature of the ordinance, but affectionately and pathetically to excite people duly to improve their baptifm. He ufually received the child immediately out of the hands of the parent that prefented it, and returned it into the fame hands again, with this or the like charge, " Take " this child, and bring it up for God." He ufed to fay, that one advantage of public baptifm was, that there were many to join in prayer for the child, in which therefore, and in blefling God for it, he was ufually very large and particular. After he had baptized the child, before he gave it back to the parent, he commonly ufed thefe words; " We receive this " child into the congregation of Chrift's church, hav- " ing wafhed it with water, in the name of the Father, " and of the Son, and of the Holy Ghoft, in token " that hereafter it fhall not be afhamed to confefs " Chrift crucified, and manfully to fight, &c."

He baptized many adult perfons, that through the error of their parents were not baptized in infancy, and fome in public.

The folemn ordinance of the Lord's fupper he conftantly celebrated in his congregation once a month, and always to a very confiderable number of communicants. He did not ufually obferve public days of preparation for that ordinance, other than as they fell in courfe in the weekly lectures: nor did he ever appropriate

priate any particular subject of his preaching to Sacrament-days, having a great felicity in adapting any profitable subject to such an occasion : and he would say, What did the primitive christians do, when they celebrated the Lord's supper every Lord's day ? His administration of this ordinance was very solemn and affecting. He had been wont to go about in the congregation, and to deliver the elements with his own hand ; but in his latter time, he delivered them only to those near him, and so they were handed from one to another, with the assistance of one who supplied the office of a deacon, as having also the custody and disposal of the money gathered for the use of the poor ; Mr Henry taking and carefully keeping a particular account of it.

Such as desired to be admitted to the Lord's supper, he first discoursed with concerning their spiritual state ; and how the case stood between God and their souls; not only to examine them, but to instruct and teach them, and to encourage them as he saw occasion ; gently leading those whom he discerned to be serious, though weak and timorous ; he usually discoursed with them more than once, as finding precept upon precept, and line upon line necessary : but he did it with so much mildness, and humility, and tenderness, and endeavour to make the best of every body, as did greatly affect and win upon many. He was herein like our great Master, who " can have compas-
" sion on the ignorant," and doth not " despise the
" day of small things."

But his admission of young people out of the rank of catechumens into that of communicants, had a peculiar solemnity in it. Such as he catechized, when they grew up to some years of discretion, if he observed them to be intelligent and serious, and to set their faces heaven-wards ; he marked them out to be admitted to the Lord's supper ; and when he had a competent number of such, twelve or fifteen perhaps, or more ; he ordered each of them to come to him severally,

rally, and difcourfed with them of the things belonging to their everlafting peace; put it to their choice whom they would ferve; and endeavoured to affect them with thofe things with which by their catechifms they had been made acquainted; drawing them with the cords of a man, and the bands of love, into the way which is called holy. For feveral Lord's days he catechized them, particularly in public, touching the Lord's fupper, and the duty of preparation for it, and their baptifmal covenant, which in that ordinance they were to take upon themfelves, and to make their own act and deed. Often telling them upon fuch occafions, that they were not to oblige themfelves to any more than what they were already obliged to by their baptifm, only to bind themfelves fafter to it. Then he appointed a day in the week before the ordinance; when in a folemn affembly on purpofe, he prayed for them, and preached a fermon to them, proper to their age and circumftances: and fo the following Sabbath they were all received together to the Lord's fupper. This he looked upon as the right confirmation, or tranfition, into the ftate of adult church-memberfhip. The more folemn our covenanting with God is, the more deep and the more durable the impreffions are likely to be. He hath recorded it in his diary, upon one of thefe occafions, as his heart's defire and prayer for thofe who were thus admitted, " That it might " be as the day of their efpoufals to the Lord Jefus, " and that they might each of them have a wedding " garment."

3. The difcipline he obferved in his congregation was, not fuch as he could have wifhed for, but the beft he could get, confidering what a fcattered flock he had, which was his trouble, but it could not be helped. He would fometimes apply to the circumftances he was in, that of Mofes, Deut. xii. 8, 9. However, I fee not but the end was effectually attained by the methods he took, though there wanted the formality of officers and church-meetings for the purpofe.

If

If he heard of any that walked diforderly, he fent for them, and reproved them, gently or fharply, as he faw the cafe required. If the fin had fcandal in it, he fufpended them from the ordinance of the Lord's fupper, till they gave fome tokens of their repentance and reformation. And where the offence was public and grofs, his judgement was, that fome public fatisfaction fhould be made to the congregation before re-admiffion. But whatever offence did happen, or breaches of the chriftian peace, Mr Henry's peculiar excellency lay in reftoring with the fpirit of meeknefs; which, with his great prudence, and love, and condefcenfion, did fo much command the refpects of his people, and win upon them, that there was a univerfal fatisfaction in all his management; and it may truly be faid of him, as it was of David, 2 Sam. iii. 36. that " what-" foever he did pleafed all the people." And it is an inftance and evidence, that thofe minifters who will rule by love and meeknefs, need no laws or canons to rule by, other than thofe of the holy fcripture. " How forcible are right words! Job vi. 25.

4. He was very ftrict and very ferious in obferving the public fafts appointed by authority, and called them a delight. He had feldom any one to affift him in carrying on the duties of thofe days, but performed the fervice of them himfelf alone. He began at nine of the clock, or quickly after, and never ftirred out of the pulpit till about four in the afternoon, fpending all that time in praying and expounding, and finging, and preaching, to the admiration of all that heard him, who were generally more on fuch days than ufual. And he was fometimes obferved to be more warm and lively towards the latter end of the duties of a faftday, than at the beginning; as if the fpirit were moft willing and enlarged when the flefh was moft weak. In all his performances on public faft-days, he did, *hoc agere*, attend to that which was the proper work of the day; every thing is beautiful in its feafon. His prayers and pleadings with God on thofe days, were

epfecially

especially for national mercies, and the pardon of national sins : how excellently did he order the cause before God, and fill his mouth with arguments in his large and particular intercessions for the land, for the king, the government, the army, the navy, the church, the French Protestants, &c. He was another Jacob, a wrestler, an Israel, a prince with God. Before a fast-day he would be more than ordinarily inquisitive concerning the state of public affairs, as Nehemiah was, Neh. i. 2. that he might know the better how to order his prayers and preaching : for on such a day (he hath sometimes said) " as good say nothing, as no-" thing to the purpose." He made it his business on fast-days, to shew people their transgressions, especially the house of Jacob their sins. " 'Tis most proper (said " he) to preach of Christ on Lord's-days, to preach of sin on fast-days, and to preach duty on both. He went over the third chapter of the Revelation, in the fast-sermons of two years. Another year he preached over the particulars of that charge, Zeph. iii. 2. Hypocrisy in hearers, and flattery in preachers (as he would sometimes say) is bad at any time, but it is especially abominable upon a day of humiliation.

5. He preached a great many lectures in the country about, some stated, some occasional, in supplying of which he was very indefatigable. He hath sometimes preached a lecture, ridden eight or nine miles, and preached another, and the next day two more: to quicken himself to diligence he would often say, " our opportunities are passing away, and we must " work while it is day, for the night cometh." Once having very wet and foul weather to go through to preach a lecture, he said, he comforted himself with two scriptures ; one was 2 Tim. ii. 3. " Endure hard-" ness as a good soldier of Jesus Christ." The other (because he exposed and hazarded his health, for which some blamed him) was 2 Sam. vi. 21. " It was before " the Lord." He took all occasions in his lectures abroad, to possess the minds of people with sober and
moderate

moderate principles, and to ſtir them up to the ſerious regard of thoſe things wherein we are all agreed. " We are not met here together (ſaid he once in an exhortation, with which he often began at his lecture) " becauſe we think ourſelves better than others, " but becauſe it is our deſire to be better than we " are."

He was very happy in the choice of his ſubjects for his week-day lectures. At one which was ſtated, he preached againſt errors in general, from James i. 16. " Do not err, my beloved brethren;" particularly from divers other ſcriptures he ſhewed, that we muſt not err, concerning God and Chriſt, and the Spirit; concerning ſin and repentance, faith and good works; concerning God's ordinances; concerning grace and peace, and afflictions and proſperity, and the things of the life to come.

At the monthly lectures he delivered at his own houſe, he choſe to preach upon the four laſt things, death and judgment, heaven and hell, in many particulars, but commonly a new text for every ſermon. When he had in many ſermons finiſhed the firſt of the four, one that uſed to hear him ſometimes, enquiring of his progreſs in his ſubjects, aſked him if he had done with death? meaning that ſubject concerning death; to which he pleaſantly replied, " No, I have not done " with him yet; I muſt have another turn with him, " and he will give me a fall; but I hope to have the " victory at laſt." He would ſometimes remove the lectures in the country from one place to another, for the benefit of thoſe that could not travel. Once having adjourned a lecture to a new place, he began it there with a ſermon on Acts xvii. 6. " Theſe men that " have turned the world upſide down, are come hither " alſo;" in which he ſhewed how falſe the charge is, as they meant it; for religion doth not diſturb the peace of families or ſocieties, doth not cauſe any diſorder or unquietneſs, &c. And yet, that in another ſenſe there is a great truth in it; that when the goſpel comes in power to any foul, it turns the world upfide down in that foul; fuch is the change it makes there.

All this he did gratis, and without being burthenfome to any; nay, he was beft pleafed, when at the places where he preached, nothing was got for his entertainment, but he came home (though fome miles) fafting; as in other places it was a trouble to him to fee his friends careful about much ferving, though it was out of their refpect to him.

Laftly, As he was an excellent preacher himfelf, fo he was an exemplary hearer of the word, when others preached, though every way his inferiors; fo reverent, ferious, and attentive, was he in hearing, and fo obfervant of what was fpoken. I have heard him tell, that he knew one (and I fuppofe it was as Paul knew a man in Chrift) who could truly fay, to the glory of God, that for forty years he had never flept at a fermon. He was diligent alfo to improve what he heard afterwards by meditations, repetition, prayer, and difcourfe; and he was a very great encourager of young minifters that were humble and ferious, though their abilities and performances were but mean. He hath noted in his diary, (as that which affected him,) this faying of a godly man, a hearer of his, "I find it eafier " to go fix miles to hear a fermon, than to fpend one " quarter of an hour in meditating and praying over " it in fecret (as I fhould) when I come home."

As to the circumftances of his family in the laft nine years of his life, they were fomewhat different from what they had been; but the fame candle of God which had fhined upon his tabernacle, continued ftill to do fo. In the years 1687, and 1688, he married all his five children; the three eldeft in four months time, in the year 1687, and the other two in a year and a half after; fo many fwarms (as he ufed to call them) out of his hive; and all not only with his full confent, but to his abundant comfort and fatisfaction. He would fay, he thought it the duty of parents to ftudy to oblige their children in that affair. And tho' never could children be more easy and at rest in a father's house than his were, yet he would sometimes say concerning them, as Naomi to Ruth, Ruth iii. 1. " Shall I not seek rest for thee ?" Two advices he used to give, both to his children and others, in their choice of that relation : One was, " Keep within the " bonds of profession," such as one may charitably hope is from a good principle. The other was, " Look " at suitableness," in age, quality, education, temper, &c. He used to observe from Gen. ii. 18. " I will make " him a help meet for him;" that where there is not meetness, there will not be much help. And he would commonly say to his children, with reference to that choice, " Please God, and please yourselves, and you " shall never displease me ;" and greatly blamed those parents, who conclude matches for their children, and do not ask counsel at their mouth. He never aimed at great things in the world for his children, but sought for them in the first place the kingdom of God, and the righteousness thereof. He used to mention sometimes the saying of a pious gentlewoman, that had many daughters : " The care of most people, is how to " get good husbands for their daughters ; but my care " is to fit my daughters to be good wives, and then " let God provide for them." In this, as in other things, Mr Henry steered by that principle ; That " a " man's life consisteth not in the abundance of the " things that he possesseth." And it pleased God so to order it, that all his children were disposed of, into circumstances very agreeable and comfortable, both for life and godliness. He was greatly affected with the goodness of God to him herein, without any forecast or contrivance of his own. " The country (saith " he in his diary) takes notice of it, and what then " shall I render ?" Surely this is a token for good.

All his four daughters were married at Whitewellchapel, and he preached a wedding sermon for each of them, in his own family, after. He would often tell his friends, that those who desire, in the married condition,

dition, to live in the favour of God, muſt enter upon that condition in the fear of God. For it's an ill omen to ſtumble at the threſhold : and an error in the firſt concoction, is ſeldom amended in the ſecond.

While he lived, he had much comfort in all his children and their yoke-fellows, and ſomewhat the more, that by the Divine Providence, four of the five families which branched out of his, were ſettled in Cheſter.

His youngeſt daughter was married April 26, 1688, the ſame day of the year (as he obſerves in his diary) and the ſame day of the week, and in the ſame place that he was married to his dear wife, twenty-eight years before ; upon which this is his remark, "I can-
" not deſire for them, that they ſhould receive more
" from God than we have received, in that relation
" and condition; but I would deſire, and do deſire,
" that they may do more for God in it than we have
" done." His uſual compliment to his new-married friends, was, Others wiſh you all happineſs, I wiſh you all holineſs, and then there is no doubt but you will have all happineſs.

When the marriage of the laſt of his daughters was about to be concluded on, he thus writes ; " But is
" Joſeph gone, and Simeon gone, and muſt Benjamin
" go alſo ? we will not ſay that all theſe things are
" againſt us, but for us : if we muſt be thus in this
" merciful way bereaved of our children, let us be be-
" reaved ; and God turn it for good to them, as we
" know he will. if they love and fear his name." And when, ſome time after ſhe was married, he parted with her to the houſe of her huſband, he thus writes ; " We
" have ſent her away, not as Laban ſaid he would
" have ſent his daughters away, with mirth, and with
" ſongs, with tabret, and with harp, but with prayers
" and tears, and hearty good wiſhes :" " And now
" (ſaith he in his diary) we are alone again, as we
" were in our beginning ; God be better to us than
" twenty children." Upon the ſame occaſion he thus

writes

writes to a dear relation: " We are now left as we
" were, one and one, and yet but one; the Lord, I
" truft, that has brought us thus far, will enable us
" to finifh well; and then all will be well, and not till
" then."

That which he often mentioned, as the matter of his great comfort that it was fo, and his defire that it might continue fo, was, the love and unity that was among his children; and that (as he writes) the tranfplanting of them into new relations, had not leffened that love, but rather increafed it; for this he often gave thanks to the God of love; noting from Job i. 4. That the childrens love to one another is the parents comfort and joy. In his laft will and teftament, this is the prayer which he puts up for his children, " That
" the Lord would build them up in holinefs, and con-
" tinue them ftill in brotherly love, as a bundle of
" arrows which cannot be broken."

When his children were removed from him, he was a daily interceffor at the throne of grace for them and their families. Still the burnt-offerings were offered according to the number of them all. He ufed to fay,
" Surely the children of fo many prayers will not mif-
" carry." Their particular circumftances of affliction and danger, were fure to be mentioned by him with fuitable petitions. The greateft affliction he faw in his family was the death of his dear daughter-in-law, Catharine, the only daughter of Samuel Hardware, Efq. who, about a year and a half after fhe was tranfplanted into his family (to which fhe was the greateft comfort and ornament imaginable) died of the fmall pox in child-bed, upon the thankfgiving day for king William's coming in. She died but a few weeks after Mr Henry had married the laft of his daughters, upon which marriage fhe had faid, " Now we have a full
" leafe, God only knows which life will drop firft." She comforted herfelf in the extremity of her illnefs with this word, " Well, when I come to heaven, I
" fhall fee that I could not have been without this af-
" fliction."

"fliction." She had been for some time before under some fears as to her spiritual state, but the clouds were through grace dispelled, and she finished her course with joy, and a chearful expectation of the glory to be revealed. When she lay ill, Mr Henry (being in fear not only for her that was ill, but for the rest of his children in Chester, who had none of them past the pikes of that perilous distemper) wrote thus to his son, on the evening of the Lord's day, "I have "just done the public work of this day, wherein, be- "fore many scores of witnesses, many of whom I dare "say, are no little concerned for you: I have abso- "lutely, freely, and unreservedly given you all up to "the good will and pleasure of our heavenly Father, "waiting what he will do with us, for good I am sure "we have received, and shall we not receive evil also? He preached at Chester, upon occasion of that sad breach in his family, on Job x. 3. "Shew me where- "fore thou contendest with me."

When two of his children lay ill, and in perilous circumstances, after he had been wrestling with God in prayer for them, he wrote thus in his diary: "If "the Lord will be pleased to grant me my request "this time concerning my children, I will not say as "the beggars at our door use to do, I'll never ask any "thing of him again; but, on the contrary, he shall "hear oftner from me than ever; and I will love God "the better, and love prayer the better, as long as I "live." He used to say, trades-men take it ill, if those that are in their books go to another shop: while we are so much indebted to God for past mercies, we are bound to attend him for further mercies.

As he was an intercessor for his children at the throne of grace, so he was upon all occasions a remembrancer to them, both by word and letter, to quicken them to that which is good. How often did he inculcate this upon them? "Love one another, and the God of love "and peace will be with you. Do all you can, while "you are together, to help one another to heaven, that
"you

"you may be together there, for ever, and with the Lord." When the families of his children were in health and peace, the candle of God fhining upon their tabernacles, he wrote thus to them, "'Twas one of Job's comforts in his profperity, that his children loved one another, and feafted together: the fame is ours in you, which God continue. But you will not be offended, if we pray that you may none of you curfe God in your hearts. Remember, the wheel is always in motion, and the fpoke that is uppermoft will be under, and therefore mix tremblings always with your joy."

He much rejoiced in the vifits of his children, and made that as other things, which were the matter of his rejoicing, the matter of his thankfgiving. His ufual faying at parting, was, " This is not the world we are to be together in, and 'tis well it is not; but there is fuch a world before us :" and his ufual prayer was, " that our next meeting might be either in heaven, or further on in our way towards it."

He had in eight years time twenty-four grand-children born, fome by each of his children; concerning whom he would often blefs God, that they were all " the fealed ones of the God of heaven, and enrolled " among his lambs." On the birth of his fecond grand-child, at a troublefome time as to public affairs, he thus writes, " I have now feen my childrens children, let me alfo fee peace upon Ifrael; and then I will fay, Lord, now letteft thou thy fervant depart." Some were much affected with it, when he baptized two of his grand-children together at Chefter, publickly, and preached on Gen. xxxiii. 5. " They are the children which God hath gracioufly given thy fervant." He obferved in what a favory, pious, gracious manner Jacob fpeaks. He had fpoken good fenfe if he had only faid, they are my children; but then he had not fpoken like Jacob, like one that had fo lately feen the face of God. Though our fpeech be not always of grace, yet it muft be always with grace,

grace

grace poured into the lips. There is a kind of language, the air of which speaks it the language of Canaan; chriftians fhould fpeak like chriftians.

It was not long after his children were married from him, but his houfe was filled again with the children of feveral of his friends, whom he was, by much importunity, perfuaded to take to table with him. All that knew him, thought it a thoufand pities, that fuch a mafter of a family fhould have but a fmall family, and fhould not have many to fit down under his fhadow. He was firft almoft neceffitated to it, by the death of his dear friend and kinfman, Mr Benyon of Afh, who left his children to his care. Some he took gratis, or for fmall confideration; and when by reafon of the advances of age he could not go about fo much as he had done, doing good, he laid out himfelf to do the more at home. He kept a teacher to attend their fchool learning; and they had the benefit, not only of his infpection in that, but (which was much more) his family-worfhip, Sabbath inftructions, catechizing and daily converfe, in which his tongue was as choice filver, and his lips fed many. Nothing but the hopes of doing fome good to the rifing generation could have prevailed with him to take this trouble upon him. He would often fay, "We have a bufy houfe, but
" there is a reft remaining. We muft be doing fome-
" thing in the world while we are in it; but this fafh-
" ion will not laft long, methinks I fee it paffing a-
" way."

Sometimes he had fuch with him as had gone through their courfe of Univerfity learning, at private academies, and defired to fpend fome time in his family, before their entrance upon the miniftry; that they might have the benefit, not only of his public and family inftructions, but of his learned, pious converfe, in which, as he was throughly furnifhed, for every good word and work, fo he was very free and communicative. The great thing which he ufed to prefs upon thofe who intended the miniftry, was to ftudy the fcriptures,

tures, and make them familiar. *Bonus textuarius est bonus thelogus,* was a maxim he often minded them of. For this purpose he recommended to them the study of the Hebrew, that they might be able to search the scriptures in the original. He also advised them to the use of an interleaved Bible, wherein to insert such expositions and observations as occur occasionally in sermons or other books; which, he would say, are more happy and considerable sometimes, than those that are found in the professed commentators. When some young men desired the happiness of coming into his family, he would tell them, " You come to me as " Naaman did to Elisha, expecting that I should do " this and t'other for you; and alas, I can but say as " he did, Go wash in Jordan;—Go, study the scriptures. " I profess to teach no other learning but scripture " learning." It was but a little before he died, that in reading Isa. l. he observed from ver. 4. " The Lord " hath given me the tongue of the learned," &c. That the true learning of a gospel minister consists not in being able to talk Latin fluently, and to dispute in philosophy, but in being able to speak a word in season to weary souls. He that knows how to do that well, is a learned minister.

CHAP. IX.

His sickness, Death, and Burial.

IN the time of his health, he made death very familiar to himself by frequent and pleasing thoughts and meditations of it; and endeavoured to make it so to his friends, by speaking often of it. His letters and discourses had still something or other which spoke his constant expectations of death; thus did he learn to die daily; and it is hard to say, whether it was more easy to him to speak, or uneasy to his friends, to hear him speak of leaving the world. This minds me of a passage I was told by a worthy Scotch minister, Mr

Y   Patrick

Patrick Adair, that vifiting the famous Mr Durham of Glafgow, in his laft ficknefs, which was long and lingering; he faid to him, "Sir, I hope you have fo fet "all in order, that you have nothing elfe to do but "to die:" "I blefs God (faid Mr Durham) I have "not had that to do either thefe many years." Such is the comfort of dying daily, when we come to die indeed.

Mr Henry's conftitution was but tender, and yet by the blefling of God upon his great temperance, and care of his diet, and moderate exercife by walking in the air, he did for many years enjoy a good meafure of health, which he ufed to call "The fugar that fweet- "ens all temporal mercies," for which therefore we ought to be very thankful, and of which we ought to be very careful. He had fometimes violent fits of the cholick, which would be very afflictive for the time. Towards his latter end he was diftreffed fometimes with a pain, which his doctor thought might arife from a ftone in his kidneys. Being once upon the recovery from an ill fit of that pain, he faid to one of his friends that afked him how he did, "he hoped, by the grace of "God, he fhould now be able to give one blow more "to the devil's kingdom;" and often profeffed, "he "did not defire to live a day longer than he might "do God fome fervice." He faid to another, when he perceived himfelf recovering, "Well, I thought I "had been putting into the harbour, but find I muft "to fea again."

He was fometimes fuddenly taken with fainting fits, which, when he recovered from, he would fay, "Dy- "ing is but a little more."

When he was in the fixty-third year of his age, which is commonly called the Grand Climacteric, and hath been to many the dying year, and was fo to his father, he numbered the days of it, from Auguft 24. 1693, to Auguft 24. 1694, when he finifhed it: and when he concluded it, he thus wrote in his diary: "This day finifheth my commonly dying year, which I
"have

"have numbered the days of; and should now apply "my heart more than ever to heavenly wisdom." He was much pleased with that expression of our English liturgy in the office of burial, and frequently used it; "In the midst of life we are in death."

The infirmities of age, when they grew upon him, did very little abate his vigour and liveliness in preaching, but he seemed even to renew his youth as the eagles; as those that are planted in the house of the Lord, who still bring forth fruit in old age; not so much to shew that they are upright, as to shew that the Lord is upright, Psal. xcii. 14, 15. But in his latter years, travelling was very troublesome to him; and he would say, as Mr Dod used to do, that when he thought to shake himself as at other times, he found his hair was cut; his sense of this led him to preach an occasional sermon not long before he died, on John xxi. 18. "When thou wast young, thou girdedst thy-"self," &c. Another occasional sermon he preached when he was old, for his own comfort, and the comfort of his aged friends, on Psal. lxxi. 17, 18. "O God, "thou hast taught me from my youth," &c. He observed there, that it is a blessed thing to be taught of God from our youth; and those that have been taught of God from their youth, ought to declare his wondrous works all their days after. And those that have been taught of God from their youth, and have all their days declared his wondrous works, may comfortably expect, that when they are old he will not forsake them. Christ is a master that doth not use to cast off his old servants.

For some years before he died, he used to complain of an habitual weariness, contracted, he thought, by his standing to preach, sometimes very uneasily, and in inconvenient places, immediately after riding. He would say, Every minister was not cut out for an itinerant; and sometimes the manifest attention and affection of people in hearing, enlarged him both in length and fervency, somewhat more than his strength could well bear.

bear. It was not many months before he died, that he wrote thus to a dear relation, who inquired folicitoufly concerning his health; "I am always habitually "weary, and expect no other till I lye down in the "bed of fpices." And (bleffed be God) fo the grave is to all the faints, fince He lay in it who is the rofe of Sharon, and the lily of the vallies. When fome of his friends perfuaded him to fpare himfelf, he would fay, "Its time enough to reft when I am in the grave; "what were candles made for, but to burn."

It doth not appear that he had any particular prefages of his death; but by many inflances there were of his actual gracious expectation of it, fomewhat more than ordinary for fome time before. The laft vifit he made to his children in Chefter, was in July 1695, almoft a year before he died, when he fpent a Lord's day there, and preached on the laft verfe of the epiftle to Philemon, "The grace of our Lord Jefus Chrift be "with your fpirit." By grace he underftood not fo much the good will of God towards us, as the good work of God in us, called the grace of Chrift, both becaufe he is the author and finifher of it, and becaufe he is the pattern and famplar of it. Now "the choi- "ceft gift we can afk of God for our friend is, that "this grace of our Lord Jefus Chrift may be with "their fpirit." This is the one thing needful, the better part, the root of the matter, the whole of man, the principle thing, the more excellent way, a blefling indeed, and the thing that accompanies falvation. The grace of Chrift in the fpirit, enlightens and enlivens the fpirit, foftens and fubdues the fpirit, purifies and preferves the fpirit, greatens and guides the fpirit, fweetens and ftrengthens the fpirit, and therefore what can be more defirable. A fpirit without the grace of Chrift, is a field without a fence, a fool without underftanding; it is a horfe without a bridle, and a houfe without furniture; it is a fhip without tackle, and a foldier without armour; it is a cloud without rain, and a carcafe without a foul; it is a tree without fruit, and a

traveller

traveller without a guide. How earneſt therefore ſhould we be in praying to God for grace, both for ourſelves and for our relations! He had intended to preach upon that text, when he was at Cheſter the year before, but was then prevented, by a particular ſad occaſion, which obliged him to a funeral ſermon, divine Providence reſerving that benediction (which his heart was much upon) for his valediction. The Thurſday following being kept as a faſt in his ſon's congregation at Cheſter, he preached on Luke xix. 41. " He beheld the city, and wept over it;" which proved his farewell to the town, as the former was his farewell to his friends and relations in it.

It was not many weeks before he died, that he wrote thus to one of his children: " We are well here, thanks
" be to God, and are glad to hear that you and yours
" are well alſo, God in mercy continue it: but why
" ſhould we be well always? Do we deſerve it? Are there
" no mixtures in our obedience? Are there any perſons
" or families, at whoſe door ſickneſs and death never
" knocked? Muſt the earth be forſaken for us, or the
" rock removed out of its place? Is it not enough that
" we be dealt with according to the manner of men,
" and that we have a promiſe, that it ſhall end well,
" everlaſtingly well?"

To another of his children, about the ſame time, he writes, " We are ſenſible that we decline apace, but
" the beſt of it is, that as time goes, eternity comes;
" and we are in good hope, through grace, that it will
" be a comfortable eternity."

It was in April 1696, a few weeks before he died, that his ſon's father-in-law, Robert Warburton, Eſq; was gathered to his grave in peace, in a good old age. Upon the tidings of whoſe death, Mr Henry wrote thus to his ſon; " Your fathers, where are they? your
" father-in-law gone, and your own father going; but
" you have a God-father that lives for ever." He was wont ſometimes to ſubſcribe his letters, your ever-loving, but not ever-living father.

It was not a month before he died, that, in a letter to his very dear and worthy friend and brother, Mr Tallents of Shrewsbury, he had this paſſage : " Me-
" thinks it is ſtrange, that it ſhould be your lot and
" mine, to abide ſo long on earth by the ſtuff, when
" ſo many of our friends are dividing the ſpoil above,
" but God will have it ſo ; and to be willing to live
" in obedience to his holy will, is as true an act of
" grace, as to be willing to die when he calls, eſpeci-
" ally when life is labour and ſorrow. But when it
" is labour and joy, ſervice to his name, and ſome
" meaſure of ſucceſs and comfort in ſerving him; when
" it is to ſtop a gap, and ſtem a tide, it is to be rejoi-
" ced in ; 'tis heaven upon earth : nay, one would
" think, by the Pſalmiſt's oft repeated plea, Pſal. vi.
" xxx. lxxxviii. cxv. and cxviii. that it were better
" than to be in heaven itſelf; and can that be ?"

A little before his ſickneſs and death, being ſummer time, he had ſeveral of his children, and his childrens children about him, at Broad Oak, with whom he was much refreſhed, and very cheerful; but ever and anon ſpoke of the faſhion he was in, as paſſing away ; and often told them, he ſhould be there but a while to bid them welcome. And he was obſerved frequently in prayer, to beg of God, that " he would make us ready'
" for that which would come certainly, and might
" come ſuddenly." One aſking him how de did, he anſwered, " I find the chips fly off apace, the tree will
" be down ſhortly."

The laſt time he adminiſtered the Lord's ſupper, a fortnight before he died, he cloſed the adminiſtration with that ſcripture, 1 John iii. 2. " It doth not yet ap-
" pear what we ſhall be ;" not yet, but it will ſhortly. The Sabbath but one before he died, being, in the courſe of his expoſition, come to that difficult part of ſcripture, the xl. of Ezekiel, and the following chapters, he ſaid he would endeavour to explain thoſe prophecies to them ; and added " If I do not do it now,
" I never ſhall :" and he obſerved, that the only pro-
phetical

phetical sermon which our Lord Jesus preached, was but a few days before he died. This many of his hearers not only reflected upon afterwards, but took notice of at that time with a concern, as having something in it more than ordinary.

On the Lord's-day, June 21. 1696, he went through the work of the day with his usual vigour and liveliness. He was then preaching over the first chapter of St Peter's second epistle, and was that day on those words, " Add to your faith virtue," ver. 5. He took virtue for christian courage and resolution in the exercise of faith; and the last thing he mentioned, in which christians have need of courage, is in dying; " for (as he was often us'd to say) it is a serious thing to die, and to die is a work by itself." That day he gave notice, both morning and afternoon, with much affection and enlargement, of the public fast, which was appointed by authority the Friday following, June, 26. pressing his hearers, as he us'd to do upon such occasions, to come in a prepared frame, to the solemn services of that day.

The Tuesday following, June 23, he rose at six o'clock, according to his custom, after a better night's sleep than ordinary, and in wonted health. Between seven and eight o'clock he performed family worship, according to the usual manner; he expounded very largely the former half of the civ. Psalm, and sung it; but he was somewhat shorter in prayer than he us'd to be, being then (as it was thought) taken ill. Blessed is that servant, whom his Lord, when he comes, shall find so doing. Immediately after prayer he retired to his chamber, not saying any thing of his illness, but was soon after found upon his bed in great extremity of pain, in his back, breast, and bowels; it seemed to be a complicated fit of the stone and cholick together, in very great extremity. The means that had been us'd to give him relief in his illness were altogether ineffectual; he had not the least intermission or remission of pain, neither up nor in bed, but in a continual

toss.

tofs. He had faid fometimes, that God's Ifrael may find Jordan rough; but there's no remedy, they muft through it to Canaan; and would tell of a good man who us'd to fay, he was not fo much afraid of death as of dying. We know they are not the godly people, part of the defcription of whofe condition it is, that there are no bands in their death, and yet their end is peace, and their death gain, and they have hope in it. In this extremity he was ftill looking up to God, and calling upon him, who is a prefent help in the needful hour. When the exquifitenefs of his pain forced groans and complaints from him, he would prefently correct himfelf with a patient and quiet fubmiffion to the hand of his heavenly Father, and a cheerful acquiefcence in his heavenly will. "I am afhamed (faith he) of thefe groans, I want virtue: O for virtue now when I have need of it (referring to his fubject the Lord's-day before) forgive me that I groan thus, and I will endeavour to filence them; but indeed my ftroke is heavier than my groaning." It is true, what Mr Baxter faid in his pain, There's no difputing againft fenfe. It was his trouble, as it was Mr Baxter's that by reafon of his bodily pain, he could not exprefs his inward comfort; however that was it, with which God gracioufly ftrengthened him in his foul. He faid to thofe about him, They muft remember what inftructions and counfels he had given them when he was in health, for now he could fay but little to them, only to refer them to what he had faid, as that which he would live and die by.

It was two or three hours after he was taken ill, before he would fuffer a meffenger to be fent to Chefter for his fon, and for the doctor, faying, he fhould either be better, or dead, before they could come; but at laft he faid, as the prophet did to his importunate friends, Send. About eight o'clock that evening they came, and found him in the fame extremity of pain which he had been in all day. And nature being before fpent with his conftant and indefatigable labours in the work

of

of the Lord, now funk, and did perfectly fuccumb under its burthen, and was quite difabled to grapple with fo many hours inceffant pain. What further means were then us'd proved fruitlefs, and did not anfwer the intention. He apprehended himfelf going apace, and faid to his fon when he came in, " O fon, you are " welcome to a dying father : I am now ready to ' " offered, and the time of my departure is at han His pain continued very acute, but he had peace u in. I am tormented (faid he once) but bleffed be God. not in this flame ; and foon after, " I am all on fire," (when at the fame time his extreme parts were cold) but he prefently added, Bleffed be God it is not the fire of hell. To fome of his next neighbours who came in to fee him (for thofe at a diftance had not notice of his illnefs) he faid, " O make fure work for your fouls " by getting an intereft in Chrift while you are in " health ; for if I had that work to do now, what would " become of me ? but I blefs God I am fatisfied." It was a caution he was often wont to give ; See to it, that your work be not undone, when your time is done, left you be undone for ever.

Towards ten or eleven o'clock that night, his pulfe and fight began to fail ; of the latter he himfelf took notice, and inferred from it the near approach of his diffolution.

He took an affectionate farewell of his dear yoke-fellow, with a thoufand thanks for all her love and care, and tendernefs ; left a bleffing for all his dear children, and their dear yoke-fellows and little ones, that were abfent. He faid to his fon, who fat under his head, " Son, the Lord blefs you, and grant that. " you may do worthily in your generation, and be " more ferviceable to the church of God than I have " been ;" fuch was his great humility to the laft. And when his fon, replied, O Sir, pray for me that I may but tread in your fteps ; he anfwered, Yea, follow peace and holinefs, and let them fay what they will. More he would have faid to bear his dying teftimony to the way in which he had walked, but nature was spent, and he had not strength to express it.

His understanding and speech continued almost to the last breath, and he was still in his dying agonies calling upon God, and committing himself to him. One of the last words he said, when he found himself just ready to depart, was, " O death, where is thy----?" with that his speech faultered, and within a few minutes (after about sixteen hours illness) he quietly breathed out his precious soul, into the embraces of his dear Redeemer, whom he had trusted, and faithfully served in the work of the ministry, about forty-three years. He departed betwixt twelve and one o'clock in the morning of June 24. midsummer-day, in the sixty-fifth year of his age. Happy, thrice happy he, to whom such a sudden change was no surprize, and who could triumph over death, as an unstung disarmed enemy, even when he made so fierce an onset. He had often spoke of it as his desire, that if it were the will of God, he might not outlive his usefulness; and it pleased God to grant him his desire, and give him a short passage from the pulpit to the kingdom; from the height of his usefulness, to receive the recompence of reward. So was it ordered by Him in whose hands our times are.

After the account we have given of his great usefulness, it is easy to imagine what sorrow and mourning there was among his friends, when they heard that the Lord had taken away their master from their head. One that lived so much desired, could not but die as much lamented. The surprise of the stroke put people into a perfect astonishment; and many said, The Lord removed him so suddenly, because he would not deny the many prayers that would have been put up for his recovery, had it been known that he was in peril. One thing that aggravated this severe dispensation, and made it in the apprehension of many look the more dismal, was, that this powerful intercessor was taken away just before a fast-day, when he would have been

wrestling

wreſtling mightily with God for mercy for the land. However, it proved a faſt-day indeed, and a day of humiliation to that congregation, to whom an empty pulpit was an awakening ſermon. The Broad-Oak was then like that under which Rebekah's nurſe was buried, Gen. xxxv. 8. *Allon bacuth*, the oak of weeping. They who had many a time ſitten with dry eyes, under melting ordinances, could not ſit ſo under ſuch a melting providence, by which the Lord God called ſo loudly to weeping and to mourning, and to girding with ſackcloth. But becauſe Mr Henry had been wont to give it for a rule, that weeping muſt not hinder ſowing, a mite was caſt into the treaſury of the nation's prayers, and a word ſpoken to bring the work of the day, and the event of the day together, from 2 Kings xiii. 20.

The day following being Saturday, June 27. the earthen veſſel, in which this treaſure had been lodged, was laid up in the grave in Whitchurch church, attended thither with a very great company of true mourners, all the country round; many from Cheſter and Shrewſbury, and the towns about, came to do him honour at his death: and, beſides the floods of tears that were ſhed, there were abundance of teſtimonies given to him, by perſons of all ſorts, like that to Jehoiadah, 2 Chron. xxiv. 16. That he was one that had done good in Iſrael. And there were thoſe who ſaid, he was a man that no body did or could ſpeak evil of, except for his nonconformity. He was uſed to ſay to his relations, When I am dead, make little ado about me; a few will ſerve to bring me to my grave. But his mind could not be obſerved in that; 'twas impoſſible ſuch a burning and ſhining light could be extinguiſhed, but there muſt be a univerſal notice taken of it. Multitudes came unſought; not to fill their eyes (as Mr Vines expreſſeth it) but to empty them; nor was there any other noiſe there, but that of general lamentation.

That morning before the removal of the corpſe, a
moſt

most affectionate sermon was preached in Mr Henry's meeting-place, by his dear and worthy friend Mr Tallents of Shrewsbury, who was eleven years older than he, and through God's goodness still survives him. He was willing to take that opportunity, to testify the great love and honour that he had for Mr Henry, whom he called a friend that is nearer than a brother. His text was, Rom. viii. 23. " And not only they, but
" ourselves also, which have the first fruits of the Spi-
" rit, even we ourselves groan within ourselves, wait-
" ing for the adoption, to wit, the redemption of our
" body." In his application he shewed excellently, and with much affection, how " the consideration of the
" spirit and life of this eminent servant of God, would
" greatly lead us to believe on Christ, and to have the
" spirit of Christ and live after it ; and to suffer with
" Christ, and to groan for our adoption." Several things were hinted concerning him, which have been mentioned already in this narrative, and a very honourable testimony born to him. From a long acquaintance with him, he witnessed concerning him, to those who knew his record to be true, that " he was hum-
" ble and meek, kind and peaceable, wise and chari-
" table, and one in whom the fruits of the Spirit were
" eminently: that he was a friend and a counsellor,
" and a father to many; that his expounding and
" preaching was plain and pleasant, warm and savory,
" full, and such as few could reach, and greatly blessed
" by God; and that in it he laboured more abundant-
" ly than any." And after a great encomium of him, it was excellently observed, and must be mentioned here, as that which was highly agreeable to Mr Henry's spirit, and his expressions upon all occasions : " That
" it was not his own righteousness that saved him, nor
" his own strength that quickened and upheld him, but
" Christ's righteousness and Christ's strength; for to
" him to live was Christ: and in all his discourses, ser-
" mons, and letters, he was very careful to ascribe the
" honour of all to Christ, and to make Christ his all
" in

"in all." He concluded with some words of seasonable advice to those of that society and neighbourhood:
1. "Give thanks to God that ever you had him or saw him, and that you had him so long, above thirty years in this place. Do not many of you owe even your very souls to him under God? while you mourn, give thanks to God that you ever knew him; old and great mercies must be thankfully remembered.

2. "Rejoice in the glory that he now enjoys: "weep not for him, but weep for yourselves:" 'twas the text on which he preached, not much above a year ago, at the funeral of that intelligent, holy, useful man, Mr William Lawrence of Wem. The primitive christians buried their saints with hymns and psalms of joy. Chrysostom on the Hebrews saith, We are to glorify God, and give thanks to him, that he hath crowned the deceased, and freed them from their labours; and chides those that mourned and howled. And the days of their death were called *Natalitia martyrum & sanctorum*, the birth days of the saints and martyrs. And Hierom (in his epitaph on holy Paula, and in the lives of other holy persons, writ by him) saith, that at her funeral no shrieks were heard, but multitudes of psalms and hymns were sung in divers languages.

3. "Bewail the loss, the general loss, and yours in particular, yet so as to have hope in God. I need not tell you how great your loss is, you feel it more than I am able to express. If any rejoice that he is gone, because he tormented them, say as the church Micah vii. 8, 9.

4. "Seek out for a supply; do not mourn and sit still, but up and be doing in your places; you have had a cheap gospel hitherto: God sent you one that could preach freely, and which is more, that would do so too; one that sought not yours, but you; and now God will see what you will do for yourselves; that now the shepherd is smitten, the sheep may not
be

"be scattered. Pray to God to raise up others like
"him, and graciously to give you one.

5. "Take heed of liking no preacher, now he is
"gone. This is a usual fault among many that have
"had excellent preachers, no body can please them.
"But God may bless weaker means, and make your
"souls live and thrive under them.

6. "Hold fast that which you have; it is the advice
"given to Philadelphia, the best of the Churches,
"Rev. iii. 11. Keep that good thing which is commit-
"ted to you, that favorineſs of heart, that love to Chriſt
"and to ſaints, to all ſaints, that knowledge of the
"truth. Keep to his ſober principles. Remember
"his dying counſel, Follow peace and holineſs: have
"theſe things always in remembrance. Take heed
"of falling off, take heed of falling away; the world
"will draw you, and Satan will tempt you, and your
"own buſy hearts will be apt to betray you; but go
"on humbly and honeſtly in the ſtrength of Chriſt,
"and fear not: be not like thoſe Jews that turned a-
"ſide when John Baptiſt was dead, John v. 35. The
"Lord keep you from being ſuch, and give you to go
"on to his heavenly kingdom."

It would have ſwelled this book too much, if we
inſerted the ſermon at large, and therefore we forbear it.

The next day being Lord's day, Mr Owen of Oſ-
weſtry preached a moſt excellent ſermon in the morning, agreeable to that ſad occaſion, upon that pathetical
farewell which Eliſha gave to Elijah, 2 Kings ii. 12.
"My father, my father, the chariots of Iſrael and the
"horſemen thereof, and he ſaw him no more; and he
"took hold of his own clothes, and rent them." He
obſerved, 1. "That faithful miniſters are the fathers of
"a people, and their chariots and horſemen; the for-
"mer a metaphor taken from a family, a peaceable
"ſociety; the latter from an army, a warlike body.
"Fathers to provide good things, chariots and horſe-
"men to protect from evil things. 2. There is a time
"when

"when we shall see these fathers, these chariots and
"horsemen of Israel no more. Their time is appoint-
"ed, their work cut out for them, and when those
"are finished they are removed 3. When God takes
"away our fathers, the chariots of our Israel, and the
"horsemen thereof, it is a proper season for mourn-
"ing and lamentation. Under this he did most af-
"fectionately excite us, 1. To be sensible of our loss,
"which is better felt than exprest. 'Tis the loss of
"one that was a father; a father to his family, to
"whom he was constant in unfolding the holy ora-
"cles; a father to the prophets, for counsel, and con-
"duct, and example: the sons of the prophets never
"conversed with him, but they were, or might have
"been the better for him; a father to his congrega-
"tion, now left orphans: 'tis the loss of one of the
"chariots and horsemen of our Israel, so eminent was
"he for prevalency in prayer, courage in duty, con-
"duct in affairs, constancy in religion, and a firm ad-
"herence to his ministerial vows; and, lastly, a con-
"tempt of the world, in which as he that warreth, he
"did not entangle himself. 2. To be sensible of those
"sins, which have provoked God to deprive us of
"him. Barrenness and unfruitfulness under his min-
"istry; 'tis for this that God hath a controversy with
"us. 3. To bless God that we enjoyed him so long:
"eaten bread must not be forgotten. 4. To be fol-
"lowers of him, as he was of Christ. He was a pat-
"tern for ministers, excelling in the knowledge of the
"scriptures, which made this man of God perfect, and
"industrious to advance the honour of Jesus Christ,
"whom he made the Alpha and Omega of his reli-
"gion; not addicted to controversies, but walking in
"the good old way, unwearied in the work of God.
"It was the delight of his heart, to be laying out him-
"self for the good of souls. Exemplary for humility
"and low thoughts of himself, and his own perform-
"ances, for meekness and readiness to forgive injuries,
"for candor in speaking of others, and their words
"and

" and actions, on which he ever put the best construc-
" tion, and was never apt to speak evil of any man.
" Eminent for family religion, and in that an excel-
" lent copy to all masters of families. Those things
" therefore which you have heard and seen in him do,
" and the God of peace shall be with you." These
were the heads which were copiously and excellently
enlarged upon in that sermon.

In the afternoon of that Sabbath, another sermon
was preached by a near relation of Mr Henry's on
Heb. xi. 4. " And by it, he being dead yet speak-
" eth."

The Wednesday following, July 1. being the lecture
in course at Danford in Whitchurch parish, Mr Samuel
Lawrence of Nantwich, whose turn it was to preach
that lecture, brought up the long train of mourners,
(as he expressed it) in a most savoury and pertinent discourse on Heb. xiii. 7. " Remember them which have
" (or have had) the rule over you, who have spoken
" unto you the word of God, whose faith follow, con-
" sidering the end of their conversation." " Bishops
" no doubt, (saith he) are here meant, scripture pri-
" mitive bishops, the pastors of particular congrega-
" tions, for they were such as had spoken to them the
" word of God, and watched for their souls, ver. 17.
" Such a one Mr Henry was, that great man, who is
" fallen this day in Israel, removed from us, but hath
" left behind him a good name to be remembered, a
" good example to be imitated; many a good word
" spoken to us, and many a good prayer put up for
" us. Remember him with thankfulness, that God
" has given such power, such gifts and graces unto
" men. I never knew a man (said he) in all my ac-
" quaintance, in whom I have seen so much of God
" as in good Mr Henry, whose holy, humble, heaven-
" ly, gracious conversation, hath been to me no small
" confirmation of the truth of the christian religion;
" that God gave him to you, and continued him so
" long, to see the church in a better state than he had
" some-

" sometimes seen it; that God crowned his labours
" with such great success. Many souls in heaven, and
" some on earth blessing God that ever they saw his
" face, and that God continued him in his usefulness
" to the last. Remember him with a quiet submission
" to the hand of God in his removal from us. Sensi-
" ble we must be of the stroke; 'tis a public loss, a
" loss to the ministry, our hands are this day weak;
" a loss to the nation, for which he was a powerful
" intercessor; a loss to this country, in which he was
" a burning and shining light; but yet we must ac-
" quiesce in the divine will. The treasure was in an
" earthen vessel, and God will bring us to depend
" more upon himself; and he is teaching us to live,
" and live to Christ without good Mr Henry, though
" we have sometimes said, we did not know how we
" could live without him. Remember him to pay all
" honour and respect to his name and memory; rise
" up and call him blessed. That's a foul tongue, as
" well as a lying one, that can say any thing of him
" unbecoming a disciple, servant, and minister of Jesus
" Christ. Remember him, to imitate his good exam-
" ple. Many of you will be called Mr Henry's fol-
" lowers; be so indeed. He was a pattern to minis-
" ters of diligence, zeal, humility, and great meekness
" in dealing with all people, which contributed abun-
" dantly to his success; his preaching affectionate,
" without affectation. To all people he was a pattern
" of faith and charity, and contempt of the world, of
" zeal and moderation, patience in suffering, and of
" constancy and perseverance to the end. Remem-
" ber him, and remember your sins which have pro-
" voked God to take him away. Have not we griev-
" ed this good man's spirit? &c. Remember him,
" and remember Christ's fulness, who is the same, ver.
" 8. and hath the residue of the Spirit. Instruments
" shifted, cisterns emptied, but there is the same in the
" fountain. Remember him, and remember your
" own death, and heaven where he is: we may think
" the

"the worfe of this world, which is much impoverifh-
"ed, and the better of heaven, which is fomewhat en-
"riched by the removal of this good man."

Thus we have gleaned a little out of the fermons, which very well deferved to have been publifhed at large, fome of the teftimonies that were borne to him, by fuch as had had long and intimate-acquaintance with him, that knew his excellencies very much, and knew as little to give flattering titles; nor was it any invidious piece of fervice, to fpeak thus honourably of one, who, like Demetrius, had a good report of all men, and of the truth itfelf.

Nor was it there only, but from abroad, that very honourable teftimonies were given of him. Sir Henry Ashurft (whofe great worth and ufefulnefs the world hath been made to know, by fome of the beft pens of the age) befides the perfonal acquaintance he had with Mr Henry, both at Boreatton and in London, had kept up a conftant correfpondence with him, by letter, for many years. Read the character he gave of him, in a letter to a near relation of Mr Henry's, upon the tidings of his death:—"I need not tell you how fadly I
"received the doleful news of Mr Henry's tranflation,
"who, I do think, lived the greateft example of fin-
"cere godlinefs, with prudence and fweetnefs of tem-
"per, of any I ever knew." And in another letter, not only propofing, but prefling the publication of an account of his life, he profeffeth, he thought there was none like him in his day, at leaft of his acquaintance, which is known to be both of the largeft and of the beft: "And (faith he) if Sir Fulk Grevil would have
"it infcribed upon his tombftone, that he was a friend
"to Sir Philip Sidnèv, I may well be pleafed to have
"it told to the world, that I loved and honoured blef-
"fed Mr Henry; a man of fo much prudence, and
"withal fo much fincerity, of fo good a temper, fo
"much a gentleman, and yet of fuch ftrict piety and
"devotednefs to God, that I fcarce ever knew his
"fellow."

The Life of Mr PHILIP HENRY.

The reverend Mr William Turner, now vicar of Walburton in Suffex, (of whom mention was m... before) lately sent to me a very kind letter, *ex mer tu*, with his free consent to have it inserted in t... count; some hints whereof I think fit to subjo...

Worthy Sir,

" I am glad to hear that you have been prevailed with
" to set upon so good a work, as recording the most
" remarkable passages of Mr Henry's life. I doubt
" not but you will meet with some, that will give such
" a history but a cold reception. All that part of the
" world that lies in darkness, will be offended, when
" beams of clear light and sun-shine first dart into their
" faces. *Virtutem præsentem odimus.*

" A little before I went to the university, I was up-
" on the commendation of my worthy school-master
" Mr E. (yet living) and with my father's consent, half
" a year a domestick with him; partly as a tutor to
" his young ones, and partly as a pupil to himself;
" and in some little degree as a companion; where I
" had the opportunity of informing myself more fully
" concerning the humour and principles, and conver-
" sation of a sort of people (and especially him and his
" family) whom I had heard asperfed very freely in for-
" mer companies, and represented to the world, as
" very hypocritical and disloyal people. At my first
" going, I resolved to stand upon my guard, and pry
" into the cause, which was then the great subject of
" difference and dispute; and upon the whole do say,
" that Mr Henry was a man of so clear a brain, so
" gentle a behaviour, so steady a conversation, so re-
" gular a devotion; was so courteous and condescend-
" ing to inferiors, so respectful and dutiful to superi-
" ours, so sweet and obliging to all; was so careful to
" improve his time well, to do as much good as pof-
" sible to every body, so constantly affectionate in his
" prayers for the king and government, so desirous to
" keep up a fair correspondence and communion with

"his conformable brethren, so very indifferent in mak-
"ing proselytes to his particular opinions; and with-
"al, so zealous to promote substantial goodness and
"true christianity, so inoffensive and peaceable in
"all his expressions and actions; so prudent, pure,
"pious, just, sober, charitable, chearful and pleasant,
"that I profess I am almost afraid to give him his due
"character without some correctives, lest they that
"knew him not should suspect my veracity, and ima-
"gine my pen to be managed by some mercenary
"hand. I remember the worshipful Rowland Hunt of
"Boreatten, Esq. speaking of Mr Henry, thus expres-
"sed himself to me, (and if I mistake not, the Lord
"Embassador Pagett was present) I was (said he) near
"seven years resident in the universities, and seven
"more at the Inns of court in London, and had op-
"portunity of knowing and acquainting myself with
"the most eminent divines and preachers in both these
"places; yet I never found any every way so accom-
"plished, for clearness and quickness of apprehension,
"solidity of judgement, and roundness of style, as Mr
"Henry is. I have noted in my book of providences
"the remark I made upon the temporal blessings God
"had rewarded him with; viz. a good and virtuous
"consort, who brought him a good estate, gave him
"a due reverence, loved him with an entire affection,
"an ingenious and hopeful offspring, well affected,
"well educated, and well disposed of in the world,
"the favour of men, and a quiet undisturbed habita-
"tion upon earth, in great measure, &c.

Sic testatus, sic monet, sic precatur,
Amicus mærens, anhelus, seperfles.

W. TURNER, A. M.

Another worthy conformist, of his acquaintance, having occasion to mention him in a letter to a friend, calls him "The great, good, now glorious Mr Henry,
"whose memory (saith he) shall ever be precious, and
"even sacred to me."

Such

Such as thefe were the honourable teftimonies which all that knew him, and knew how to value true excellency, attended him with. It is part of the recompence of charity and moderation in this world, that it obtains a good report of all men. The kingdom of God (faith the bleffed apoftle, Rom. xiv. 17. 18.) is not meat and drink, which were then the matters of doubtful difputation, "but righteoufnefs, and peace, and joy in the "Holy Ghoft; and he that in thefe things ferveth "Chrift, is not only acceptable to God, but approved "of men;" as, on the contrary, they that judge will be judged, and with what meafure we mete, it will be meafured to us again. And this is the excellency of a good name, that it is out of the reach of death, and is not buried in the grave, but rather grows up from the grave.

It is not for nothing Solomon hath joined this good name, which is better than precious ointment, with the day of one's death, which upon that account is better than the day of one's birth, that it compleats the character of thofe that finifh their courfe well, and are faithful unto death; whereas a great name, like the names of the great ones of the earth, is often withered and blemifhed by death. We read of thofe that " bear " their fhame when they go down to the pit, though " they were the terror of the mighty in the land of " the living." Ezek. xxxii. 35.

At a meeting of the diffenting minifters of Chefhire at Knutsford in May 1696, (a few weeks before Mr Henry died) it was agreed, that their next meeting fhould be at Chefter (though inconvenient to many of them) upon condition that he would meet them there, and give them a fermon. It was with much difficulty that he was prevailed with to promife it, but his Mafter called for him before the time appointed came. Mr Flavel of Devonfhire died when he was under a like appointment. But happy they that are come to the " General affembly, and church of the firft-born, and " to the fpirits of juft men made perfect."

As

As to his bodily prefence, he was of a middle ſtature, his complexion not approaching to any extream, of a very pleaſant afpect, and an unuſual mixture of gravity and ſweetneſs in the air of his countenance, which was the true index of his mind. When ſome of his friends have ſolicited him to have his picture drawn, he would put them off with this, that "the " beſt picture of a miniſter is in the hearts of his peo- " ple."

CHAP. X.

A miſcellaneous collection of ſome of his ſayings, obſervations, counſels and comforts, out of his ſermons, letters and diſcourſes.

MR Henry, through the exceſs of his modeſty and ſelf-diffidence, never publiſhed any of his labours to the world, nor ever fitted or prepared any of them for the preſs; and yet none more valued the labours of others, or rejoiced more in them; nor have I heard any complain leſs of the multitude of good books, concerning which he often ſaid, that ſtore is no ſore, and he was very forward to perſuade others to publiſh; and always expreſſed a particular pleaſure in reading the lives, actions, and ſayings of eminent men, ancient and modern, which he thought the moſt uſeful and inſtructive kind of writings. He was alſo a very candid reader of books, not apt to pick quarrels with what he read, eſpecially when the deſign appeared to be honeſt, and when others would find fault, and ſay, this was wanting, and t'other amiſs, his uſual excuſe was, " there is nothing perfect under the " ſun."

It will be but a ſmall repair of this want of the publiſhing of ſome of his works (but I doubt it will prove the beſt we can make,) to glean up ſome few of many of his ſayings, obſervations, and good inſtructions (as
his

his remains) which we shall not marshal in any order, but give them as they occur, besides those which have been already inserted into this narrative.

'Twas a saying he frequently used, which hath been mentioned already, that " Every creature is that to us, " and only that, which God makes it to be :" and another was, " Duty is ours, events are God's :" and another was " The soul is the man," and therefore " That " is always best for us, which is best for our souls :" and another was, " The devil cozens us of all our time, " by cozening us of the present time."

In his thanksgivings for temporal mercies, he often said, " If the end of one mercy were not the beginning " of another, we were undone :" and to encourage to the work of thanksgiving he would say, that " new " mercies call for new returns of praise, and then those " new returns will fetch in new mercies ;" and from Psal. l. 23. " He that offers praise glorifies me, and to " him that orders his conversation aright—." He observed, that thanksgiving is good, but thanks-living is better.

When he spoke of a good name, he usually described it to be a name for good things with good people. When he spoke of contentment, he used to say, " When " the mind and the condition meet, there's content- " ment. Now in order to that, either the condition " must be brought up to the mind, and that is not " only unreasonable but impossible ; for as the condi- " tion riseth, the mind riseth with it ; or else the mind " must be brought down to the condition, and that is " both possible and reasonable. And he observed, " that no condition of life will of itself make a man " content, without the grace of God ; for we find " Haman discontented in the court, Ahab discontent- " ed on the throne, Adam discontented in Paradise, " nay (and higher we cannot go) the angels that fell " discontented in heaven itself."

The three questions which he advised people to put to themselves in self-examination before the sacrament,

were,

were, What am I ? What have I done ? and What do I want ?

He ufed to recommend to his friends thefe four fcripture arguments againft fin, expreffed for memory's fake in four verfes, to be ready in an hour of temptation.

> Is this thy kindnefs to thy friend ?
> It will be bitternefs in the end.
> The vows of God upon me lye ;
> Should fuch a man as I am fly?

He faid there were four things which he would not for all the world have againft him, The word of God, his own confcience, the prayers of the poor, and the account of godly minifters.

" He that hath a blind confcience which fees noth-
" ing, a dead confcience which feels nothing, and a
" dumb confcience which faith nothing, is in as mif-
" erable a condition as a man can be in on this fide
" hell."

Preaching on 1 Pet. i. 6. "'If need be, you are in
" heavinefs----." He fhewed what need the people of God have of afflictions. " The fame that our bodies
" have of phyfick, that our trees have of pruning, that
" gold and filver have of the furnace, that liquors have
" of being emptied from veffel to veffel, that the iron hath of a file, that the fields have of a hedge, that the
" child has of the rod."

Preaching on that prayer of Chrift for his difciples, John xvii. 21. " That they all may be one," which no doubt is an anfwered prayer, for the Father heard him always, he fhewed, " That notwithftanding the many
" fad divifions that are in the church, yet all the faints,
" as far as they are fanctified, are one ; one in rela-
" tion, one flock, one family, one building, one body,
" one bread : one by reprefentation, one in image and
" likenefs, of one inclination and difpofition : one in
" their aims, one in their afkings, one in amity and
" friendfhip, one in intereft, and one in their inheritance ;

The Life of Mr PHILIP HENRY.

" ance; nay, they are one in judgement and opinion;
" though in some things they differ, yet those things
" in which they are agreed are many more, and much
" more considerable than those things wherein they
" differ. They are all of a mind concerning sin, that
" it is the worst thing in the world; concerning Christ
" that he is all in all; concerning the favour of God,
" that it is better than life; concerning the world, that
" it is vanity; concerning the word of God, that it is
" very precious," &c.

Preaching on Gal. i. 16. concerning the conversion of Paul, he began his sermon with this remark, to raise attention: much is said in story concerning the seven wonders of the world, the Temple of Ephesus, the Pyramids of Egypt, the Tomb of Mausoleus, &c. all which are now no more; but I have been sometimes thinking, whether I could not name seven things which I would call the seven wonders of the church; and what do you think of these seven? are they not wonderful? 1. Our redemption by Jesus Christ, who is called Wonderful; 2. The salvation of Noah in the Ark; 3. The faith of Abraham in offering up Isaac; 4. The patience of Job; 5. The providences of God towards the Nation and people of the Jews; 6. The pouring out of the Spirit upon the Apostles; 7. The conversion of Paul.

But it would be endless to gather up such passages as these out of his sermons, which were full of them, and we mention these only because they occur first.

He used to observe concerning the nation of the Jews, that before the captivity in Babylon, no people could be more strongly addicted to idols and idolatry than they were, to admiration, considering what clear warnings they had against it. But after that captivity, never was any people more averse to idols and idolatry than they, that the promise might be fulfilled, Ephraim shall say, What have I to do any more with idols? and he looked upon it, that the idolatry of the papists was one of the greatest obstructions to the Jews conversion, which he did expect and look for, as not apprehending

hending how the promises, Rom. xi. have yet had their full accomplishment; not that they shall again be incorporated into a people, but shall join themselves to the churches of Christ, in the several nations whither they be scattered.

The great thing that he condemned and witnessed against in the church of Rome, was their monopolizing of the church, and condemning all that are not in with their interests, which is so directly contrary to the spirit of the gospel, as nothing can be more. He sometimes said, "I am too much a catholick, to be a Roman catholick."

He often exprest himself well pleased with that healing rule, which, if duly observed, would put an end to all our divisions: *Sit in necessariis unitas, in non necessariis libertas, in omnibus charitas.* Let there be in necessary things unity, in every thing charity, and then there need not be in every punctilio uniformity.

By the institutions of the gospel (he said) he knew of no holy place, one holy day, two holy sacraments, and four holy canons. Let all things be done in charity: let all things be done to edifying: let all things be done decently and in order: and let all things be done to the glory of God.

When his opinion was asked about any doubtful matter, as playing at cards, the marriage of cousin-germans, or the like, he was very cautious in determining such things to be sinful; but he would say, It's good keeping on the safer side; and a man would not chuse to go upon a precipice, when he might go upon even ground: Prov. x. 5. "He that walks uprightly, walks "surely," in opposition to walking at all adventures.

In the observations he made of God's Providences, he frequently took notice in discourse with his friends, of the fulfilling of the scripture in them; for (saith he) the scripture hath many accomplishments, and is in the fulfilling every day. Speaking of a wicked son in the neighbourhood that was very undutiful to his mother, he charged some of his children to observe the providence

dence of God concerning him; perhaps (faith he) I may not live to fee it, but do you take notice, whether God do not come upon him with fome remarkable judgement in this life, according to the threatening implied in the reafon annexed to the fifth commandment: but he himfelf lived to fee it fulfilled not long after, in a very fignal providence.

He obferved from fcripture inftances, as well as from fome providences which he had taken notice of in his own day, That if any began well in the ways of religion and godlinefs, and afterwards caft off their profeffion, and returned to profanenefs again, ufually God fets a mark of his difpleafure upon them, by fome vifible judgement in this world; their eftates ruined, their reputation blafted, their families funk, or themfelves brought to mifery; fo that all who paffed by might fay, This was an apoftate. "If any man draw back, my "foul fhall have no pleafure in him."

He obferved from Numb. x. 12. "That all our re- "moves in this world, are but from one wildernefs to "another." Upon any change that is before us, we are apt to promife ourfelves a Canaan, but we fhall be deceived, it will prove a wildernefs.

Once preffing the ftudy of the fcriptures, he advifed to take a verfe of Pfalm cxix. every morning to meditate upon, and fo go over the pfalm twice in the year, and that (faid he) will bring you to be in love with all the reft of the fcripture; and he often faid, "All grace "grows, as love to the word of God grows."

One afking his advice, what to do when (as often unavoidably) we are in the fight and hearing of the wickednefs of the wicked, and whether we are to reprove them; why (faith he) you know what an angry countenance doth, and we may fometimes give a reproof by our looks, when we have not opportunity of giving it otherwife.

He would not bear that any fhould be evil fpoken of in his hearing, 'twas to him as vinegar to the teeth. He would mind thofe who reflected upon people behind their backs, of that law, Lev. xix. 14. "Thou shalt not curse the deaf." Those that are absent are deaf, they cannot right themselves, and therefore say no ill of them. A friend of his inquiring of him concerning a matter which tended to reflect upon some people; he began to give him an account of the story, but immediately broke off, and checked himself with these words, "But our rule is, to speak evil of no man," and would proceed no further in the story. 'Twas but the week before he died, that one desired him to lend him such a book; "Truly (saith he) I " would lend it you, but that it rakes in the faults of " some, which should rather be covered with a man- " tle of love." 'Twere easy to multiply instances of this.

To quicken people to diligence and liveliness in the worship of God, he would sometimes observe, that the temple was built upon a threshing-floor, a place of labour. He would also urge, that in answer to those who turned it to his reproach, that his meeting-place had been a barn; no new thing (would he say) to turn a threshing-floor into a temple.

When some zealous people in the country would have him to preach against top-knots, and other vanities in apparel, he would say, that was none of his business; if he could but persuade people to Christ, the pride and vanity, and excess of those things would fall of course; and yet he had a dislike to vanity and gaiety of dress, and allowed it not in those that he had influence upon. His rule was, that in such things we must neither be owls nor apes; not affect singularity, nor affect modishness; nor (as he used to observe from 1 Pet. iii. 3.) make the putting on of apparel our adorning, because christians have better things to adorn themselves with. When some complained to him of a relation of theirs, that would not let them dress his children with ribbands, and other fine things, "why truly " (said Mr Henry) those things are fit for children;" thereby reproving both him that would not allow them

to

to his children, and them that perhaps minded them too much themselves.

He often, both in sermons and discourses, would press people to fix to themselves some good principles, and to come off from the corrupt and carnal principles that worldly people go by. He took all occasions to recommend such principles as these: " That God who is " the first and best, should have the first and best; " that a part in Christ is a good part; that soul pros- " perity is the best prosperity, and that it is well " or ill with us, according as it is well or ill with " our souls; that honesty is the best policy; that " those that would have the comfort of relations, must " be careful to do the duty of them; that all is well " that ends everlastingly well; that time and the things " of time, are nothing compared with eternity and " the things of eternity; that it is better to suffer the " greatest affliction than to commit the least sin; that " it highly concerns us to do that now, which we shall " most wish we had done when we come to die; that " ' work for God is its own wages; that it is folly for " a man to do that which he must certainly undo a- " gain by repentance, or be undone to all eternity." Such as these were the principles he would have christians to govern themselves by.

Speaking of the causes of atheism, he had this observation; " That a head full of vain and unprofitable " notions, meeting with a heart full of pride and self- " conceitedness, disposes a man directly to be an atheist."

A gentlewoman, that upon some unkindness betwixt her and her husband, was parted from him, and lived separately near a twelve-month, grew melancholy, and complained of sin, and the withdrawing of the light of God's countenance, and the want of assurance; he told her she must rectify what was amiss between her and her husband, and return into the way of duty, else 'twas in vain to expect peace. Her friends were against it; but he said, he was confident it would prove so.

He

He said he had observed concerning himself, that he was sometimes the worse for eating, but never for abstinence; sometimes the worse for wearing too few cloathes, but never for wearing too many; sometimes the worse for speaking, but never for keeping silence.

As to his letters, he was very free in writing to his friends. A good letter, he would say, may perhaps do more good than a good sermon, because the address is more particular, and that which is written remains. His language and expressions in his letters were always pious and heavenly, and seasoned with the salt of grace; and when there was occasion, he would excellently administer counsels, reproofs, or comforts by letter. He kept no copies of his letters, and it is impossible if we should attempt it, to retrieve them from the hands into which they were scattered. Mr Rutherford's and Mr Allen's letters, that (like some of the most excellent of Paul's epistles) bore date out of a prison, have a mighty tincture of their peculiar prison comforts and enlargements; we have none such to produce of Mr Henry's, no pastoral letters or prison letters; he was himself, in his whole conversation, an epistle of Christ: But we shall only glean up some passages out of such of his letters as are in our hands, which may be affecting and edifying.

To his son, when he was abroad for improvement at London, in the year 1685, and 686, with the common business of his letters, which was always written with a favor of religion, he would intermix such lines as these: " We are all well here, thanks be to God,
" the divine providence watching about our taber-
" nacle, and compassing us about with favour, as with
" a shield. Our great inquiry is, What shall we ren-
" der? alas! our renderings are nothing to our receiv-
" ings; we are like the barren field, on which much
" cost is bestowed, but the crop is not accordingly.
" Our heavenly Father is loading us with his benefits,
" and we are loading him with our sins; grieving him
" that comforts us; and how long shall it be so? O
" that

"that it might be otherwise! that our mercies might
"be as oil to the wheels, to make us so much the
"more active and lively in our Master's work, especi-
"ally considering how it is with our fellow servants;
"they empty and we fill, they Marah and we Naomi.
"There may a day come, when it may cost dear to
"be honest, but after all, to fear God and keep his
"commandments, is the whole of man. I therefore
"commend it to you, and you to God, who is a shield
"and buckler to them that fear him.

"We are well, but in daily expectation of that
"which we are born, and born again to, and that is
"trouble in this world, yet rejoicing in hope of the
"glory of God, which we are reaching after, and
"pressing towards, as we trust you are also. Where
"you are, you see more of the glittering vanities of
"this world in a day, than we here do in an age; and
"are you more and more in love with them, or dead
"and dying to them? I hope dead and dying to them,
"for they are poor things, and perish in the using;
"make many worse that enjoy them, but none better.
"What is translated Vexation of spirit, Eccl. i. 2. may
"be read, Feeding upon wind, Hos. xii. 1. and
"can wind satisfy? the Lord preserve and keep you
"from all evil, the Lord preserve and keep your soul.
"We both send you our love, and bless you together,
"and apart, every day, in the name of the Lord. A-
"men and Amen.

"Be sincere, and humble, and choice in your com-
"pany, always either getting good or doing good,
"gathering in or laying out. Remember to keep the
"heart with all diligence and above all keepings, for
"there the fountain is, and if that be well kept and
"clean, the streams will be accordingly.

"'Tis some short refreshment to friends and rela-
"tions, to see and hear from one another, but it pas-
"seth away, and we have here no continuing city, no
"abiding delights in this world; our rest remains else-
"where; those we have, lose much of their sweetness,

"from

"from the thoughts of parting with them while we
"enjoy them, but the happiness to come is eternal.
"After millions of millions of ages (if we may so speak
"of eternity) as far from an end as the first moment;
"and the last of glory will be glory (so some read
"Prov. xxv. 27. keep that in your eye (my dear child)
"and it will as much as any thing dazzle your eyes,
"to all the fading deceiving vanities of this lower
"world; and will be a quickening motive to you, to
"abound always in the work of the Lord, forasmuch
"as you know your labour shall not be in vain in the
"Lord. The Lord bless you, who blesseth indeed.

"See that you walk circumspectly, not as the fools,
"but as the wise; many eyes are upon you, his espe-
"cially, who is all eye; *Cave, Deus videt. Memento
"hoc agere*; our blessing with 1 Chron. xxviii. 9.

"The same which is yet the prologue of yours, is
"of ours also. *Omnia bene, laus Deo!* but he that
"girdeth on the harnass, must not boast as he that
"puts it off. While the world we live in is under
"the moon, constant in nothing but inconstancy; and
"such changes are made in other families, why should
"we alone promise ourselves immunity from the com-
"mon lot? there would be no need of faith and pa-
"tience, which are Winter graces, if it should be al-
"ways Summer time with us. We have three un-
"changeables to oppose to all other mutabilities; an
"uncheangeable covenant, an unchangeable God, and
"an unchangeable heaven: and while these three re-
"main the same, yesterday, to day, and for ever; wel-
"come the will of our heavenly Father in all events
"that may happen to us: come what will, nothing can
"come amiss to us.

"Keep the invisible things of the other world al-
"ways in your eye. He that ventures the loss of an
"eternal crown and kingdom, for a cup or two of
"puddle water (such as all terrene pleasures in com-
"parison are) makes a bargain, which no less a space
"than that which is everlasting will be sufficient to
bewail

"bewail and repent of. How much better is it to
"lay up in ſtore now a good foundation for time to
"come, and to lay hold on eternal life? doing thoſe
"works which we would be willing ſhould hereafter
"follow us, yet ſtill making the bleſſed Jeſus our all
"in all.

"The further progreſs you make in your ſtudies,
"you will find them the eaſier; 'tis ſo with religion,
"the worſt is at firſt: It is like the picture that frown-
"ed at firſt entrance, but afterwards ſmiles and looks
"pleaſant. They that walk in ſinful ways, meet with
"ſome difficulties at firſt, which cuſtom conquers, and
"they become as nothing. 'Tis good accuſtoming
"ourſelves to that which is good. The more we do,
"the more we may do in religion. Your acquaint-
"ance (I doubt not) increaſeth abroad, and accord-
"ingly your watch muſt be; for by that oftentimes,
"ere we are aware, we are enſnared. He that walk-
"eth with wiſe men ſhall be wiſe.

"The return of the Spring invites our thankſgiving
"for the mercy of it. The birds are ſinging early
"and late, according to their capacity, the praiſes of
"their Creator; but man only, that hath moſt cauſe,
"finds ſomething elſe to do. 'Tis redeeming love
"that is the moſt admirable love; leſs than an eter-
"nity will not ſuffice to adore it in. Lord, how is it!
"Lord, what is man! as the ſtreams lead to the foun-
"tain, ſo ſhould all our mercies lead us to that. We
"both of us ſend you our moſt affectionate love and
"bleſſing: bleſſing? that is, we pray and beſeech the
"moſt bleſſed God, even our own God, to give you
"his bleſſing, for he only can command the bleſſing;
"and thoſe whom he bleſſeth are bleſſed indeed. Let
"us ſtill hear to our comfort, that you walk in the
"truth, living above the things of the world, as
"dead to them. The Lord in mercy fit us for his
"will in the next providence, public and perſonal, for
"time is always teeming.

"Your improvement is our joy. Be ſincere and ſeri-
"ous,

"ous, cloathed with humility, abounding always in
"the work of the Lord; and when you have done
"all, saying I am an unprofitable servant. 'Twas the
"good advice of the moral philosopher, In your con-
"verse with men, *distrust*; but I must add, In every
"thing towards God, *believe*. Expect temptation and
"a snare at every turn, and walk accordingly. We
"have a good cause, a vanquished enemy, a good se-
"cond, and extraordinary pay; for he that overcomes
"needs not desire to be more happy than the second
"and third of the revelation speaks him to be. The
"God of all mercy and grace compass you about al-
"ways with his favour as with a shield!

"I would have you redeem time, for hearing the
"word in season, and out of season; your other stu-
"dies will prosper never the worse, especially if you
"could return immediately from it to the closet
"again, with cooling divertisements by the way.

"See your need of Christ more and more, and live
"upon him; no life like it, so sweet, so safe. *Christus
"meus mihi in omnia.* We cannot be discharged from
"the guilt of any evil we do, without his merit to sa-
"tisfy: we cannot move in the performance of any
"good required, without his Spirit and grace to assist
"and enable for it; and when we have done all, that
"all is nothing, without his mediation and interces-
"sion to make it acceptable; so that every day, in eve-
"ry thing, he is all in all. Though you are at a dis-
"tance from us now, we rejoice in the good hope we
"have through grace, of meeting again in the land of
"the living, that is, on earth, if God see good; how-
"ever in heaven, which is the true land of the truly
"living, and is best of all. The Lord God everlast-
"ing be your sun and shield in all your ways: see time
"hasting away apace towards eternity, and the Judge
"even at the door, and work accordingly, wherever
"you are, alone or in company; be always either do-
"ing or getting good, sowing or reaping. As for me,
"I make no other reckoning, but that the time of my
"depart-

" departure is at hand, and what trouble I may meet
" with before, I know not, the will of the Lord be
" done: one of my chief cares is, that no iniquity of
" mine may be laid up for you, which God grant for
" his mercy's fake in Chrift Jefus. Amen.

" Be careful of your health. Remember the rule,
" *Venienti occurrere*; but efpecially neglect not the
" main matter. The foul is the main; if that do
" well, all's well. Worfhip God in the fpirit; rejoice
" in Chrift Jefus, and have no confidence in the flefh.
" God be gracious unto thee, my fon; redeem time,
" efpecially for your foul: expect trouble in this world,
" and prepare for it; expect happinefs in the other
" world, and walk worthy of it, unto all pleafing.

" A good book is a good companion at any time,
" but efpecially a good God, who is always ready to
" hold communion with thefe that defire and feek
" communion with him. Keep low and humble in
" your thoughts and opinion of yourfelf; but aim
" high in your defires and expectations, even as high
" as the kingdom of heaven itfelf, and refolve to take
" up with nothing fhort of it. The Lord guide you
" in all your ways, and go in and out before you,
" and preferve you blamelefs to his heavenly king-
" dom."

Immediately after his fon was ordained to the work
of the miniftry at London, in the year 1687, he thus
wrote to him: " Are you now a minifter of Jefus
" Chrift? hath he counted you faithful, putting you
" into the miniftry? then be faithful; out of love to
" him feed his lambs; as a workman that needs not
" to be afhamed, rightly dividing the word of truth. I
" hope what you experienced of the prefence of God
" with you in the folemnity, hath left upon you a tru-
" ly indelible character, and fuch impreffions, as neith-
" er time nor any thing elfe fhall be able to wear out.
" Remember Pfalm lxxi. 16. It is in the eye of fenfe
" a bad time to fet out in; but in fowing and reaping,
" clouds

"clouds and wind muſt not be heeded. The work
"is both comfortable and honourable, and the re-
"ward rich and ſure: and if God he pleaſed to give
"opportunity and a heart, though there may be
"trouble attending it, 'twill be eaſily borne. If we
"ſuffer with him we ſhall alſo reign with him. I am
"and ſhall be, according to my duty and promiſe,
"earneſt at the throne of grace on your behalf, that
"the Lord will pour out upon you of his Holy Spirit,
"that what he calls you to, he would fit you for; eſ-
"pecially that he would take you off your own bot-
"tom, and lay you low in the ſenſe of your own un-
"worthineſs, inability and inſufficency, that you may
"ſay with the evangelical prophet, Wo is me, I am un-
"done! and with Jeremiah, I am a child; and with
"Paul, I am nothing. Where this is not, the main-
"thing is wanting; for God reſiſts the proud, but
"gives grace to the humble. Now the Lord give
"you that grace to be humble; and then, according
"to his promiſe, he will make you rich in every other
"grace."

It were very eaſy to tranſcribe many more ſuch lines as theſe, out of his letters to his ſon, but theſe ſhall ſuffice.

We ſhall next gather up ſome few paſſages out of ſome of his letters to a perſon of quality in London, (ſuch of them as are come to our hands, which are but few of many) the beginning of his correſpondence with that gentleman, (which continued to his death, and was kept up monthly for a great while) was in the year 1686, and the following letter broke the ice:—

Honoured Sir,

"HOPING you are by this time, as you intended,
" returned to London, to your home and habi-
"tation there, I make bold, according to my pro-
"miſe, to ſalute you in a few lines. In the firſt place,
"to be your remembrancer of the vows of God which
"are upon you, upon the account of the many mer-
"cies

" cies of your journey, both in your going out, and
" in your coming in. Was not every ſtep you took
" hedged about with ſpecial providence? Had not
" the angels charge over you? Did not they pitch
" their tents where you pitched yours? Did not good-
" neſs and mercy follow you, and ſhould it not then
" be had in thankful remembrance? Where mercy
" goes before, ſhould not duty follow after? If you
" have Mr Anger's life, you will find there, page 88,
" 89. a collection out of his diary, of ten heads of
" mercies, acknowledged in a journey, to heighten
" God's praiſes, and to quicken his own and others
" hearts therein, and they are certainly very affecting.
" Next (Sir) I am to acquaint you, that I have faith-
" fully diſpoſed of the money you left with me at part-
" ing, to eight poor praying widows in this neighbour-
" hood, as you appointed. And this among all the
" reſt of your alms-deeds is had in memorial before
" God; 'tis fruit that will abound to your account,
" bread ſent a voyage upon the waters, which you
" and yours will find again after many days; for he is
" faithful that hath promiſed. The apoſtle's prayer
" ſhall be mine, 2 Cor. ix. 10. Now he that miniſter-
" eth feed to the ſower, doth miniſter bread for your
" food, and multiply your feed ſown, and increaſe the
" fruits of your righteouſneſs. Amen.

And ſome time after he writes, "Your acknowledg-
" ing·God in all your affairs, I cannot but rejoice in,
" as an evidence of the uprightneſs of your heart to-
" wards him; 'tis the life and ſoul of all religion; 'tis
" indeed to walk with God: that includes as much as
" any other ſcripture command in ſo few words, In all
" thy ways acknowledge him; in every thing thou
" doſt have an eye to him; make his word and will
" thy rule, his glory thy end; fetch in ſtrength from
" him; expect ſucceſs from him; and in all events
" that happen, which are our ways too (whether they
" be for us or againſt us) he is to be acknowledged,
                                            " that

" that is adored: if profperous, with thankfulnefs; if
" otherwife, with fubmiffion: as Job, " The Lord hath
" given, and the Lord hath taken, and bleffed be the
" name of the Lord." This is to fet the Lord always
" before us, to have our eye ever towards the Lord:
" where this is not, we are fo far without God in the
" world."

In another letter, " As to the acceffion lately made
" to your eftate, much good may it do you; that is
" much good may you do with it, which is the true
" good of an eftate. The lady Warwick would not
" thank him, that would give her a thoufand a year,
" and tye her up from doing good with it. I rejoice
" in the large heart which God hath given you with
" your large eftate, without which heart the eftate
" would be your fnare."

I have lately met with a letter of Mr Henry's, to a couple related to him, who in a very fhort time had buried all their children of the fmall-pox, to their great grief, 'twas in the year 1679. What comfort and counfels he adminiftered to them, may be of ufe to others in their afflictions, and therefore I fhall tranfcribe the whole letter, though it be long.

Dear Coufins,
" THIS is to you both, whom God hath made
" one in the conjugal relation, and who are one alfo
" in the prefent affliction; only to fignify to you, that
" we do heartily fympathize with you in it. The tri-
" al is indeed fharp, and there will be need of all the
" wifdom and grace you have, and of all the help of
" friends you can get, both to bear and to improve it
" aright. You muft bear it with " filence and fubmif-
" fion. Surely it is meet to be faid unto God, I have
" born chaftifement." He is fovereign Lord of all,
" and may do with us and ours as pleafeth him. It
" is not for the clay to quarrel with the potter. It
" was mercy you had children, and comfort in them
" fo

"so long; it is mercy that yet you have one another,
" and your children are not lost, but gone before, a
" little before, whither you yourselves are hasting af-
" ter. And if a storm be coming, (as God grant it
" be not) it is best with them that put first into the
" harbour. Your children rae taken away from the
" evil to come, and you must not mourn as they that
" have no hope. Sensible you cannot but be, but
" dejected and sullen you must not be; that will but
" put more bitterness into the cup, and make way for
" another, perhaps a sharper stroke. You must not
" think, and I hope you do not, that there cannot be
" a sharper stroke, for God hath many arrows in his
" quiver; he can heat the furnace seven times hotter,
" and again and again seven times hotter, till he hath
" consumed us; and if he should do so, yet still we
" must say, he hath punished us less than our iniquities
" have deserved. For examples of patience in the like
" kind we have two eminent ones in the book of God,
" those are Job and Aaron; of the latter it is said,
" Lev. x. 13. " He held his peace;" and that which
" quieted him, was what his brother Moses said to
" him, " This is that which the Lord hath said, I will
" be sanctified;" and if God be sanctified, Aaron is
" satisfied; if God have glory from it, Aaron hath
" nothing to say against it. Of the former it is said,
" Job i. 20. he fell down, but it was to worship; and
" we are told how he expressed himself, The Lord gave,
" &c. He acknowledgeth God in all: and indeed, af-
" ter all, this is it (my dear cousins) that you must
" satisfy yourselves with under this sad providence,
" that the Lord hath done it, and the same will that
" ordered the thing itself, ordered all the circumstan-
" ces of it; and who are we that we should dispute
" with our Maker? " Let the potsherds strive with
" the potsherds of the earth; but let not the thing for-
" med, say to him that formed it, Why hast thou
" made me thus?" and as for the improvement of this
" affliction, (which I hope both of you earnestly de-
" fire,

"fire, for it is a great lofs to lofe fuch a providence,
"and not be made better by it) I conceive there are
"four leffons which it fhould teach you, and they are
"good leffons, and fhould be well learned, for the ad-
"vantage of them is unfpeakable. 1. It fhould for
"ever imbitter fin to you; you know what fhe faid to
"the prophet, 1 Kings xvii. 18. "Art thou come to
"call my fins to remembrance, and to flay my fon?"
"'tis fin, fin that is the old kill-friend, the Jonah that
"hath raifed this ftorm, the Achan that hath troubled
"your houfe; then how fhould you grow in your hat-
"red of it, and endeavours againft it? that you may
"be the death of that which hath been the death of
"your dear children; I fay the death of it, for noth-
"ing lefs will fatisfy the true penitent, than the death
"of fuch a malefactor. 2. It fhould be a fpur to you
"to put you on in heaven's way: it may be you were
"growing remifs in duty, beginning to flack your for-
"mer pace in religion, and your heavenly Father faw
"it, and was grieved at it, and fent this fad providence
"to be your monitor, to tell you, you fhould remem-
"ber whence you were fallen, and do your firft works,
"and be more humble and holy, and heavenly and
"felf-denying, and watchful, abounding always in the
"work of the Lord. O blefied are they that come
"out of fuch a furnace thus refined, they will fay
"hereafter, 'twas a happy day for them that ever they
"were put in. 3. You muft learn by it as long as
"you live, to keep your affections in due bounds to-
"wards creature-comforts, How hard is it to love
"and not to over-love, to delight in children or yoke-
"fellows, and not over-delight: now God is a jealous
"God, and will not give his glory to any other; and
"our excefs this way doth often provoke him to re-
"move that mercy from us, which we do thus make
"an idol of; and our duty is to labour when he doth
"fo, to get that matter amended, and to rejoice in all
"our enjoyments with trembling, and as if we rejoi-
"ced not. 4. It fhould be a means of drawing your
"hearts

"hearts and thoughts more upwards and homewards;
"I mean your everlasting home. You should be look-
"ing oftner now than before into the other world. I
"shall go to him, faith David, when his little son was
"gone before. It is yet but a little while ere all the
"things of time shall be swallowed up in eternity;
"and the matter is not great, whether we or ours die
"first, whilst we are all dying: in the midst of life we
"are in death: what manner of persons then ought
"we to be? Now our Lord Jesus Christ himself, and
"God, even our Father, be your support under, and
"do you good by this dispensation, and give you a
"name better than that of sons and daughters. We
"are daily mindful of you at the throne of grace, in
"our poor measure, and dearly recommended to
"you," &c.

We shall next gather up some passages out of his letters to his children, after they were married and gone from him.

To one of his daughters with child of her first child, he thus writes, " You have now one kind of burthen
" more than ever you had before to cast upon God,
" and if you do so, he will sustain you, according to
" his promise."

And when the time of travail was near, thus; "You
" know whom you have trusted, even Him who is
" true and faithful, and never yet did, nor ever will
" forsake the soul that seeks him. Though he be Al-
" mighty, and can do every thing, yet this he cannot
" do, he cannot deny himself, nor be worse than his
" word; but what is his word? Hath he promised
" that there shall be always a safe and speedy delive-
" ry? that there shall be no Jabez, no Benoni? No,
" but if there be, he hath promised it shall work to-
" gether for good: hath promised, if he doth not
" save from, he will save through: if he call to go,
" even through the valley of the shadow of death, (and
" what less is child-bearing?) he will be with you,
" his

"his rod and his staff shall comfort you, and that's well: therefore your faith must be in those things as the promise is, either so or so, and which way soever it be, God is good and doth good. Therefore (my dear daughter) lift up the hands that hang down, cast your burthen upon him, trust also in him, and let your thoughts be established. We are mindful of you in our daily prayers, but you have a better Intercessor than we, who is heard always."

To another of them, in the same circumstance, he thus writes; "Your last letter speaks you in a good frame; which rejoiced my heart, that you were fixed, fixed waiting upon God; that your faith was uppermost, above your fears; that you could say, Behold the handmaid of the Lord, let him do with me as seemeth good in his eyes. We are never fitter for a mercy, nor is it more likely to be a mercy indeed, than when it is so with us; now the Lord keep it always in the imagination of the thoughts of your heart. And he concludes, forget not 1 Tim. ii. last.

When one of his daughters was safely delivered, in a letter to another of them that was drawing near to that needful hour, he observed, that when David said, Psal. cxvi. 12. What shall I render? he presently adds, ver. 13. "I will call upon the name of the Lord." "As if (faith he) calling upon the name of the Lord for mercy for you, were one way of rendering unto the Lord, for the great benefit done to your sister."

On occasion of affliction in their families by the sickness or death of children, or otherwise, he always wrote some word in season.

"In the furnace again? (faith he) but a good friend fits by, and it is only to take away more of the dross. If less fire would do, we should not have it so much and so often. O for faith to trust the Refiner, and to refer all to his will and wisdom, and to
"wait

The Life of Mr Philip Henry.

" wait the issue.---for I have been young, and now
" am old, but I never yet saw it in vain to seek God,
" and to hope in Him."

At another time he thus writes : " Tough and knot-
" ty blocks must have more and more wedges ; our
" heavenly Father, when he judgeth, will overcome.
" We hear of the death of dear S. T. and chide our-
" selves for being so often pleased with his little pret-
" ty fashions, lest we offended therein, by being too much
" so. No rival must sit with Him in his throne, who
" deserves all our love and joy, and hath too little of
" it."

At another time, upon the death of another little
one : " The dear little one (saith he) made but a short
" passage through this to another world, where it is
" to be for ever a living member of the great body,
" whereof Jesus Christ is the ever-living head ; but
" for which hope there were cause for sorrow indeed.
" If he that gives takes, and it is but his own, why
" should we say, What dost thou ?

At another time upon the like occasion ; " Our
" quiver of childrens children is not so full, but God
" can soon empty it : O for grace, grace at such a
" time, which will do that that nature cannot. The
" God of all grace supply your need and ours, accor-
" ding to his riches in glory. The Lord is still train-
" ing you up in his good school ; and though no af-
" fliction for the present be joyous, but grievous, never-
" theless afterwards it yields well ; your work is
" in every thing to bring your will to the will of
" God."

To one of his daughters concerning her little ones,
he thus writes ; " They are but bubbles : we have
" many warnings to sit loose; the less we rely upon
" them in our joys and hopes, the more likely to have
" them continued to us. Our God is a jealous God,
" nor will he suffer the creature to usurp his throne
" in our affections."

Upon the death of a little child but a few days old,

he thus writes: "The tidings of the death of your little one were afflicting to us, but the clay muſt not ſay to the potter, What doſt thou? If he that took be the ſame that gave, and what he gave and took was his own, by our own conſent, it becomes us to ſay, Bleſſed be the Name of the Lord. I hope you have been learning to acknowledge God in all events, and to take all as from his hand, who hath given us to know, I ſay, to know (for Paul ſaith ſo) that all things do work together, (not only ſhall, but do) for our good, that we may be more and more partakers of his holineſs. He can make the two left as comfortable to you as all the three, as all your five could have been. However, if all the ciſterns were drawn dry while you have your fountain to go to, you are well; you may alſo by faith look forward, and ſay, it was a covenant-child, and through mercy, we ſhall ſee it again in a better world."

Upon the ſickneſs of a dear child, he thus writes to the parent: "You and we are taught to ſay, It is the Lord; upon his will muſt we wait, and to it muſt we ſubmit in every thing; not upon conſtraint, but of choice: not only becauſe he is the potter and we the clay, and therefore in a way of ſovereignty he may do what he pleaſeth with us and ours;—but becauſe he is our Father, and will do nothing but what ſhall be for good to us. The more you can be ſatisfied in this, and the more willing to reſign, the more likely to have. Be ſtrong therefore in the grace which is in Chriſt Jeſus; it is given for ſuch a time of need as this. I hope your fears and ours will be prevented, and pray they may; but thanks be to God, we know the worſt of it, and that worſt hath no harm in it, while the better part is ours, which cannot be taken away from us."

To one of his children in affliction he writes thus; "'Tis a time of trial with you, according to the will
of

"of your and our heavenly Father. Though you see
" not yet what he means by it, you shall see. He
" means you good, and not hurt; he is shewing you
" the vanity of all things under the sun, that your
" happiness lies not in them, but in himself only:
" that they and we are passing away, withering flow-
" ers; that therefore we may learn to die to them,
" and live above them, placing our hope and happi-
" ness in better things, trusting in Him alone who is
" the rock of ages, who fails not, neither can fail, nor
" will fail those that fly to Him. I pray you, think
" not a hard thought of him, no not one hard thought,
" for he is good, and doth good in all he doth, and
" therefore all shall work for good: but then, as you
" are called according to his purpose (blessed be his
" name for it) so you must love him, and love (you
" know) thinks no evil, but puts the best construction
" upon all that the person loved faith or doth, and
" so must you, though now for a season, if need be,
" you are in heaviness."

At another time: " Your times, and the times of
" yours, are in the Lord's good hand, whose will is
" his wisdom. 'Tis one thing (as we read and ob-
" served this morning, out of Ezek. xxii.) to be put
" into a furnace and left there as dross to be consum-
" ed; and another thing to be put in as gold or silver
" to be melted for use, and to have the refiner set by.
" You know whom you have believed, keep your
" hold of the everlasting covenant: he is faithful that
" hath promised. We pray for you, and we give
" thanks for you daily, for the cup is mixed, there-
" fore trust in the Lord for ever, and rejoice in the
" Lord always; again I say rejoice."

To one of his sons-in-law that was a little engaged
in building, he thus writes: " Be sure to take God
" along with you in this, as in all your other affairs;
" for except he build the house, they labour in vain
" that build it. Count upon troublesome occurrences
" in it, and keep the spirit quiet within: and let not
" God's

"God's time nor dues be entrenched upon, and then all will be well."

'Twas but a little before he died that he wrote thus to one of his children; "We rejoice in God's goodnefs to you, that your diftemper hath been a rod fhaken only, and not laid on. He is good, and doth good; and fhould we not love him, and reft in our love to him? He faith, he doth in his to us, and rejoiceth over us with finging, Zeph. iii. 17. And have not we much more caufe? What lovelinefs in us? What not in him? I pray let me recommend him to your love: love him, love him with all the powers of your foul, and out of love to him pleafe him. He is pleafed with honeft endeavours to pleafe him; though, after all, in many things we come fhort, for we are not under the law, but under grace."

To one of his children recovered from ficknefs he gives this hint: "Remember that a new life muft be a new life indeed: reprieves extraordinary call for returns extraordinary."

The laft journey he made to London was in Auguft 1690; before he went, he fent this farewell letter to his fon at Chefter: "I am going forth this morning towards the great city, not knowing but it may be Mount Nebo to me: therefore I fend you this as full of bleffings as it can hold, to yourfelf, my daughter your wife, all the reft of my daughters, their hufbands, and all the little ones, together and feverally. If I could command the bleffings, I would; but I pray to Him that hath and doth, and I truft will. The Lord blefs you, and keep you, and lift up the light of his countenance upon you. As you have received, and you for your part preached Chrift Jefus the Lord, fo walk in him: keeping confcience always void of offence, both towards God, and towards all men. Love your mother, and be dutiful to her, and live in love and peace

"among

"among yourselves, and the God of love and peace
"that hath been, will be with you. Amen."

To one who desired his direction for the attaining of the gift of prayer, he wrote the following letter of advice:

"If you would be able in words and expressions of your own, without the help of a form, to offer up prayers to God, observe these following rules of direction, in the use whereof, by God's blessing, you may in time attain thereunto.

"1. You must be throughly convinced, that where such a gift is, it is of great use to a christian; both very comfortable and very profitable, and therefore very desirable, and worth your serious endeavours: this must first be, or else all that follows will signify nothing: for it is as the wise man saith, Prov. xviii. 1. "Through desire a man having separated himself, "seeketh and intermeddleth with all wisdom;" that is, till we are brought in some good measure to desire the end, we shall never in good earnest apply ourselves to the use of means for the obtaining of it. It is a gift that fits a person to be of use to others in the duty of prayer, according as there is occasion, either in a family or in christian communion. It is also of great advantage to ourselves; for how can any form (though ever so exact) be possibly contrived, so as to reach all the circumstances of my particular case, and yet it is my duty, in every thing to make my requests known to God.

"2. As you should be perswaded of the excellent use of it, where it is attained, so also you should believe, that where it is not, it may be attained, and that without any great difficulty. No doubt, but many are discouraged from endeavouring after it, by an opinion they have that it is to no purpose; they think it a thing so far above their abilities, that they had as good sit still and never attempt it: this is of very bad consequence, as in other matters of religion, so particularly in this, and therefore watch againſt this ſuggeſtion, and conclude, that (though it may be harder to ſome than others) yet it is impoſſible to none: nay, this wiſdom is eaſy to him that underſtandeth, where means are uſed in the fear of God.

" 3. You muſt rightly underſtand and conſider who it is with whom you have to do in prayer, for your encouragement to come to Him, though in the midſt of many infirmities and imperfections. He is your Father, your loving, tender-hearted Father, who knows your frame, and remembers you are but duſt; who is not extreme to mark what we do amiſs, in manner and expreſſion, where the heart is upright with him. You may judge a little concerning his love, by the diſpoſition that is in you towards your children, when they come to aſk things needful of you; and believe him to be infinitely more merciful and compaſſionate, than the moſt merciful and compaſſionate of fathers and mothers are or can be; eſpecially remembering that we have an Advocate with the Father Jeſus Chriſt the righteous, who is the great High Prieſt of our profeſſion, and whom he heareth always.

" 4. You muſt pray that you may pray; beg of God, the Father of lights, from whom every good and perfect gift comes, to beſtow this gift upon you. We read, Luke xi. 1. that one of the diſciples came to Jeſus Chriſt upon this errand, " Lord, teach us to " pray," and he had his requeſt granted preſently: go you to Him on the ſame errand. You may plead the relation of a child, from that ſcripture, Gal. iv. 6. " And becauſe you are ſons, God hath ſent forth the " Spirit of his Son into your hearts, crying, Abba, " Father:" and the promiſe alſo from that ſcripture, Zech. xii. 10. " I will pour upon the houſe of David, " and the inhabitants of Jeruſalem, the ſpirit of grace, " and of ſupplication;" which two, relation and a promiſe, if they be not ſufficient to encourage your faith and hope in this addreſs, what is, or can be?

5. It is good, before you addreſs yourſelf to the duty,

ty, to read a portion of holy fcripture, which will be of great ufe to furnifh you both with matter and words for prayer, efpecially David's Pfalms, and Paul's Epiftles. The Holy Spirit hath provided for us a treafury, or ftorehoufe, of what is fuitable for all occafions, and where both the word and the matter are his own, and of his own framing, and inditing: if affections be ftirring in us accordingly, we have great reafon to believe he will accept of us. In divers places he hath himfelf put words into our mouths for the purpofe, as Hof. xiv. 2. " Take with you words." Matth. vi. 9. " After this manner therefore pray ye," and often elfewhere.

6. There muft be fome acquaintance with our own hearts, with our fpiritual ftate and condition, our wants and ways, or elfe no good will be done in this matter. 'Tis fenfe of need, hunger, thirft, cold, nakednefs, that fupplies the poor beggar at your door with pertinent expreffions and arguments, he needs not the help of any friend or book to furnifh him; fo if we know ourfelves, and feel our condition, and fet God before us as our God, able and ready to help us, words will eafily follow wherewith to offer up our defires to him, who underftands the language even of fighs and tears, and groanings which cannot be uttered, Rom. viii. 26.

7. It is of ufe in ftated prayer, ordinarily to obferve a method, according to the feveral parts of prayer, which are thefe four:

1. Compellation or adoration, which is the giving of due titles to God in our addreffes to him, and therein abfcribing to him the glory due unto his name. With this we are to begin our prayers, both for the working of a holy awe and dread upon our hearts towards him, on the account of his greatnefs and majefty; as alfo for the ftrengthening of our faith and hope in him, upon the account of his goodnefs and mercy.

2. Confeffion; fin is to be confeffed in every prayer:

original sin as the root, spring-head and fountain; and actual sin as the fruit and stream proceeding from it. Herein you must not rest in generals, as the most do, but especially when you are in secret before the Lord, you must descend to particulars, opening the whole wound, hiding nothing from him, also aggravating the fault from the circumstances of it, judging and condemning yourself for it in the sight of God; and for your help herein, you must acquaint yourself with the divine law, the precepts and prohibitions of it, especially their extent and spiritual nature, as the rule, and then bring your own thoughts, words, and actions to it daily, to be tried by it.

3. Petition, for such good things as God hath promised, and you have need of, both concerning this life and that which is to come. As to the latter, you are to pray for mercy to pardon, and grace to help in time of need. As to the former, for bread to eat, and raiment to put on, and a heart to be therewith contented. You are to pray for others also, the church of God, the land of your nativity, magistrates, ministers, relations, and friends, not forgetting the afflictions of the afflicted.

4. Thanksgiving, which should have a considerable share in every prayer; for our duty is, in every thing to give thanks for mercies received, public and personal, which is the will of God in Christ Jesus concerning us.

This rule of method is not so necessary to be observed in prayer, as in no case to be varied from; but it is certainly very useful and expedient, and a great help to young beginners in that duty.

8. My advice is, that you would delay no longer, but forthwith apply yourself, in the strength of Jesus Christ, to this sweet and excellent way of praying; and I dare say, in a short time you will find, through the aids and supplies of divine grace, what is at first hard and difficult, will by degrees be easy and delightful. The promise is, that to him that hath, *i. e.* that

hath,

hath, and useth what he hath, more shall be given. Though you cannot do what you would, yet fail not to do what you can, wherein the Lord will accept of you, according to his everlasting covenant in Christ Jesus, for we are not under the law, but under grace.

CHAP. XI.

A short Account of some of his Friends, especially his brethren in the ministry, that died before him.

WE think ourselves obliged to add this account out of his own papers, partly as an evidence of the great esteem he had of the gifts and graces of others to whom he delighted to do honour; (an instance of that humility which he was in all respects a great example of;) and partly that we may preserve the remembrance of some in that country, whose names ought not to be buried in oblivion. It is part of that honour which we owe to them that fear the Lord: to mention them with respect when they are dead and gone, that we may contribute something to the fulfilling of the promise, that the righteous, and especially they who turn many to righteousness, shall be had in everlasting remembrance. While their glorified souls shine as the stars in the firmament of our Father, it is fit that their embalmed memories should in these lower regions go forth as a lamp that burneth. The Jewish rabbins read Prov. x. 7. as a precept, " Let the " memory of the just be blessed." We will take them in the order wherein we find them in his diary, according to the time of their death, premising only this note of his, occasioned by a particular instance; " Such a " day I read the life of old Mr Bruen of Stapleford, " in which I met with some things that shame me, " some things that confirm me, and some things that " quicken me." Blessed be God for that cloud of witnesses we are encompassed about with.

Mr John Machin was buried at Newcaftle, Sept. 8. 1664, a worthy inftrument in gofpel work: laborious, faithful, and fuccefsful above his fellows; taken away in the midft of his days; the firft candle I have heard of put out by God, among the many hundreds put under a bufhel by men. [An account of his holy exemplary life was printed many years after, drawn up, I think by Mr Newcome.]

Mr Heath, late minifter of Alkmans church in Salop, was buried May 28, 1666. He was of Chrift's College in Cambridge, where he was much valued for his great learning, efpecially in the Oriental tongues, in which he was one of the greateft mafters of his age. He was employed to correct the Syriac and Arabick of the Polyglot bible, which was fent down to him in fheets for that purpofe, for which bifhop Walton gave him a copy. He read the liturgy till Auguft 24, 1662, and then was filenced, becaufe he could not come up to the impofed terms of conformity. When the five-mile act commenced, March 25, 1666, he removed to Wellington, and there within a few weeks died, and was buried. When he lay upon his death-bed, Mr Lawrence afked him what reflections he had upon his nonconformity; " Truly (faid he) I would not but " have done as I did for a thoufand worlds." He had great confidence, that God would provide for his widow and children, according to promife. (The character Mr Baxter gives of him is, that he was moderate, fedate, quiet, and religious.)

Much about the fame time Mr York died in Salop, a holy good man, and well approved in the miniftry, who wafted his own candle in giving light to others, even after he was removed out of the candleftick. Lord! is this the meaning of Rev. xi. 12. concerning the witneffes?

Mr Thomes Porter, late minifter of Whitchurch, died at Salop in a good old age, June 19, 1667; he was born in Northamptonfhire, bred in Cambridge; he was fettled minifter of Hanmer in Flintfhire, long

before

before the wars, by the means of Sir John Hanmer, the patron, who was a very worthy, pious gentleman, and a great promoter of religion in that parish (but died in the midst of his days.) Here Mr Porter's miniftry was bleffed with wonderful acceptance and fuccefs, both in that and the neighbouring parifhes; and a great harveft of fouls was there gathered in to Chrift. After the wars were over (during the heat of which he was forced to withdraw) he procured Mr Steel for Hanmer, and he removed to Whitchurch, where he continued an inftrument of much good, till the king came in, and then he gave way to Dr Bernard, a worthy moderate man. He preached his farewell fermon at Whitchurch, Auguft 28, 1660, on Col. i. 24. and fpent the reft of his days in filence and affliction. He was exercifed long with pain upon his bed, and the multitude of his bones with ftrong pain. If this be done to the green tree, what fhall be done to the dry? His dying counfel to the Lord's people was, to " ftick " to Chrift, and not to let him go, come life come " death."

The worthy Colonel Thomas Hunt died at his houfe in Shrewfbury, April 12, 1669, a true Nathaniel, an Ifraelite indeed, in whom was no guile: one that, like Caleb, followed the Lord fully in difficult trying times; he was a member of the long Parliament for Shrewfbury, and very active for God in his generation, abounding in good works, and his memory is bleffed. I was going to Shrewfbury upon an appointment of his, and by the way met the fad news of his death, which was fudden, but not furprifing, to one that was always ready. He was twice at public ordinances the day before, being Lord's day, worfhipped God with his family in the evening, went to bed well as at other times; but about two or three o'clock in the morning wak'd very ill, and before five fell afleep in the Lord. " Help, Lord, for the godly man ceafeth."

Mr George Mainwaring a faithful minifter of Jefus Chrift, and my worthy friend, died in a good old age, March

March 14. 1669-70, gathered as a fhock of corn in his feafon. He was born in Wrenbury parifh in Chefhire, fupported at the Univerfity by Mr Cotton of Cumbermere, where he had the reputation of a good fcholar; he was brought acquainted with the ways of religion by means of Mr Buckly his uncle, a ftrict puritan. He was firft chaplain to Sir Henry Delves, afterwards rector of Baddely, and chaplain to Sir Thomas Mainwaring. After the wars he was removed to Malpas, whence he was ejected upon the King's coming in. His converfation was exemplary, efpecially for plainnefs and integrity; he was eminent for expounding fcripture. While he was at Malpas, he conftantly gave all the milk which his dairy yielded on the Lord's day to the poor.

Mr John Adams of Northwood, was buried at Ellefmere, April 4, 1670, he was a faithful minifter of the gofpel.

Mr Zechariah Thomas, my worthy friend, died of a confumption at Nantwich, November 14, 1670, in the forty-firft year of his age. He was bred up for a tradefman in Suffolk, but always addicted to his book, and was ordained a minifter after the King came in, and entertained curate at Tilftock, under Dr. Bernard, but by reafon of his nonconformity could not continue there long. On the Monday before he died, he faid to thofe about him, that towards Wednefday he fhould take his leave of them, and did fo. He was buried at Acton, Mr Kirkes, vicar of Acton preached, and gave him a worthy character (and fuch as he deferved) for uprightnefs, humility, moderation, prayer, faithfulnefs in reproving, patience under affliction; and in faying he was an Ifraelite indeed without guide, he faid all. The Lord make me a follower of him, and of all the reft, who through faith and patience inherit the promifes!

Mr Jofhua Richardfon, my truly worthy friend and brother, died at Alkinton in Whitchurch parifh, September 1. 1671: blefled be God for his holy life and happy

happy death. He was several years minister of Middle in Shropshire, and was turned out thence for nonconformity. He was a holy, loving, serious man. Dr Fowler preached his funeral sermon at Whitchurch, on Dan. xii. 3. highly praising him (as he deserved) for wisdom, piety, and peaceablenefs.

Mr Samuel Hilderfham died near Bromicham in April 1674, the only son of Mr Arthur Hilderfham of Afhby (whose works praise him in the gates) fellow of Emmanuel college in Cambridge, batchelor of divinity, 1623, fettled rector of Weft-Felton in Shropshire, in the year 1628, and continued there till silenced by the act of uniformity. He was one of the aſſembly of divines; a father to the sons of the prophets in and about Shropfhire. He was learned, loving, and charitable, an excellent preacher, an eminent expofitor, and very much a gentleman; he was about fourfcore years of age when he died. He ordered by his will this infcription upon his grave-ftone: Samuel Hilderfham, B. D. rector of Weft-Felton, in the county of Salop, 34 years, till Auguft 24, 1662.

Mr Richard Sadler, my worthy friend and fellow-labourer, died at Whixal in Prees parifh, April---1675. He was born in Worcefter: went, when young, with his father into New-England; after the wars he returned into England; was ordained at Whixal-chapel, May 16. 1648, and was removed thence to Ludlow. Being turned out there upon the King's coming in, he fpent the reft of his days in privacy at Whixal: a man of great piety and moderation.

Mr Rowland Nevet died at his houfe near Ofweftry December 8. 1675, and was buried at Morton-chapel. I preached his funeral fermon at Swinny, on 2 Pet. i. 14. "Knowing that I muft fhortly put off this my ta-" bernacle:" thence fhewing that the minifters of Chrift muft certainly and fhortly die. He was born in Hodnet parifh, *Anno Dom.* 1609, brought up at Shrewfbury fchool, was afterwards of Edmund-hall in Oxford, commenced mafter of arts in the year 1634,

he

he was episcopally ordained; and *Anno* 1635, he was presented to the vicarage of Stanton in Shropshire, where he continued many years, with great success in his ministry. While he was single, he kept house, judging that more for the furtherance of his work among his people, than to table. After the war he removed to Ofweftry, where he laboured abundantly in the work of the Lord; and even after he was silenced for nonconformity, he continued among his people there to his dying day, doing what he could, when he might not do what he would. He would say, he thought most of his converting work was done at Ofweftry, the first seven years of his being there. He loved to preach, and to hear others preach concerning the great things of religion, Redemption, Reconciliation, Regeneration, &c. for thefe (faid he) are the main matter. When the plague was at Ofweftry, he continued with his people, and preached to them, and it was an opportunity of doing much good.

His conversation from his youth was not only blamelefs, but holy and pious; he was exemplary for family religion, and great care and induftry in the education of his children. He was looked upon as congregational in judgement and practice, and was not fatisfied to join in the common prayer; but he was free to communicate with those that did. It was his judgement, that ministers fhould be ordained by ministers; and that a minister is not only a minister of the particular congregation in which he labours. He greatly bewailed the divifions of the church, and the intemperate heats of fome of all persuafions. He was exceeding kind and loving to his friends, very frequent in pious ejaculations to God. Being often distempered in body, he would say, he was never better than in the pulpit, and that it was " the beft place he could wish to die " in." He often blessed God for a fit of sickness which he had, which he faid he would not have been without for a world, the foundation of his comfort, and hope of heaven being laid then. When he was sometimes

much

much spent with his labours, he would appeal to God, that, " Though he might be wearied in his service, he " would never be weary of it." His dying prayer for his children (after many sweet exhortations) was, " That the Mediator's blessing might be the portion of " every one of them:" adding, " I charge you all, see " to it, that you meet me on the right hand of Christ, " at the great day." A little before he died he had this expression, " Go forth, my Soul, go forth to meet " thy God;" adding by and by, " It is now done; " come, Lord Jesus, come quickly." One present saying to him, that he was now going to receive his reward, he replied, " It is free grace." [Mr Henry was much importuned to print his sermon at Mr Nevet's funeral, with some account of his life and death, which he was somewhat inclined to do, but was discouraged by the difficulties of the times, and it was never done. But some materials he had for it, out of which we have collected these hints.]

Mr Robert Fogg, my old dear friend, was buried at Acton near Nantwich, April 21. 1676, he died in a good old age, about eighty. He was minister of Bangor in Flintshire, till after the King came in, and thenceforward to his death was a poor silent nonconformist, but of a bold and zealous spirit. Giving good counsel to those about him a little before he died, he had this weighty saying among others, " Assure yourselves, the " Spirit of God will be underling to no sin."

Mr Andrew Parsons, some time minister of Wem, died at London, October 1. 1684. He was born in Devonshire, and was minister there some years before the war; being driven thence to London, he became well known to Mr Pym, who sent him down to Wem, when that town was garrisoned for the Parliament; there he continued in the exercise of his ministry, till the year 1660. He was an active, friendly, generous man, and a moving, affecting preacher. Mr Baxter, in his life, part 3. page 94, commends him for a moderate man, and speaks of his being in trouble, for seditious words sworn against him, which were these: preaching from 2 Tim. iii 13. he said, " The devil was " like a king, that courted the soul, and spoke fair till " he was gotten into the throne, and then played " pranks." The witnesses deposed contrary to the coherence of his discourse, that he said the king was like the devil. He was tried at Shrewsbury before my Lord Newport, Mr Serjeant Turner and others, May 28. 1662. It was also charged upon him, that he had said, " There was more sins committed now in England " in a month, than was heretofore in seven years;" and " That there had been more and better preaching in " England for twenty years past, than was ever since " the apostles days." He had counsel assigned him, who pleaded that the time limited by the statute in which he was indicted was expired: the Court yielded it was so, allowing twenty-eight days to a month; but they would understand it of thirty days to a month, so he was found guilty, and fined two hundred pounds, and ordered to be imprisoned till it should be paid.

Mr Hugh Rogers, a worthy faithful minister of Jesus Christ, turned out for nonconformity, from Newtown in Montgomeryshire, was buried at Welshpool, March 17, 1679-80, he was looked upon as congregational but his declared judgment was, " That mini- " sters ought to be ordained by ministers, and to give " themselves wholly to that work; and that none but " ministers have authority to preach and govern in a " constituted church; and that Christ's ministers are " his ministers in all places; and that where the word " of Christ is preached, and his Sacraments adminis- " tered, there is a true church." He was a man of excellent converse, and whose peculiar felicity lay in pleasant and edifying discourse.

July 2d and 3d, 1680, these two days brought tidings of the death of Mr Haines, some time minister of Wem in Shropshire, and since at New-chapel in Westminster; and of Mr Richard Edwards minister at Oswestry, both worthy conformists, pious, peaceable and good

good men, whom I hope, through grace, to meet shortly in heaven. The Lord raife up others in their room to be and do better.

Mr Robert Bofier, my dear friend and kinfman, having juft compleated the twenty-third year of his age, died of a fever, September 13, 1680, at Mr Doolittle's houfe in Iflington, whither he was gone but a few weeks before for improvement in learning; being formerly a commoner of Edmund-hall in Oxford, and fince having fpent fome years in my family, and defigned himfelf for the fervice of Chrift, in the work of the miniftry. He was a young man of pregnant parts, great induftry, and exemplary ferioufnefs and piety, and likely to be an eminent inftrument of good in his day. His friends and relations had promifed themfelves much comfort in him, but we know who " per-
" formeth the thing that is appointed for us, and giv-
" eth not account of any of his matters."

Mr John Malden, my dear and worthy friend, turned out from Newport in Shropfhire for nonconformity, died at Alkington near Whitchurch, May 23, 1681, a man of great learning, an excellent Hebrecian, and of exemplary piety, and a folid preacher: as he lived fo he died, very low in his own eyes; efteeming himfelf good for nothing, though really good for every thing, which was manifeftly a prejudice, both to his comfort, and to his ufefulnefs. He faid, he was far from repenting his being a fufferer againft conformity. The relicks of fo much learning, piety, and humility, I have not feen this great while laid in a grave, but bleffed be God we had fuch a one fo long.

Dr Jofhua Maddocks, a beloved Phyfician, our very dear friend and kinfman, died of a fever at Whitchurch, in the midft of his days, July 27th, 1682, a very pious man, and efpecially eminent for meeknefs; an excellent fcholar, and particularly learned in the mathematicks: he lived much defired, and died as much lamented.

Mr Thomas Bridge, who had been rector of the
higher

higher rectory of Malpas about fifty-seven years, being aged about eighty-two years, was buried at Malpas, Octob. 7, 1682. In his last sicknefs, which was long, he had appointed Mr Green, one of the curates there, to preach his funeral fermon on 1 Tim i. 16 "How-"beit, for this caufe I obtained mercy, that in me firft, "Jefus Chrift might fhew forth all long-fuffering:" and to fay nothing in his commendation, but to give a large account of his repentance upon his death-bed, &c. He was a taking, popular preacher, preaching often and almoft to the laft. When old, he could read the fmalleft print without fpectacles.

Mr William Cook, an aged, painful, faithful minifter of Jefus Chrift in Chefter, finifhed his courfe with joy, July 4, 1684, in the midft of the cloudy and dark day. [See Mr Baxter's character of him in his life, Part 3. page 98.] and an honourable account given of him by Mr Samuel Bold, of Steeple in Dorfetfhire, in a large preface to his book of Man's great duty. He was eminent for great induftry, both in public and private work; great felf-denial, mortification, and contempt of the world, and a ftrict adherence to his principles in all the turns of the times. He was firft minifter at Wroxal in Warwickfhire; there he publifhed two treatifes againft the Anabaptifts. From thence he was, by the advice of the London minifters, removed to Afhby in Leicefterfhire, whence he was turned out for refufing the engagement, and afterward fettled in Chefter, where he was minifter of Michael's church, till he was outed by the act of uniformity. He was an active man for Sir George Booth, when he made that attempt to bring in the King, in 1659, for which he was brought up a prifoner to London, and continued long under confinement in Lambeth-houfe; and had not the times turned had been tried for his life. During the ufurpation, his frequent prayer was, "That " God would pull down all ufurped power, and re- " ftore the banifhed to their right." After he was filenced by the Bartholomew act, he continued to his
                                                    death.

death in a paftoral relation to a fociety of many worthy eminent Chriftians in Chefter; though during the heat of the five-mile act, he was forced to withdraw to Puddington in Wirral, where (as in Chefter, till King Charles's indulgence) he conftantly attended on the public miniftry, and he himfelf preached in the intervals. He would fay fometimes to his friends, when he was in that retirement, that he thought "What lit-" tle peace and quietnefs there was in this world, " God's people enjoyed it in their corners." Soon after he was filenced, he was committed to the common goal of Chefter for preaching in his own houfe, by the Mayor, at inftigation of the then Bifhop Hall. He was very indefatigable in his minifterial labours, in which he never fought the afliftance of any other minifter; though while he had liberty he conftantly kept a public faft in his congregation every month, as he did alfo a private faft in his own clofet and family every week. He ufually fet apart one afternoon every week, to vifit the families of his congregation, and to catechife their children and fervants, and difcourfe with them perfonally about their fouls; his vifits were fhort and edifying (and he managed them as one that was a great hufband of his time) and he feldom or never parted without prayer. He was not free to join in the common-prayer, and bore his teftimony againft prelacy and the ceremonies with fomething of zeal; but his great piety, integrity, mortification, and charity, recommended him to the refpects even of many that differed from him. If any afked his advice to any thing which might draw fuffering upon them, he would be very tender, and defire them not to depend upon his judgement; but fince it was a matter of fuffering, to be fully perfuaded in their own minds.

He was a great fcholar, and a hard ftudent to the laft, and was far from entangling himfelf in the affairs of this life, not knowing ought he had, fave the bread that he did eat. In worldly matters he was not very converfable, but in difcourfe of the things of God,

none

none more free and affable, or more ready to do good.

He lived and died a great example of strict and close walking with God, and a heavenly converfation; and his memory is very precious with many. He died in the seventy-third year of his age. When he lay on his death-bed, an aged friend of his asking him if he had not comfort in reflection upon his labours in the work of God, he presently replied, " I have nothing " to boast of." He was buried in Michael's church in Chester; and though for some time before he died, such was the heat of the persecution, that he durst not shew his face in the city, yet many considerable persons were very forward to do him honour at his death.

Mr Jonathan Roberts of Llanvair in Denbighshire, my dear and precious friend, and a faithful minister of Christ, died at Mr Titus Thomas's house in West-Felton, and was buried there Sept. 26. 1684. A true Nathaniel, an Israelite indeed, for plainness and integrity; a silent sufferer for his nonconformity, for which he quitted a good living in Denbighshire. He was a learned man, a Master of Arts of Oxford; he died with comfort in his nonconformity, and with confidence of a return of mercy in God's due time. The summer before he died, he had been at Oxford, Cambridge, and London, where he heard and saw that which much confirmed him in his dissent.

Mr Zechariah Cawdrey, Minister of Bartomley in Cheshire, a learned and godly divine, was buried December 24. 1684. a conformist, and formerly a great sufferer for the king, but in his later times much maligned and reproached by some people for his moderation towards dissenters, for his book of preparation for martyrdom, and for his zeal in keeping up the monthly lectures at Nantwich and Tarvin. But he is gone to the world of peace, and love, and everlasting praises.

Mr Titus Thomas, minister of the independent congregation in Salop, was buried at Felton, December 10,

10, 1686. He was a worthy good man, and not so strait-laced as some others; we were six nonconformist ministers there at the funeral, and the seventh dead in the midst of us, saying to us, " Therefore be " ye also ready."

Mr John Cartwright, my worthy friend and brother, a faithful minister of Jesus Christ, was buried at Audlem in Cheshire, Feb. 17. 1687-8. formerly minister of West-Kerby in Wirral, afterwards chaplain to the pious Lady Wilbraham at Woodbey.

Mr Edward Gregg of Chester, a worthy gentleman, and my dear friend, died July 9. 1689. of a fever, in the midst of his days. He was one that feared God above many, of a meek and quiet spirit, and eminently active and useful in his generation. The Lord is pulling our earthen props from under us, that we might lean upon, and trust in himself alone, and might learn to cease from man.

Mr Daniel Benyon of Ash, my dear friend and kinsman, died June 25. 1690. a very serious, pious gentleman, and an Israelite indeed, a true lover, and ready benefactor to all good men, especially good ministers. He told me a little before he died, God had made use of me (though most unworthy) as an instrument of his conversion, for which I bless his holy name. He had a long and lingering sickness, which he bore with great patience.

Mrs Crew of Otkinton in Cheshire, an aged servant of the Lord, was buried July 8. 1690. She kept her integrity, and abounded in works of piety and charity to the last, and finished well; to God be praise.

Mrs Hunt of Shrewsbury, the relict of Colonel Hunt, another rare pattern of zealous piety, abounding charity, and eminent usefulness in her place, finished her course, October 23. 1690. after two days sickness.

The reverend, and learned, and holy Mr Richard Baxter, died at London, December 8. 1691. aged seventy-six, and one month; as much vilified by some, and magnified by others, as most men that ever were;

bu

but it is a small thing to be judged of man's day. He was buried at Christ-church, London, with great honour.

Mr John Wood, my good friend, died September 19. 1692. at Mitton in Shropshire, aged about seventy; he was sometime fellow of Magdalen-College in Cambridge, where he was outed for nonconformity; a learned man, but wanted the faculty of communicating: one that feared God, and walked in his integrity to the last; had no certain dwelling-place on earth, but I trust hath one in heaven. *Hic tandem requiescit.*

Mr Richard Steel, my old and dear friend, and companion in tribulation, and in the kingdom and patience of Jesus Christ, died at London, November 16. 1692. in the sixty-fourth year of his age. A man that had been greatly useful in his generation, both in the country and at London.

Mr Thomas Gilbert died at Oxford, July 15. 1694. formerly minister of Edgmond in Shropshire, aged eighty-three, a learned good man.

Luke Lloyd, Esq; of the Bryn in Hanmer Parish, my aged, worthy friend, finished his course with joy, March 31. 1695. being Lord's day. He was in the eighty-seventh year of his age, and had been married almost sixty-nine years to his pious wife (of the same age) who still survives him. He was the glory of our little congregation, the top-branch in all respects of our small vine, and my friend indeed.

When he made his will, under the subscription of his name he wrote, Job xix. 25, 26, 27. On which text of Scripture (I know that my Redeemer liveth, &c.) Mr Henry, at the request of some of his relations, preached a sermon at the licenced house near Hanmer, sometime after his funeral; in which sermon, he bore a very honourable testimony to that worthy gentleman, who (as he saith) went to heaven without a blot, held fast his integrity, and was lively and zealous in the Christian profession to the end of his days. He was very exemplary for his love to the ordinances of God,

God, and his delight in attending on them, his living upon Chrift for ftrength and righteoufnefs, his great humility, and condefcending obliging carriage in all his converfe. He was a man of great courage and refolution: and yet in prayer, tender and felf-abafing, to admiration, often melting into tears in the confeflion of fin; and his charity and moderation were known unto all men.

He lived and died a pattern of piety, and primitive Chriftianity, and ftill brought forth fruit in old age; his vigor, both of body and mind, being wonderfully preferved to the laft; and by the grace of God he finifhed well, and his fun fet under no cloud. Such good men are intended to be to us, as the ftar that led the wife men to Chrift; and as far as they do fo, we are to follow them. " Mark the perfect man, and behold the upright, for the end of that man is peace."

Mr Samuel Taylor, an aged minifter of Jefus Cnrift, and my true friend and fellow-labourer, died at Wem, June 26, 1695. He was turned out from Edftaftonchapel near Wem, by the act of uniformity; chufing rather to beg his bread than to wrong his confcience. He continued in Wem ever fince, and preached there as his ftrength and liberty would permit. He had his houfe burnt in the dreadful fire that was there in 1676, and had a child born that very night. He was a man of a very tender fpirit, humble and low in his own eyes, of approved integrity, and finifhed well. (Mr Henry preached his funeral fermon at Wem, on 2 Cor. iv. 7. " We have this treafure in earthen veffels.)

September 21, 1695. I heard of the death of two holy, aged Bartholomew-witneffes, Mr Richard Mayo of London, and Mr Henry Newcome of Manchefter, Pfal. xii. 1.

Mr Edward Lawrence of London, my dear and worthy friend, and a faithful minifter and witnefs of the Lord Jefus, died November---1695, about the feventieth year of his age; born at Mofton in Shropfhire, of Magdalen-College in Cambridge, turned out from Bafchurch in Shropſhire by the act of uniformity in 1662, was driven from Whitchurch by the violent proſecution of the conventicle Act, in 1670, when he removed to London, and there ſpent the reſt of his days.

He had many children, but great affliction in ſome of them, which gave occaſion to his book entitled, " Parents Groans over their wicked Children." It is a very high, but juſt character, which Mr Vincent hath given of him in his ſermon at his funeral; of which let me take leave to add ſome few inſtances that occur to us, which may be inſtructive, beſides thoſe which we have already mentioned occaſionally. At his meals, he would often ſpeak of uſing God's creatures as his witneſſes that he is good ; and we cannot conceive how much good our God doth every moment.

An expreſſion of his great regard to juſtice, was that common caution he gave his children, Trem-" ble to borrow two pence;" and of his meekneſs and tenderneſs this, " Make no man angry nor " ſad." He often ſaid, " I adore the wiſdom of God, " that hath not ſeen meet to truſt me with riches." When he ſaw little children playing in the ſtreets, he would often lift up his heart in an ejaculatory prayer to God for them, calling them " the ſeed of the next " generation." When his friend choſe to ride the back way into town, he pleaſantly checked him, telling him, that his heart hath been often refreſhed, when he hath looked out at the window and ſeen a good man go along the ſtreets. He uſed to ſay, that Cromwell did more real prejudice to religion by his hypocriſy, than king Charles the Second did, that never pretended to it. As alſo, that he feared the ſins of the land more than the French.

A friend of his in the country, writing to him not long before he died, deſired his thoughts concerning the

the differences among the London diffenters, to which he returned this anfwer : " I can fay little concerning " our divifions ; which, when fome men's judgments " and tempers are healed, will be alfo healed. But " when will that be ? They that have moft holinefs " are moft peaceable, and have moft comfort."

M. S.

M. S.
PHILIPPUS HENRY,
De Broad-Oak, in Comitatu Flint, A. M.
Sacri Minifter Evangelii ; Paftor olim Worthenburi-
enfis ;
In Aula Regia natus piis & honeftis Parentibus ;
Scholæ Weftmonafterienfis, indeq. Ædis ChriftiOxon.
Alumnus Regius :
Vir prifca Pietate & vere Chriftiana,
Judicio fubacto & limato,
Memoria præftanti, magno & fœcundo Ingenio,
Eruditione perpolita, fummo Animi Candore, Morum
Venuftate
Imprimis Spectabilis, & in Exemplum natus:
Cui Sacra femper fua fides aliorumque Fama :
Divini Numinis Cultor affiduus ;
Divini Verbi Interpres exquifitiffimus ;
Aliorum Affectus movere non minus pollens,
Quam fuis moderari :
Concionando pariter ac Vivendo palam exhibens
Chrifti Legem & Exemplar Chriftum :
Prudens peritufque rerum ; Lenis, Pacificus, Hofpi-
talis,
Ad Pietatis omnia Charitatifque officia ufque paratus ;
Suis Jucundus ; Omnibus Humanus ;
Continuis Evangelii Laboribus fuccumbens Corpus,
Nec tantæ jam par amplius Animæ,
In Dormitorium hic juxta pofitum, demifit,
Jun. 24º. Anno Dom. MDCXCVI, Ætatis LXV.

Viro opt. multumque defiderato
mœrens pofuit Gener ejus J. T. M. D.

F I N I S.

www.ingramcontent.com/pod-product-compliance
Lightning Source LLC
Chambersburg PA
CBHW031737230426
43669CB00007B/378